S Y M B O L   C O N T E X T   O R N A M E N T

	1	2	3	4	5
SOCIAL DIMENSION	●		●	●	●
FORMAL DIMENSION		●		●	●
WIT AND IRONY = OK					
IDEALISM = YES					
REPRESENTATION OF MATERIAL: FAUX NO	●	·	●	·	●
REPRESENTATION OF MATERIAL: FAUX YES					
EXPRESSION OF MATERIAL: SYMBOLIC			●	·	?
REFERENTIAL ORNAMENT · FORMAL	·				?
ABSTRACT ORNAMENT			●	·	?
ORNAMENT AS PATTERN		·			?
ORNAMENT AS ARTICULATION			●	●	?
ORNAMENT APPLIED	·	●			?
ORNAMENT AS EXPRESSION					?
ORNAMENT ON THE BUILDING			●		?
ORNAMENT AS THE BUILDING			●	●	
ORNAMENT IS GOOD		●			●
ORNAMENT IS BAD	●	·	●		·
DESIGN FROM THE OUTSIDE IN			●		
DESIGN FROM THE INSIDE OUT	●	·	●	·	?
VOCABULARY · ACCOMMODATED	●	·	●	●	
VOCABULARY · UNIVERSAL			●	·	
PLACE AND ETHOS · YES	●	·	●	●	●
PLACE AND ETHOS · NO					
CONTEXT · HURRAY	●	●		●	●
CONTEXT · FORGET IT			●		
CHANGE	●	●	·		●
PROGRESS			●		
EVOLUTIONARY	●	·			
REVOLUTIONARY			●	·	
CONVENTIONAL ELEMENTS			●		●
ORIGINAL ELEMENTS			●	·	
ELEMENTAL SHELTER	·	●			
ABSTRACT FORM			●	·	●
LITERARY / RUSSIAN CONSTRUCTIVIST	·	●		·	
LITERARY · HISTORIC			●		●
CULTURAL · NEO-CLASSICAL				●	
VOCABULARY · INDUSTRIAL VERNACULAR			●		
SYMBOLISM · ECLECTIC			●		
SYMBOLISM · CONSISTENT	●	·			
SYMBOLISM · VERNACULAR - POP			●		
SYMBOLISM · ELITIST				●	●
SYMBOLISM · CULTURALLY RELEVANT			●	·	
SYMBOLISM · IDEOLOGICALLY BASED				·	·
SYMBOLISM · AESTHETICALLY BASED			●		
SYMBOLISM · EXPLICIT				●	
SYMBOLISM · UNADMITTED					·
SYMBOLISM			●	·	
REPRESENTATION	●	·			
LITERALISM			●	·	·
MEANING	●	●			
EXPRESSION			●	·	●
REFERENCE	●	●			
ABSTRACTION			●	●	·
SYMBOL PREDOMINATES	●	●			
FORM PREDOMINATES			●	·	·

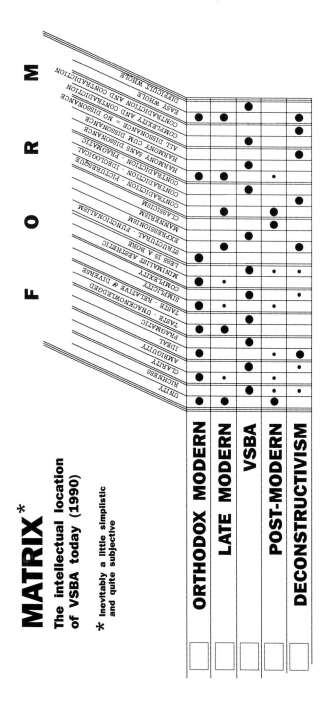

MATRIX*

The intellectual location of VSBA today (1990)

* Inevitably a little simplistic and quite subjective

Diagram designed for a lecture in Tokyo,
1990; published in the exhibition catalogue
Venturi, Scott Brown and Associates
(Seoul: Plus Publishing Co., 1992), p. 48

ICONOGRAPHY AND ELECTRONICS

UPON A

GENERIC ARCHITECTURE

A VIEW FROM THE DRAFTING ROOM

ROBERT VENTURI

The MIT Press
Cambridge, Massachusetts
London, England

This book was set in Bembo by Graphic Composition, Inc.
Printed on recycled paper and bound in the United States of America.

Library of Congress Cataloging-in-Publication Data

Venturi, Robert.
    Iconography and electronics upon a generic architecture : a view from the drafting room / Robert Venturi.
      p.   cm.
    ISBN 0-262-22051-2 (alk. paper)
    1.   Architecture, Modern—20th century.
    NA680.V44   1996
    724'.6—dc20   95-26027
                                                           CIP

To those clients without whose challenges,
understanding, and trust we could not be artists

CONTENTS

PREFACE

I have intended these essays and aphorisms to derive from informed experience—that of living and working—and not from researched knowledge, so often among architects composed to impress. Their manner is American—that is, simple and direct, in the tradition, I hope, of Franklin, Lincoln, or Hemingway—in their intention if not in their attainment.

Because these essays tend to be immediate responses to particular circumstances and therefore to become wholes in themselves more than parts of a greater whole, they tend to include occasional repetitions among themselves. But there is meant to be, of course, a general approach that they represent—and the first two essays are intended to establish the tone of the whole.

A few of these essays are jointly authored by me and Denise Scott Brown, and reflect thereby our beautiful partnership of almost 30 years which enriches our work and our thinking.

———

My special thanks go to Lynda Payne for her skill, sensitivity, and patience over many years of working together on this work, to Eric Johnson for his understanding, commitment, and literary grace in helping edit and arrange the material, and to Roger Conover and Matthew Abbate of the MIT Press for their understanding and guidance, all beyond any calls of duty.

ICONOGRAPHY AND ELECTRONICS
UPON A
GENERIC ARCHITECTURE

SWEET AND SOUR

SWEET AND SOUR

As a Comparative Method of Analysis and a Way of Design That Accommodates Mannerist Duality

An Argument for a Generic Architecture Defined by Iconography and Electronics

Originally published in *Architecture,* May 1994, pp. 51–52.

SWEET

A gentle manifesto that acknowledges the demise of a universal architecture defined as expressive space and industrial structure:

Let us acknowledge architecture for now that is not ideologically correct, rhetorically heroic, theoretically pretentious, boringly abstract, technologically obsolete.

Let us acknowledge the elemental quality of architecture as shelter and symbol—buildable and usable shelter that is also meaningful as a setting for living. Shelter and symbolism that are inevitable, admitted, and explicit elements of an architecture that embraces signs, reference, representation, iconography, scenography, and trompe-l'oeil as its valid dimensions: that makes manifest evocation. Let us acknowledge these elements as the genesis and basis of the art of architecture:

> • Shelter that admits within its imagery form *and* symbol—and whose symbolism can be explicitly juxtaposed on generic form, sometimes independent of it and sometimes contradictory to it so we should say that in our time form *followed* function while form accommodates functions—and shelter as a medium for symbolism that accommodates technical realities of our time and that acknowledges cultural context and cultural variety in our world, that promotes a vivid background for living and not a dramatic setting for acting.

• Symbolism that evolves *not* out of Renaissance tradition, whose architecture of form abstracts references to a Classical order from an ideal past—*not* out of recent Modern and current Modern Revival tradition, whose architecture of form incorporates veiled references to an industrial order from an ideal past—*not* out of Postmodernism, whose architecture of symbols promotes a nineteenth-century kind of eclecticism involving irrelevant Romantic-historical stylistic associations—and *not* incidentally out of Disneyworld architecture whose evocative representation derives from three-dimensional ducks rather than two-dimensional iconography.

• But a symbolism that derives perhaps from ancient Egyptian, Early Christian and Byzantine, and Baroque traditions whose generic architectures of surface project ornamental images—hieroglyphic bas-relief on masonry Egyptian temples, iconographic murals and mosaics in Early Christian basilicas and Byzantine domes, and scenographic or trompe-l'oeil effects inside Baroque churches. These images are signs as well as ornament—explicit sources of information virtually independent of the planar forms and sheltering surfaces of the generic architecture they are applied to all over—they evoke video projections where, projected onto independent architectural surfaces, the foot of a saint on the wall of a basilica might be amputated by the opening of an arch.

• And an iconography that suggests the relevance for us of the ornamental surfaces of temple exteriors and basilican interiors—and I should include other precedents like that of super-graphics that adorn the Constructivist designs of Konstantin Melnikov of the 1920s or the *faux* ornament depicting three-dimensional architectural elements on the surfaces of country architecture in northern Europe and representing expensive materials on cheap furniture of peasant cultures. But it demonstrates as well a difference in our electronic age when computerized images can change over time, information can be infinitely varied rather than dogmatically universal, and communication can accommodate diversities of cultures and vocabularies, vulgar and tasteful, Pop and highfaulting—from here and there. In this context the grand advertising Jumbotrons atop buildings in Tokyo and Osaka can, along with temple hieroglyphics and mosaic iconography, work as precedent for a generic architecture employing video display systems—where the sparkle of pixels can parallel the sparkle of tesserae and LED can become the mosaics of today. What S. Apollinare Nuovo does inside we can do inside and/or outside.

Here is architecture as iconographic representation emitting electronic imagery from its surfaces day and night rather than architecture as abstract form reflecting light from its surfaces only in the day—an architecture that embraces human dimensions over those of abstract expression—that celebrates the beginning of an age of virtually universal literacy and embraces meaning over expression.

There are dangers in an architecture of representation that makes art out of information. Didacts can exploit it to promote ideology within art. Abstract expressionism is safer. But techniques available now can help us achieve change and balance via flexibility, and promote richness through variety. *Our* iconography will not be etched in stone.

And it is important to remember that it is a GENERIC architecture that acknowledges symbolism and iconography for our time, that represents ornament and projects detail rather than engages them—is this virtual detail?—and whose flexibility—spatial, mechanical, and iconographic—can accommodate change explicitly. And it is this generic quality that can dominate over the iconographic where appropriate.

What are explicit implications for this vivid but incipient approach to design? Who knows for sure? Perhaps guidance concerning this artistic medium can come from our children—certainly not from our aging avant-garde, but from those who are attuned to computer techniques of our time, who can exploit the substance of a real electronic technology that is growing by leaps and bounds rather than depict the image of an old engineering technology—make of architecture kids' stuff, not *ancienne garde*. Let us explore electronics rather than exalt engineering.

Architecture was late in stylistically acknowledging the industrial revolution in the vocabulary of the Fagus Shoe Works around 1910: let us acknowledge not too late the technology of now—of video electronics over structural engineering: let us recognize the electronic revolution in the Information Age—and proclaim ourselves iconoclasts for iconography! Viva virtual architecture, almost!

SOUR

A complementary sour—or saucy—description of fin-de-siècle architecture:

Multiple oxymorons may best identify the *retardataire* avant-garde that dominates American architecture today:

An establishment avant-garde that is self-proclaimed, academic, journalistic, and, above all, heroic,

Proclaiming outré is OK when outré is passé,

Promoting a Modern Revival style as the latest thing aesthetically, technologically, theoretically, sentimentally, and heroically — promoting warmed-over leftovers overseasoned with wire-framed spice,

Which consists of, in fact, fin-de-siècle versions of Russian Constructivism and German Expressionism,

Promoting hyped and askew versions of architectural sculpture, paradoxically garbed in decoration representing heroic-functionalist exposed-frame structure symbolizing nineteenth-century engineering—while everybody knows the Industrial Revolution is dead,

Promoting what is really industrial rocaille stuck onto Cubist abstraction—that's going to be hard to maintain,

Proclaiming a Modern Revival style promoting a monocultural ideal for a universal context for fear of exposing a lack of education necessary for engaging historical symbolism and multiculturalism: could it be Neo-Modernism is the last resort of illiterates?

Justifying a conceptualization, a dematerialization, of architecture via pompous-esoteric transformations of theory, inapplicable inanities questionably borrowed from other disciplines,

Substituting polemics for theory, ideology for sensibility, where content and relevance in the end evoke the emperor's lack of clothes (not to mention create a void in the social dimension in architecture),

While amply meeting today's journalistic qualifications as it promotes architecture as trend, poster, and slogan.

But there is a way that this particular and ironical form of Postmodernism (meaning stylistic-revival-with-a-twist—a twist that perhaps disguises the inherent historicism of this Neo-Modern architecture) does connect in a way, a tiny way, with real high-tech of our Electronic Age,

Does connect via its CAD rocaille based on wire frame imagery,

Does connect in that it twists, and these twists—the characteristic formalist distortions dominating this architecture—do derive from computer technology,

From the graphic opportunity afforded by the CAD system and exploited by Deconstructionist designers who simply punch ROTATE and STRETCH on their computers to project forced-decorative geometric expressions of complexity and contradiction that weirdly exploit a deference toward the forms of classic Modern architecture while really profaning its principles,

As in the last decades we've had to suffer decennially the dry arrogance of
late Modernism, the urbanistic heroics of megastructures, the idiotic
applications of semiotics, the parvenu historicism of Postmodernism,
and now sado-masochistic expressionist applications of
Deconstructionism as complexity and contradiction gone rampant—
of modish juxtapositions of expressionistic Cubism and industrial
rocaille and recently what can be called curvaceous-organic
industrial,

While complexity becomes picturesquely motival and contradiction
becomes paradoxically consistent and ambiguity becomes pompously
arch.

Oh, for a complexity and contradiction that derive complexity from
modern experience rather than from Modern ideology which
projects spatial fantasy as a picturesque whole: down with
complexity and lunacy in architecture.

It was *so* much easier in the old days when the establishment was
conservative rather than cutting-edge.

Viva evolutionary as well as revolutionary but *à bas* pseudo-revolutionary
in architecture!

Down with fin-de-siècle Mies-mash gingerbread-Modern where organic
becomes orgasmic, where Complexity and Contradiction becomes
contradiction and contradiction, where engineering imagery as
ornamental frames sticks out of incidental shelter—all of which is
less relevant than ancient Egyptian pylons.

What an irony that we honor Modern architecture too much to distort it
decoratively.

Oh, to be bored in our Neo-Modern age of Minimalist hype!

———

The illustrations that accompany this essay indicate historical precedent for architectural iconography and then evolutions and continuity within the work of our firm, which from the beginning (I now realize) acknowledged the validity of symbolism, convention, representation, and evocation via iconography and signage—starting with the FDR Memorial Competition design where the promenade evolves into a billboard teeming with graphics, to the buildingboard of the Football Hall of Fame which electronically projects images and messages toward the parking lot–picnic ground, to Copley Square in Boston which represents an American grid-iron street configuration with a statue of Trinity Church in it, and then our early houses looked like houses. I like it that what I am proclaiming is what we have been doing.

A NOT SO GENTLE MANIFESTO

Written 1994.

That employs the comparative method to illustrate an architecture for now
in the context of an architecture of now,

That makes a plea for an architecture whose elemental dimensions
embrace generic shelter, symbolic content, electronic technology,
scenographic imagery, and flexible iconography that itself celebrates
pluralities of cultures and contexts over time,

That suggests the demise of a twentieth-century aesthetic which promoted
a universal architecture as expressive space, industrial structure, and
functional form and which has lately been spiced with chic
distortion, hype coloration, cute symbolism, and heroic theory:

Hey, what's for now is a generic architecture whose technology is
electronic and whose aesthetic is iconographic—and it all works
together to create decorated shelter—or the electronic shed!

Oh, for an architecture:

Whose aesthetic and social bases are pragmatically real—rather than
ideologically correct,

Whose universal dimension is valid generic—rather than passé industrial; whose regional dimension is iconographic—rather than passé industrial,

Whose spatial and formal bases are generic and conventional—rather than heroic and original or obsoletely innovative,

Whose architect is an anti-hero—rather than a signature,

Whose content embraces human dimensions—rather than promotes abstract forms,

Whose rhetorical basis is iconographic surface—rather than heroic form,

Whose compositional basis is rhythm with exceptions—rather than exceptions skewering exceptions,

Whose content embraces pragmatic convention via reference or symbol—rather than industrial fanfare ornamenting Cubist abstraction,

Whose electronic ornament is dynamic—rather than whose metallic rocaille is static,

Whose symbolic basis is representational and iconographic—rather than surreptitious and arbitrary,

Whose symbolic content is relevant and vital—rather than arbitrary-historical or stylistic-Modern,

Whose sheltering surfaces project ornamental pattern—rather than whose abstract planes project colorless texture,

Whose ornament is explicit appliqué—rather than unconscious essence—remembering Pugin: it's all right to decorate construction but never construct decoration,

Whose essential technical basis is twentieth-century electronic
   technology—rather than nineteenth-century engineering rhetoric,

Whose wording consists of iconographic information up front—rather
   than esoteric theorizing up front: whose content accommodates our
   Information Age—rather than our aged theorists,

Whose electronic-iconographic aesthetic accompanies generic space and
   form—rather than whose industrial-abstract aesthetic derives from
   expressive space and form,

Whose electronic surfaces can be defined as sources of light—rather than
   whose sculptural forms are defined as reflections of light, solely by
   old-fashioned shades and shadows no different from those of archaic
   Greek temples—acknowledging a 24-hour architecture for now:
   down with the infamous definition of architecture as "the masterly,
   correct and magnificent play of masses brought together in light";
   down with "forms in light; . . . cubes, cones spheres, cylinders or
   pyramids [as] the great primary forms,"[1]

Whose aesthetic pixels define a medium for architecture—rather than
   whose wire frame rotations promote ennui,

Whose forms promote scenographic-trompe-l'oeil wonder—rather than
   abstract sculptural gesture,

Whose juxtapositions of form and symbol engage the extraordinary and
   the ordinary—rather than the extraordinary ad nauseam,

Whose agonized complexity comes naturally—rather than whose willful
   picturesqueness bores in the end,

Whose aesthetic basis is iconographic representation—rather than
   sculptural expression,

Whose sheltering form creates a meaningful background for living—
    rather than a dramatic setting for acting,

Whose inherent flexibility deriving from generic form accommodates
    functions—rather than follows function: sometimes form finds
    function,

Whose originality derives from iconographic content—rather than space
    and form—as architects become poetic builders rather than
    pompous theoreticians,

Whose symbolic appliqué upon generic form accommodates the cultural
    variety of now,

Whose symbolism applied to and in combination with its generic form
    can accommodate valid complexity and contradiction—lyricism and
    dissonance—rather than picturesquely consistent complication,

Whose construction is realistically buildable and whose electronic
    technology is excitingly not obsolete,

Whose computers engage architecture as depiction—as well as depict
    architecture as image,

Whose generic shelter is adorned via electronic technology—rather than
    whose dramatic space is adorned with industrial imagery,

Whose essence is defined by electronic iconography—as well as by space
    and form,

Whose aesthetic explores electronics—rather than exalts engineering,

Whose aesthetic promotes evocative scenography—over purist abstraction
    and wire frame rocaille,

Whose content projects human meaning—rather than abstract expression.

Aren't we tired of our subjection to boring esoterica promoting arconcepture involving cuckoo sculptural form defined by old-fashioned shadow and archaic engineering which is really decoration?

Viva valid, vivid, and varied representation in architecture—rather than the constant obsolete imagery of wire frame CAD rocaille,

Viva an art that accommodates dissonance *and* lyricism and ends up tense—and sometimes enigmatic,

Viva an electronic aesthetic—over the machine aesthetic,

Viva functional guy wires—over sagging guy wires,

Viva virtual architecture—over virtuous ideology,

Viva explicit ornament—over engineered ornament,

Viva natural complexity—over engineered complication,

Viva architecture with content—rather than architecture as abstract.

A *bas* gingerbread-Modern with sagging guy wires—*viva* iconographic post-Neo-Modern (I don't really know what to call it because I wouldn't dream of naming a style—that is for historians to do ultimately).

Viva an authentic modern architecture over a revivalist Modern architecture—modernism over Modernism: down with Modernesque architecture.

Viva evocation—*à bas* abstraction.

Enfin: iconography over expression: generic over spatial: electronic over
industrial.

---

1. Le Corbusier, *Towards a New Architecture,* trans. Frederick Etchells (New York: Holt, Rine-
hart and Winston, 1976), p. 31.

2
Basilica S. Apollinare Nuovo, Ravenna
Photo credit: Fotocelere, Turin, from *Early Christian and Byzantine Architecture* by Richard Krautheimer (Baltimore: Penguin, 1965), plate 61a

1
Ancient Egyptian pylon, detail
Photo from *A History of Architecture,* 9th ed., by Banister Fletcher (New York: Scribner's, 1931), p. 35

4
Facade, Amiens cathedral
Photo credit: Jean Robier, Paris

3
Lunette, San Vitale, Ravenna
Photo credit: Anderson, from *Attraverso l'Italia,* vol. 16, *Emilia e Romagna* (Milan: Touring Club Italiano, 1950), p. 213

5
Palazzo Rucellai, Florence
Photo from *An Outline of European Architecture* by Nikolaus Pevsner (New York: Scribner's, 1948), plate LI.

6
Peter Thumb, Pilgrimage Church, Birnau

7
Pennsylvania German chest
Photo credit: The Reading Public Museum and Art Gallery, from *The Pennsylvania Germans,* edited by Beatrice B. Garvan and Charles F. Hummel (Philadelphia: Philadelphia Museum of Art, 1982), p. 30

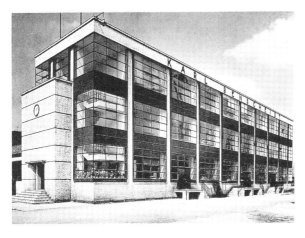

8
Fagus Shoe Works, 1910
Photo credit: Lucia Moholy, from *Modern Architecture* by Vincent Scully, Jr. (New York: George Braziller, 1961), p. 73.

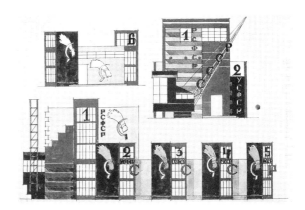

9
Facade, Constructivist period
Ilia Golosov, competition project for the USSR Pavilion for the 1925 Exposition des Arts Décoratifs, Paris; from *Architectural Drawings of the Russian Avant-Garde* (New York: Museum of Modern Art, 1990), p. 77

10
Strip, Las Vegas, 1970
Photo credit: Venturi, Scott Brown and
Associates

11
View, Tokyo
Photo credit: Masayuki Hayashi, "Neons
of Shibuya," from *The Hybrid Culture* by
Mitsukuni Yoshida (Hiroshima: Mazda,
1984), p. 128

12
View, small town, USA

13
Facade, Philadelphia

14
Sketch, Robert Venturi, 1970

15
Competition for FDR Memorial Park,
section-perspective, Washington, D.C.,
1960

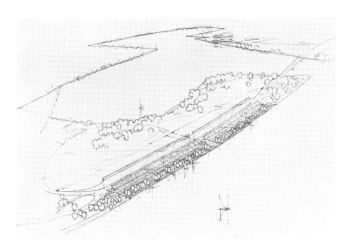

16
Competition for FDR Memorial Park, perspective, Washington, D.C., 1960

17
Headquarters building, North Penn Visiting Nurses Association, Ambler, Pennsylvania, 1961
Photo credit: George Pohl

18
Guild House, Friends Housing for the Elderly, in association with Cope and Lippin-
cott, Philadelphia, 1965
Photo credit: Skomark Associates

19
Renovation of restaurant in West Philadelphia, exterior, Venturi & Short, Philadelphia, 1961
Photo credit: Lawrence S. Williams, Inc.

22

20
Renovation of restaurant in West Philadelphia, interior, Venturi & Short, Philadelphia, 1961
Photo credit: Lawrence S. Williams, Inc.

21
Residence in Chestnut Hill (mother's
house), Chestnut Hill, Pennsylvania, 1962
Photo credit: Rollin R. La France

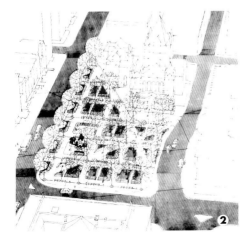

22
Competition for Copley Square, Boston,
1966

23

23
Fire Station No. 4, Columbus, Indiana,
1968
Photo credit: Venturi, Scott Brown and
Associates

24
Dixwell Fire Station, New Haven, Con-
necticut, 1974
Photo credit: Venturi, Scott Brown and
Associates

25
Lieb House, Loveladies, New Jersey, 1978
Photo credit: Stephen Hill

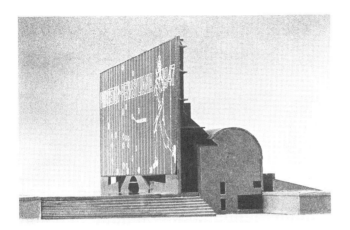

26
Competition for National College Football
Hall of Fame, New Brunswick, New Jer-
sey, 1967
Photo credit: George Pohl

27
Competition for National College Football
Hall of Fame, interior, New Brunswick,
New Jersey, 1967

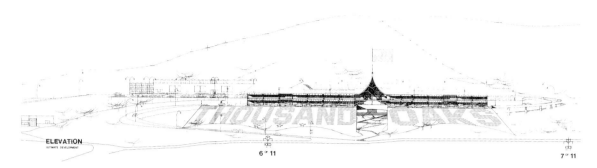

28

Competition for Thousand Oaks Civic
Center, Thousand Oaks, California, 1969

29

Project for Bicentennial, master plan for
proposed International Exposition, section,
Philadelphia, 1972

30

Franklin Court, Independence National
Historic Park, Philadelphia, 1976
Photo credit: Mark Cohn

31
City edges study, Philadelphia, 1973
Photo credit: Venturi, Scott Brown and
Associates

33
"200 Years of American Sculpture" exhibi-
tion, Whitney Museum of American Art,
New York, 1975
Photo credit: Venturi, Scott Brown and
Associates

32
Addition to Allen Memorial Art Museum,
detail, Oberlin College, Oberlin, Ohio,
1973
Photo credit: Tom Bernard

34
Basco showroom, Philadelphia, 1976
Photo credit: Tom Bernard

35
"Signs of Life: Symbols in the American
City" exhibition, Renwick Gallery, Smith-
sonian Institution, Washington, D.C., 1976
Photo credit: Tom Bernard

36
Project for Charlotte Science Museum, preliminary design, Charlotte, North Caro-
lina, 1977

37
Western Plaza, Pennsylvania Avenue, Wash-
ington, D.C., 1977
Photo credit: Tom Bernard

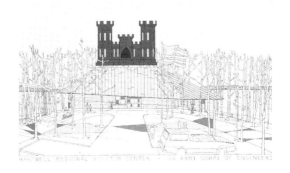

38
Competition for a Regional Visitors Cen-
ter for the U.S. Army Corps of Engineers,
Hartwell Lake, Georgia, 1978

39
Best Products Catalog Showroom, Oxford
Valley Mall, Langhorne, Pennsylvania,
1978
Photo credit: Venturi, Scott Brown and
Associates

40
Corporate Headquarters Office Building,
Institute for Scientific Information, Univer-
sity City Science Center, Philadelphia,
1978
Photo credit: Tom Bernard

41
Furniture designs for Knoll International,
Chippendale style, 1979
Photo credit: Matt Wargo

42
Gordon Wu Hall, Butler College,
Princeton University, Princeton, New Jersey, 1980
Photo credit: Tom Bernard

43
Hennepin Avenue transit and entertainment planning study, Minneapolis, 1981

VIEW OF HENNEPIN AVENUE ENTERTAINMENT CENTRUM LOOKING NORTH

44
"High Styles: 20th Century American Design" exhibition, Whitney Museum of American Art, New York, 1985
Photo credit: Matt Wargo

45
Project for symbolic element for Times
Square, New York, 1984

46
The Seattle Art Museum, Seattle, 1990
Photo credit: Matt Wargo

47
The Clinical Research Building, School of
Medicine, University of Pennsylvania, Phil-
adelphia, 1985
Photo credit: Matt Wargo

48
The Sainsbury Wing of the National Gallery, London, 1991
Photo credit: Matt Wargo

49
Renovation and addition to La Jolla Museum of Contemporary Art, rear elevation, La Jolla, California, 1990

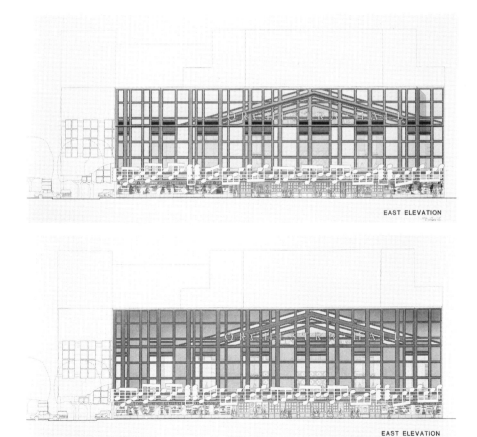

EAST ELEVATION

EAST ELEVATION

50
The Philadelphia Orchestra Hall project, revised day and night elevations, Philadelphia, 1987

51
Design competition for United States Pavilion, Expo '92, model section, Seville, Spain, 1989
Photo credit: Matt Wargo

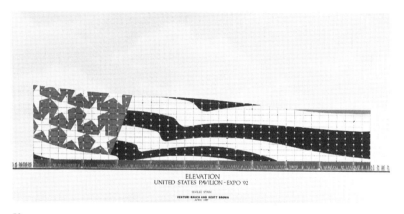

ELEVATION
UNITED STATES PAVILION-EXPO 92
SEVILLE SPAIN
VENTURI RAUCH AND SCOTT BROWN

52
Design competition for United States Pavilion, Expo '92, Seville, Spain, 1989

53
The Children's Museum of Houston, in association with Jackson & Ryan Architects, Houston, 1989
Photo credit: Matt Wargo

54
Monument to Christopher Columbus,
Philadelphia, 1992
Photo credit: Matt Wargo

55
Competition for an addition to the National Museum of Scotland, Edinburgh,
1991

56
Winning competition design for the Whitehall Ferry Terminal, New York, 1992
Photo credit: Matt Wargo

57
Winning competition design for the Whitehall Ferry Terminal, interior, New York,
1992
Photo credit: Panoptic Imaging

58
Winning competition design for the extension of the Stedelijk Museum, Amsterdam,
1992

59
Reedy Creek Improvement District Emer-
gency Services Headquarters (Fire House),
Walt Disney World, Orlando, Florida,
1993
Photo credit: Matt Wargo

60
Restoration and renovation of Memorial
Hall, Harvard University, interior, Cam-
bridge, Massachusetts, 1993

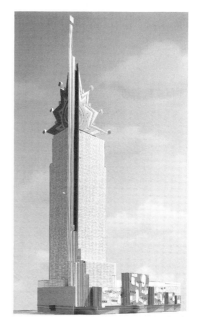

61
Project for Site 7, 42nd Street Redevelop-
ment Project, study model, 1994
Photo credit: Matt Wargo

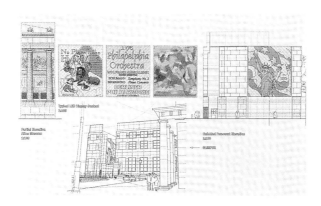

62
Competition entry for the U.S. Embassy at
the Brandenburg Gate (Pariser Platz), front
elevation and various elevations of the
LED board in entrance court, Berlin, 1995

63
Competition entry for the U.S. Embassy at the Brandenburg Gate (Pariser Platz), the LED board in entrance court from the Pariser Platz, Berlin, 1995

64
Competition entry for the U.S. Embassy at the Brandenburg Gate (Pariser Platz), view from the entrance court, Berlin, 1995

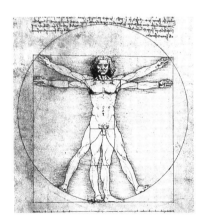

65
Renaissance concept of man with possible Mannerist and Decon reinterpretations.

GROWING UP

HOMAGE TO VINCENT SCULLY AND HIS *SHINGLE STYLE,* WITH REMINISCENCES AND SOME OUTCOMES

Written 1987.

Henry-Russell Hitchcock wrote of the art historian's particular sensibility—that of knowing what to write about and when. He showed how the art historian's timely focus, scholarly and critical, could reveal significant directions for architects to follow or learn from. And by seeing old things in new ways, by adjusting historical perspectives, the art historian whose perceptions become significantly relevant and incisive can also invent a style. Vincent Scully's perception of the Shingle Style in the early fifties became such an achievement.

It is important that "style" here is historical and created by historians and critics, not contemporary and proclaimed by practitioners. It does not concern the naming and promotion of contemporary styles by architects that has been typical in our so-called Postmodernist era: the Abbot Suger's Île de France masons weren't Gothic in the thirteenth century, and Bernini didn't know he was Baroque; the highly proclamatory Futurists in our century are an exception. And this historian's style should not define rigid or simplistic systems that discourage richness and diversity; rather it should fascinate and illuminate and direct current sensibilities toward a coherence that may become a style someday. Meanwhile, architects focus on their work, absorbing what they can from their world, including new perspectives on history but eschewing ideology.

Vincent Scully's depiction of the Shingle Style was, for me, a thrilling and significant revelation, both focusing and freeing my vision. I first read the book in Rome while a Fellow at the American Academy in the mid-fifties. As a temporary expatriate, reveling in the Baroque splendors of the city beyond my studio windows and steeping myself in the ambience of all Italy beyond the horizon, I was at the same time peculiarly sensible to visions of my own land—visualizing old things in new ways and from different angles. The American in Europe, especially the young artist, finding an American identity through absorbing a European heritage can be a most pompous cliche, but here I think it fits.

Through Vince's eyes and words and in the context of Rome, those gloomy old houses in shabby old suburbs could suddenly represent America's first significant contribution to the history of architecture—through their originality and potential. Among the many things revealed in this now-coherent group of houses were their mannerist qualities. These corresponded to those of the Mannerist architecture I was getting to know in Italy. Mannerism as a tendency and a style in Renaissance Italy and Shingle Style America illuminated my perceptions about complexity and contradiction in architecture, as I was later to call it. After my return from Rome my first commission was a shingled beach house. It was never built, but its design sent me on my architectural way—as well as others on their way whose mannered rather than mannerist versions of the Shingle Style have tended to plague the Hamptons ever since.

Many of the shingled houses from our office have in common a contradiction in their design characteristic of historical Shingle Style houses, especially the late examples by H. H. Richardson (which are sometimes of masonry, *if* in the Shingle Style) and the early work of Bruce Price at Tuxedo Park: they are picturesque and holistic at once. Their plans are quite regular in their exterior outlines but their elevations are quite irregular in their overall silhouettes. Their asymmetrically placed towers, wings, and dormers seem to be emergent—gestural or suggestive—rather than substantive or complete. In this way the houses embody a Romantic-picturesque aesthetic and accommodate interior functional complexities while their almost melting forms, reinforced by low-relief details, create a diversity of parts that are separately perceived but are becoming one: here is perhaps picturesqueness abstracted.

DONALD DREW EGBERT—A TRIBUTE

Originally published as a foreword to Egbert's *The Beaux-Arts Tradition in French Architecture,* edited by David Van Zanten (Princeton: Princeton University Press, 1980).

I took Donald Drew Egbert's course on the History of Modern Architecture four times. I sat in on it as a freshman, was the slide projectionist as a sophomore, took it for credit as a junior, and taught in it as a graduate student teaching assistant. Other architecture students at Princeton over several decades were also drawn to it, became devotees, and were influenced by it. What attracted us was not a dramatic style or arresting pronouncements— Egbert virtually read his lectures from his very complete notes while sitting down—but his lack of jargon, the clarity and elegance of his plain talk, and the balance and common sense of his approach. We were attracted also by the rich range yet meticulous order of his material, by his conviction, but also by his openness. We were thrilled by the discoveries he led us to, not to mention the lessons we learned in architectural composition that we directly applied to our work in the drafting room.

As a historian of Modern architecture, Egbert saw it as a part of the complex of nineteenth- and twentieth-century civilization, and his eyes were open to realities of that time that more doctrinaire historians, bent on proving points, couldn't see. For Egbert the influence of the Ecole des Beaux-Arts, for instance, was an important part of the complicated architectural history of the nineteenth and twentieth centuries. On the other hand for Sigfried Giedion, famous Harvard historian of the time, the Beaux-Arts was a "transitory fact." Although history was not bunk for Giedion—as it was for most Moderns from the forties through the sixties—it was subject to simplified and personal interpretation that allowed as "constituent facts"—again Giedion's phrase—some of the historical antecedents of Modern architecture (for example, some Baroque architecture and certain early industrial forms) but excluded, as transitory facts, other antecedents, the main ones being the architecture of the Ecole des Beaux-Arts. (Henri Labrouste Giedion acknowledges mostly for his cast iron.) Egbert's history of Modern architecture was inclusive—a complex evolution rather than a dramatic revolution, made up of social and symbolic as well as formal and technological imperatives.

Never doctrinaire, he was seldom in the mainstream. He focused in the forties on Beaux-Arts architecture when Giedion's spatial-technological, Bauhaus-oriented view predominated in art history. His *Social Radicalism and the Arts* (Alfred A. Knopf, 1970) countered another important trend in Modern architectural history, that pressed by Henry-Russell Hitchcock and Philip Johnson, whose influential introduction of the International Style had deemphasized the radical social content of the Modern movement and set the stage for the dominance of formalism in Modern architecture in America. Egbert studied history to search for truth, never to prove points. How unusual this is was borne out for me when I learned from a European friend that the fame of *Social Radicalism and the Arts* among Europeans is matched by their surprise that its author was not a Marxist.

Another irony of Egbert's position is that the Museum of Modern Art later acknowledged the significance of the Ecole des Beaux-Arts in the history of modern architecture. In the takeover the original protagonist, whose unpopular stand was ignored for decades by the Modern architectural establishment, was not recognized, although two of the three historians who assisted in the exhibition were David Van Zanten and Neil Levine, former students of Egbert at Princeton.

Egbert did not prescribe ideology: he opened up directions—directions not dreamt of in my philosophy, where I could perceive Modern architecture not as an end but as the current and latest part within an evolution. We students were truly students within a liberal process of education, not seminarians being given "the word." Architecture for us would evolve beyond our time and by implication through our own creativity. And there is something Egbert's teaching did *not* imply—that architecture as an academic discipline is superior to architecture as a professional discipline, an attitude prevalent today—despite his own focus on scholarship. And this accommodation could make of us knowing workers whose talents were enriched by knowledge.

I now realize Egbert became my mentor during my postgraduate years at Princeton and the early years of my practice—whom I often visited in his McCormick Hall office crammed with books—whom I could expect understanding and support from. During those visits he might ask profoundly difficult questions about architecture—some that would haunt me and that I might find answers to only years later—so that his influence on me has been active all my life.

As a Princeton graduate who had majored in architecture as an undergraduate, Egbert wrote knowingly and lovingly of his university campus and its ethos, and this kind of perception that acknowledges the significance of the familiar made us students aware of the everyday and not necessarily the ideal as a stimulus for art.

Egbert's openness had a later, gratifying effect on me. I have learned almost always to expect, when I meet an author whose works have influenced me or a former teacher who has meant much to me, that he will be unable to accept the direction my work has taken and will not see himself in it. This was never the case with Egbert, and I value very much a letter he wrote me soon before he died as a former teacher in appreciation of a work of mine.

He also wrote in that letter: "Of course the difference between a historian and an artist is that the historian has to try to be objective (though he never can succeed completely), whereas the good artist-architect has to be a man of utter conviction." Donald Egbert combined these traits.

NOTES FOR A LECTURE CELEBRATING THE CENTENNIAL OF THE AMERICAN ACADEMY IN ROME DELIVERED IN CHICAGO

Written 1993.

I am delighted to be here even though I am obliged to lecture—I am an architect first, a lecturer thirty-first. In between, I am, as a practicing architect—during the process of getting the job, doing the job, and administering the construction—a lawyer, business administrator, psychiatrist, salesman, socialite, and world traveler/victim of vagabondage. I must be also a referee among consultants, each of whom wants to make his part perfect at the cost of the whole, and a supplicant to bureaucrats representing clients or agencies, each of whom focuses on enhancing his image, to historical commissions who fear making history in their time, to design review boards who promote deadening urbanity (while expounding my partner's and my ideas of some decades ago), to goody-goody community boards with too much time on their hands, and to contractors who measure their success not by the quality of their skills but the number of their claims. At the same time, like any artist, the architect must engage in the details that God is in and that good design entails.

My talk might be rambling, but I intend it to be understandable, which is unusual for architects today who define success as talkers in terms of their obliqueness. Also I intend to ramble not too long!

But more specifically I am happy to be here in this building—a Prairie School house containing Barcelona chairs—this institution, the Graham Foundation, which supported the publication of my book *Complexity and Contradiction in Architecture* when I was outrageous, and this city, Chicago, which might be the architectural Rome of our continent. And I am happy and grateful to participate in this occasion: the Academy is the Academy.

I shall talk about connections within this century which is the focus of this centennial celebration of the American Academy in Rome—connections as I see them that involve Rome, the American Academy, Americans in Rome, Classicism in architecture, and Modernism in architecture.

These categories will be intermingled—I hope not mixed up.

The subject sounds grandiose but I think I can make it simple yet not simpleminded.

And I speak, of course, not as a historian or scholar, but, as I've said, as an architect—even though I shall show no slides. What I say will involve some reminiscing and a great deal of subjectivity, with maybe a touch of egotism.

I shall mention that this summer, on August 8, I hope to have a luncheon party in Rome to celebrate the forty-fifth anniversary of my first day in Rome—when I learned the city was really colored orange—and corresponding to my similar celebration on the same day in '88 on the fortieth anniversary—because that experience was so significant for me as an architect.

And soon after that day in '48 I resolved to become a Fellow of the American Academy in Rome—which I did several years later, after applying three times incidentally—by the third try my friends said "Can't you take a hint?," "Have you no pride?" It was the most wonderful Mary Williams, then Secretary of the Academy in New York, who kept encouraging me.

————

First, ROME:

Rome as the eternal city—but, significantly, eternal in terms of its relevance, not in terms of its consistency.

In terms of inconsistent relevance—its relevance continually changing every generation, every era, every century.

Rome for the first generation of American architectural academicians 100 years ago meant something different, of course, from what it means now and what it meant between then and now.

And we must acknowledge the richness of Rome's meaning as well as the variety, or its meanings over time—not the consistency or the purity of its lessons but the richness of them: in Rome, within the context of time, it is richness that precludes purity.

In the early days of the Academy it is obvious that the Fellows in Architecture focused on Classical Roman architecture with dashes of Renaissance and appreciated it for its literal relevance—the relevance of Classical architecture in terms of its order and vocabulary involving form and symbol—for the relevance of these elements representing ideals appropriate for an America finding itself when it was young and confident—a very different America from that of today.

Here was Classical Rome as the way to achieve unity and civic dimension in the architecture of its fast-growing cities—to be manifest in the City Beautiful.

Here is Classicism as a vehicle for universal order—especially relevant for Daniel Burnham, a founder of the Academy—exemplifying his ideals in general and his work for Chicago in particular and at the Columbian Exposition.

This architectural ideal is manifest in the work of John Russell Pope, the early American Academician in Rome whose interpretation of Classicism became quite literally correct.

And there was Philip Schutze, a later Academician, whose use of a Classical vocabulary was also quite literal but more Romantic in its eclectic range which included Baroque Classicism—specifically Borrominian—in his exquisite work in Atlanta in the twenties and thirties.

———

Now for some reminiscing concerning my time at the American Academy in the richly but inconsistently eternal city:

My time there represented perhaps another major phase within the century when we absorbed not the formal vocabulary or the symbolic dimension of historical Roman architecture—heaven forbid—in those days of confident, progressive, explicitly innovative Modernism. The relevance of Roman architecture for us then involved its spatial dimensions—Space with a capital S—that was *the* word; you would not be caught dead referring to style—and symbolism was a word that had been forgotten in architecture.

We looked at two things:

First, civic Space—especially as manifest in piazzas—the space between buildings, as we called it: research into this kind of urbanism was fun as it could involve legitimately sitting in outdoor cafes in piazzas looking at leisure at architecture—and people.

Second, Baroque architecture—but not in terms of its form or symbol—not as style—but in terms of its complex and dynamic Space within its urban context: Sigfried Giedion oriented us architects toward this limited slice of history it was OK to acknowledge in this limited way.

More recently some architects have returned via so-called Postmodernism to an eclectic-symbolic approach paralleling that of earlier decades—involving, very often, quite literal adaptations of stylistic form.

And of course there may recently have been another form of Roman architectural relevance whose esotericism only the Neo-Modernists—or Deconstructivists—could comprehend.

This leads perhaps to the subject of variety and richness in Classicism—or should we say, in Classicisms. There is, of course, that Classicism that is essentially UNIVERSAL—for all times, for all places. The three Classical orders are consistently relevant in ancient Roman architecture and in the Renaissance adaptation of Roman Classicism as a universal ideal.

Then you say there is Classical order that is broken—that is there, so to speak, to be broken—that admits contradiction—that is MANNERIST. But broken by circumstance—not for the picturesque or arty reasons that are characteristic today of Decon, for instance, but by circumstance—a manifestation of order that acknowledges the ultimate complexity and contradiction in experience. Mannerism that pragmatically acknowledges the limitations of universal order in terms of form and symbol—that acknowledges urban context and promotes aesthetic tension—and in the end exalts the element of dissonance.

Then there is Classical order that is complex—that promotes in its order rich complexity over pure simplicity—BAROQUE Classicism that promotes not only spatial-formal complexity but also complexities ornamental and symbolic.

We should recognize another kind of relevance of Rome at a moment in the mid-twentieth century when Modernism as a movement was dominant; this embraces the period when I was there in the mid-fifties.

Conventionally Rome in that era was considered irrelevant in terms of its historical architecture—certainly the ancient Classical vocabulary of Roman architecture was irrelevant—Classical orders were out with a vengeance—down with history in general and Classicism in particular—you might be a little more historically at home with structuralist Gothic up north or Zen gardens in the East.

But, as manifest in the International Style—a term rejected by practitioners but really very apt—Modernism promoted an ideal universality—ironically no different from that of Roman and Renaissance Classicism—in the universal application of *its* order—not based on historical reference or ornamental appliqué, of course, but on its industrial vocabulary relevant universally all over—with essentially no reference to context—and with quite a lot in common in its minimalist-purist dimension with that of pure Roman Classicism.

Thus there was a symbolism within the classic Modernist order exemplified in the International Style—that based on the imagery of the indigenous American factory rather than that of the Mediterranean Roman temple— that existed symbolically but was unacknowledged. Let us not forget Le Corbusier's infatuation with the forms of Midwestern grain elevators. And then there was his Ville Radieuse which was universally for anywhere— Paris or Chandigarh. And there's Mies van der Rohe's minimalist-purist order which was appropriate for a Midwestern institute, a monumental sky-scraper, a Berlin museum, and a house on the bank of a river.

What a sad irony: Rome and the American Academy and the International Style could have been in tune except for the intrusion of the anti-historicist Modernist ideology—an anti-historicism that still exists—with an ironical vengeance—in our era of askew structural expressionism based on the forms of old-time industrial engineering and constructivist vocabularies that by our time are truly historical.

———

Now to return specifically to some ideas about the Academy:

We are aware of its significance as a place for groups of artists and scholars to live and work together—as a community to communicate within.

And as a place for introspection—during an interlude in your life when you can prepare for future action in a period of inaction, when your sensibilities and intuitions can be nurtured.

But also, less acknowledged: there is the Academy as a place where artists— architects—can be expatriates for a while.

Expatriates—perhaps in the traditional manner of American literary artists, of writers like Henry James, Ernest Hemingway, and James Baldwin who could see their own world from new perspectives—perceive their origins with new eyes—see where they have come from and assess where they can go to.

Where they could define themselves uniquely as Americans while following Ralph Waldo Emerson's quest for individualism and American essence. Perhaps that's how Denise Scott Brown and I would be able to go from Rome to Las Vegas.

And this "academian" way can involve irony as you perceive, via perspective, new ways within the aura of old ways.

But hereby you learn not so much *from* Rome, as *by means of* Rome.

For me, I went there looking for SPACE—among forms and in piazzas—but I fell in love with Borromini, became enamored of Michelangelo and discovered Mannerism and, later, symbolism.

And I loved reading Americana in the setting of Rome—Vincent Scully's *Shingle Style* and Charles Moore's biography of Charles Follen McKim, for instance, and recalling daily the photograph in that book of McKim's mother from Lancaster, PA, dressed in Quaker (or Mennonite) garb as I would pass the Latin inscription on the rosy marble plaque dedicated to Carlus Follen McKim in the Academy vestibule in papal Rome.

It was in my last few weeks at the Academy that I realized Mannerism was what turned me on—and made Michelangelo relevant—relevant for an American architect of my time.

And out of that intuition several years later evolved *Complexity and Contradiction in Architecture*—where my ideas had to be expressed in words rather than in work because of the radicalism of those ideas in their time—hard as that is to believe in our time. I could not get big commissions nor feel at home for long in an establishment firm and so I had to write rather than do.

Also in Rome, as I immersed myself in Medieval and Baroque city planning, I perceived, via perspective and comparison, the genius of the American gridiron plan. It became no longer ordinary but special—as the democratic or egalitarian configuration of streets was explicitly devoid of hierarchy and where buildings derived significance not from where they were, not from their relative positions, but from their inherent character: the mayor's house could theoretically sit across from a deli. There was no Ducal Palace terminating an axial boulevard—rather, there was space at the end of the streets, infinite space leading toward the frontier, eternally open to opportunity, as Vincent Scully has put it.

Next I was taken to Las Vegas in 1966 by Denise Scott Brown—prepared a little by Tom Wolfe and a lot by Baroque Rome. Out of that trip came our studio at Yale and then our book *Learning from Las Vegas*.

I don't celebrate my first day in Las Vegas but that city turned us on—a kind of love-hate relationship developed where we were appalled and fascinated by validity and vitality.

The main thing is we learned about symbolism within this despised city of urban sprawl—symbolism to be perceived from the moving automobile and within the scale of space the automobile had created—a symbolism manifest in commercial signs whose hype quality acknowledged late twentieth-century sensibility as it was read from a distance at the speed of a car.

So we went from Rome to Las Vegas, as we then said, and from Las Vegas to Rome—when we returned to that other homeland in our Western culture and could see Rome with new eyes and from a reverse perspective this time—take in a greater range of its dimensions; that is, we could acknowledge its symbolism—and the iconography and scenography which are essential to its architecture. So there was now for us in Rome space *and* symbolism.

———

And finally, to return to Rome:

It is the home of Classicisms in the plural. It is the Rome of evolving juxtapositions—of eternal incompleteness. It is Rome whose essence lies not in some historic sense of a whole that goody-goody historical preservationists promote for American cities: thank God old buildings sometimes could be demolished in the past to build new buildings that we revere today!

But there are not only the layers of Classicisms—there is Early Christian, Medieval, Romantic-eclectic-19th-century, 20th-century-Fascist, International Style-Rationalist-Modern within its architectural evolutions.

It is a Rome acknowledging evolutions of many kinds and juxtaposing contexts of many kinds, a Rome that is never complete, a Rome that I love that is ultimately significant for our time.

For instance, I am currently enjoying the Early Christian apse of Santa Prudenziana, whose iconographic mosaic I read as the electronic Jumbotron of that day and which exemplifies architecture as sign—and I think thereby illuminates for us a valid architectural aesthetic and insinuates a valid architectural technology for our time. Viva electronic technology in the service of integral ornament and dynamic iconography for a generic architecture of surface!

But also we can compare the multiple Classicisms of our old Rome with the multiple cultures of our new time—involving appropriately and with relevance juxtapositions of old cultures in new contexts and new cultures in new contexts. Here is Rome as the multicultural phenomenon par excellence!

And this leads to my favorite city of now: Tokyo. Here today the vivid juxtapositions of evolving cultures parallel those of evolved Classicisms—where the multicultural urban juxtapositions of Rome are sequential, they are in Tokyo simultaneous!

Ours can be not a pure environment, but a rich environment, embracing the extraordinary *and* the ordinary—it is not to be the universal environment promoting unity *über alles* but, if you will, a multiple environment where *mess is more*.

From Rome to Las Vegas to Tokyo—but eternally back to Rome.

So the eternal city is eternal by means of its eternal relevance—its constant *and* dynamic relevance—ever changing—as each generation of artists perceives and learns from the variety and richness of this city in different ways. There's no place like Rome.

————

Alas, the patina of Rome as vivid orange, almost Canaletto in its sublime aura, and the immaculate condition and civic pride characteristic of the city of the late forties and mid-fifties exist no more—the former the victim of decades of exhaust fumes absorbed by the surfaces of stucco and travertine, and the latter the result of social and physical deterioration now universal in the cities of the Western world. So I can't resist saying to young people today: you should have known Rome when I was young—while acknowledging when that was said to me when I was young my reaction under my breath was: shut up you old fart, Rome is perfectly good enough for me as it is.

Significant addendum: but perhaps I must come to terms with this generation's Rome and acknowledge its late-twentieth-century manifestations as the aura of patina is replaced by the aesthetic of grunge—as the blackish smudge unites poetically with the blackish attire and the punk chic of today's youth in the foreground.

ADORABLE DISCOVERIES WHEN I WAS A SEMI-NAIVE FELLOW AT THE AMERICAN ACADEMY IN ROME THAT I NEVER FORGET

Written 1994.

Reading Vince Scully's *Shingle Style* in my studio above Rome where I learn about the essence of architectural America from the perspective of Rome—when the ordinary becomes extraordinary.

Discordant juxtapositions of the layered facades of arcades of Armando Brasini's EUR Forestry Building (now demolished) which significantly revealed Mannerism to me.

Sublime tension of scale juxtapositions via the pilaster-capital as big as the adjacent window atop the apse of St. Peter's.

Sublime aura in the narrow streets of Rome deriving from, then, orange facades creating "the golden air of Rome" of Henry James.

Sublime complexity and ambiguity and richness within generic spatial systems articulated via sublime details in Borromini—especially in the interior of the chapel of I Tre Magi.

Buildings as inflection in the Piazza S. Ignazio!

The Sforza Chapel in S. Maria Maggiore where the implied whole extends beyond the immediate whole!

And early Christian apses whose figurative mosaic surfaces convert us space-nuts to iconography.

Accommodating pedestrian piazzas that illuminate via contrast the validity of vehicular commercial strips, promoting urban iconography over urban space.

ARMANDO BRASINI REVISITED

Written 1993.

My fascination with the church of Il Cuore Immacolato di Maria Santissima in the Parioli section of Rome by Armando Brasini began in the mid-fifties and I have continued to learn from this building as my sensibilities have evolved since then. It is easy to see how this fascination is a bit strange now, but it is hard to comprehend how very strange it was almost forty years ago. Believe me, you didn't like architecture of the Fascist period, especially that alluding to historical forms, in that era of Modernism in its most strident phase—and then a church was a not significant building type. But that building haunted me as did other work of Brasini, whom I had the pleasure of meeting in 1956 in his studio and home in Rome—itself a fascinating and instructive fragment of architecture at the foot of the Ponte Milvio. And I have realized since that time how glad I am I have resisted conforming to swings of taste and accommodated to liking things via intuition rather than ideology.

But one's fascination for Brasini is tempered as you recall his grandiose urban schemes for the center of Rome in the thirties where the Campo Marzio, for instance, was to be Parisified via vast demolition of existing architectural fabric for the creation of axial boulevards that were to terminate at buildings originally designed for the piazzas they are in. And I well recall my horror while doing research for my master's thesis in the late forties at discovering Brasini's scheme for changing the context of the Trevi Fountain by means of demolition from that of an enclosed Roman piazza to that of a Parisian axial termination where the Roman fountain was to become a Fontaine

St.-Michel. Thank goodness Benito Mussolini and Armando Brasini did not prevail in their potential roles as the Napoleon III and Baron Haussmann of Fascist Rome!

In *Complexity and Contradiction in Architecture,* written in the early sixties, I referred to the spatial layerings characteristic of the plan of this church of the thirties which was aesthetically fortunate, in my opinion, never to be completed. Since then I have enjoyed and been enlightened by other qualities of this significant building.

First of all, my favorite view of this church is from the front and from across the Piazza Euclide while sipping an espresso in a cafe under an arcade as gas pumps protrude in the immediate foreground as it holds its own behind intervening Roman traffic—as you learn from it and enjoy it. What you see is a harmonious *and* dissonant architectural symphony of complexly layered elements—formal and symbolic, masterfully defined by shade and shadow, combining rhetoric and substance, Baroque fanfare in Palladian drag, and whose juxtapositions—or rather, collisions—of curves, rectangles, diagonals—as squat columns, gross piers, useless buttresses, eloquent walls and voids, domeless drum, protruding *and* receding segmented pediment—must in the end compose in the Fascist era a glorious final gesture of what can be considered Baroque survival.

The plan—or plans—combine layers and juxtapositions inside that at once compose a central-circular plan and a Greek cross plan, and then there is a beautifully tense suggestion of a longitudinal nave via an additional bay toward the east and toward the west that creates eloquent ambiguity as the whole of the interior barely hangs together. A sense of the whole derives in the end mostly from four outer zones in plan that articulate the almost-circular central plan. But then there are the four chapels attached to the outside of these fragmental curves that are virtually pure circles in plan with no inflection toward the whole! And then there is in plan the layered front facade cum pedimented porch whose curve works to contain the complex overall plan in front and reinforce the perception of the whole; this element acknowledges also the curving configuration of the street in this otherwise urbanistically freestanding central-form church.

The section of this building is equally complex in its compositions of vaults reflecting various parts of the plan; a particularly surprising form of vault occurs in the final eastern bay of the "nave" which creates its span in a very shallow manner.

Thank God—or Maria Santissima—the church, as I've said, was never finished: the dome is missing and this circumstance diminishes the historical literalism of the architecture and establishes the building, in my opinion, as a grand and fortuitous fragment—as an unfinished symphony. And it makes the rhetoric of the now functionless buttresses more poignant and eloquent in their effect.

The facade I have already described in terms of its rich complexity whose each part works to promote the perception of the whole through its inflection as form or its position relative to other parts.

A last word concerning the ironical use of the squat Classical proportions of a Palladian vocabulary in the creation of elegant Baroque fanfare. In the end this spare, indeed rather puritanical imagery of the parts makes more impactful the complexly Baroque composition of the whole—and the resultant tension is eloquent.

In the very end here is fanfare with substance.

FURNESS AND TASTE

Originally published as the introduction to *Frank Furness: The Complete Works,* by George Thomas, Michael J. Lewis, and Jeffrey A. Cohen (New York: Princeton Architectural Press, 1991).

I come to Furness as an architect and I write as a rather old architect. I signify the latter because most younger critics cannot comprehend how the work of Furness, as I shall describe, was hated before their time. (I refer to the period *after* his thriving practice when he *was* appreciated by lots of people, as indicated by all the work he got in his heyday.) When I was young you hated Victorian architecture—especially the particularly perversely distorted forms and their gross juxtapositions in the work of *this* Victorian—and then his work was sometimes banal rather than repulsive when his budget was low. Even Lou Kahn once told me the interior stair in the Pennsylvania Academy of the Fine Arts descended too closely to the main entrance—it was to him awkwardly big for the space it occupied in the lobby rather than grandly tense. As a polite youth of my time I did not admit my disagreement with him.

But I can remember loving to hate those squat columns as I was driven as a boy by my father past the Provident Life and Trust Company on Chestnut Street in the thirties; and yet in the forties loving the distraction of those looming, almost menacing hammer beam trusses during sermons as I sometimes attended services in the First Unitarian Church with my parents; and then I well remember the serious debate in one of my first faculty meetings at the School of Fine Arts at Penn as late as the early sixties on the subject of should the School take a stand concerning the contemplated demolition of the Furness Library on that campus. My then future wife, Denise Scott Brown, was eloquently and courageously for saving the building; I sat there too shy to say I agreed.

All this to a great extent involves the matter of taste—your sensibility concerning what seems perceptually right—or rather, the matter of cycles of taste. You usually hate what your father loved and like what your grandfather liked, as Donald Drew Egbert pointed out, but believe me, it was only we extreme sophisticates who could take Frank Furness even as late as the mid-sixties. Thank the Lord our great Furness Library did not feel the wrecker's ball as practically all the other major work of Furness did in the various goody-goody periods of architecture that succeeded his.

But I am leading up to something else that might relate to my limitations as an older person who is subject, despite his critical hypersophistication, if I may put it that way quasi-sarcastically, to an ingrained prejudice due to taste. With me concerning Furness it is not hate-love; it is absolute, unrestrained adoration and respect for his work; it elates me by its quality, spirit, diversity, wit, tragic dimension—but my love is a little perverse—I can't help feeling it a touch kinky, my love. And the impressive critiques I now read in *Frank Furness: The Complete Works* on this subject don't contain a touch of this quality in their admiration, which can be described as squeaky clean—as utterly wholesome affairs.

But my admiration *is* OK—if I look at Furness as an American-Emersonian,[1] individualist-reformist, naturalist-artist, as one who follows at the same time the sturdy, continental, functionalist Gothicism of Viollet-le-Duc in France and the exuberant Italianate Gothicism of Ruskin in Britain. But also as a mannerist. He is a mannerist as the anguished artist described in these essays evolving beyond the America of Manifest Destiny and abolitionist idealism and toward the postwar realities of dynamic economic growth and unlimited political corruption. To me his mannerist tensions are essential. They make my kind of love respectable, out of the closet, and valid. Furness does not use totally original forms, vocabularies, ornament, or organization of these forms; he uses columns, colonnets, brackets, squinches, arches—pointed and otherwise—quoins, rustication, exposed steel, and hammer beam trusses, etc. But of course he makes these conventional elements signally original and he composes them in crazy ways; his relative sizes and scales of elements and his juxtapositions are dissonant/ambiguous, complex and contradictory. From these qualities that can be called mannerist I have learned so much from Furness. Agreed he never heard of these terms or others also that you might employ—empirical juxtapositions like ugly *and* beautiful, lyrical *and* gross. But above all these forms are tense with a feeling of life and reality.

Anyhow, I think that's how I can love the work of Furness and respect it as much as that of any architect in the history of America, and why.

---

1. I am grateful to Whitney R. Browne for illuminating the influence of Ralph Waldo Emerson in the life and work of Frank Furness in his thesis "The Architecture of Frank Furness as a Manifestation of the Writing of Ralph Waldo Emerson," Trinity College, Hartford, CT, 1991.

FRANK LLOYD WRIGHT ESSAY FOR THE
PENNSYLVANIA ACADEMY OF THE FINE ARTS

Originally published in the Pennsylvania Academy of the Fine Arts *Calendar of Events,* January/February/March 1991.

May I indulge in a reminiscence describing my own attitudes toward Frank Lloyd Wright during my life and spanning as well the cycles of taste that occur over time and affect the reputations of even established artists.

One constant within these evolutions has been that Wright—since I first learned of him when I was 16—has been for me the greatest American architect. When I was young you had to take a stand: you were for Wright or you were for Mies. I was a Wright man, which was not a popular position when I worked in Saarinen's office in the early fifties, for instance. And I refer to Wright as the greatest American architect despite my adoration of other American architects, some of whom I have learned more from than from Wright, who have influenced me more in direct ways and who in my opinion are more relevant for now; among these I include Thomas Jefferson, Frank Furness, and Henry Hobson Richardson. Concerning the latter we must remember Vincent Scully's startling insight that Richardson's abstracted version of a Romanesque architecture, along with his domestic Shingle Style architecture, represents the first direction in American art that was essentially original in the context of Western culture and that had an influence in Britain rather than the other way around.

While on this subject of influences I have come to feel that Wright was less the original genius he promoted himself as in his numerous writings (especially his autobiography) who sprang spontaneously—and organically, of course—from his Midwestern roots—by implication via immaculate conception. We now can see, because historians have recently restudied Wright within a general context of the early Modern movement and a particular context within the Midwest, that other architects were producing buildings whose designs paralleled Wright's at the time—those in the Midwest in a style that to me seems derivative Richardsonian Romanesque sans arches. But if Wright was perhaps less original than he proclaimed himself—and originality is by no means the sole test of genius—he was by far the best of these practitioners, and he was certainly most significantly original in his articulation of interior flowing space in his Prairie Houses. In fact, here he was as supremely original as he himself maintained. But we must remember Mies van der Rohe who said "I'd rather be good than original," and it is ironical that Wright's claim to greatness might fall to a significant extent in an area different from that which he proclaimed.

In the end Wright's genius resides essentially in the quality of his work, the extent of its scope, the richness of its detail, and the depth of its concept. And his self-promoting blustering in midlife is poignant and forgivable as a manifestation of his misfortune at this time deriving from inevitable swings of taste and particularly from the importation of the International Style; but perhaps out of this anguish came sublime Fallingwater and his later fantastic but meaningful proto-megastructure (the first version) for Pittsburgh Point—whose original rendering I first saw in 1949 and handled as I worked on the exhibition of Wright's work for Gimbel's Department Store in Philadelphia and the Strozzi Palace in Florence, while I worked in the office of Oscar Stonorov.

As I mentioned, I first learned of Wright in '41. I came across H. R. Hitchcock's *In the Nature of Materials* as a 16-year-old working that summer at Ballinger and Company when the other office boy pointed it out while browsing in Wanamaker's Book Department during a lunch break. That was late in my life considering I had been interested in architecture as a child, but it shows how out Wright had become in those years. That treasured tome has since disappeared from my library but I got to know it by heart; it was sad for me later to hear Wright refer to H. R. Hitchcock as a man of "much knowledge and little understanding."

I heard this during the week in the spring of 1947 as I sat next to Wright at lunch when I was a senior at Princeton and Wright was at a conference attended by all the great architects of the Western world except Le Corbusier to celebrate the bicentennial year of the university. At an informal evening session during that week in the lounge of the Princeton Inn Wright also spoke informally as the senior architect present of the superiority of the culture of the East over that of the West by drawing two diagrams each connecting two points. The Eastern approach was demonstrated by his connecting one set of two points drawn one above the other on a large pad by an S-shaped line; it exemplified the indirect and subtle philosophical approach toward a goal characteristic of the East; he connected the other set of dots, also one above the other, by a vertical straight line exemplifying the inferior approach of the West—direct, efficient, and unambiguous. Everyone in the room was speechless except George Howe who sprang up saying: "But Frank, there is a third approach, the American way, which involves a juxtaposition of your two ways," as he drew on the same pad an *S* with a vertical line through it.

This story illustrates Wright's well-known fascination with Japan: he later told an architecture student friend of mine who was crossing the Atlantic to study in Paris and found himself on the same liner as Wright, "Young man, you are going in the wrong direction." (When I visited Taliesen a few years later I warned my companion not to mention my imminent trip to Rome as a Rome Fellow.) And Wright's interpretation—along with that of other Modernists—put me off Japan for many years. This is because he and they focused on a single aspect of historical Japanese architecture—fragments of temples, villas, and shrines in Kyoto—and denied thereby the complexity behind the simplicity and next to it. He and they were extolling this architecture by abrogating its context—including the juxtapositions of rich colors and profuse patterns of the kimonos originally hovering within the spaces and of the *objets* filling the markets beyond—and the symbolism, abstraction, and stylization which the surrounding gardens represent. I later came to realize I had been visualizing this Japanese architecture through their eyes as goody-goody in its effect, and for many years focused on, and traveled toward, the other East—by this I mean Europe—especially Italy and England to learn from.

In the end, as I have said, I admire Wright for the supreme quality of his work—but I have found his philosophy, his approach, irrelevant to our time, and it is for this reason that he has influenced me via the quality of his achievement more than through the content; in this sense he discourages me because, of course, it is hard to approach his quality in your own work. The aesthetic of Wright's buildings, furniture, town planning is based on a motival order that heroically promotes an essential consistency within the whole composition—as far as the eye can see—from the andiron in the fireplace of the Prairie style or Usonian house to the far edge of Broadacre City—not to mention the design of the frock, if possible, of the lady of the house. This kind of purity, despite its aesthetic power, is unattainable within the experience of *our* world, and it is useless and profoundly inappropriate for architects to attempt to attain it. This is because Wright is distinctly of another time—the end of the era that exemplified middle-class dominance and confidence, where you could attain harmony and unity among forms and symbols in your exclusive world and experience these phenomena via your interpretations of nature—or you thought you could attain this ideal.

Also, is there no considerable irony deriving from Wright's reaction against Victorian clutter and his embrace of organic consistency, whose closest historical parallel is that ornamental motival order characteristic of an aristocratic Rococo style—as the master architect becomes the sublime individualist while the individuals in his houses and his towns become ultimate conformists?

Our era is less heroic and more pragmatic, less optimistic and more realistic, less consistent and more ambiguous—where many cultures coexist, where richness and ambiguity dominate purity and unity: there is no longer a dominant ideal culture that can promote a universal order and ultimate unity. Here Wright appears in the motival aesthetic of his Broadacre City ironically close to that universal Classical aesthetic of the Renaissance style and to an industrial universality represented by the International Style. Broadacre City and La Ville Radieuse—where there is one culture for all over—are ironically similar on this point, and they appear, only some decades later, aesthetically and culturally prehistoric. On the other hand, Broadacre City, in another dimension and in hindsight, became a visionary prototype for an American suburban ideal whose ultimate almost-universal manifestation was Levittown.

And Wright's compositions allow no exceptions to the order, much less contradictions; there is no room for dissonance as there is in Beethoven's or Michelangelo's compositions. You adore Frank Lloyd Wright for his perfection when you contemplate him today, but you have to forget him when you work.

WORDS ON THE GUGGENHEIM MUSEUM IN RESPONSE TO A REQUEST BY THOMAS KRENS

Originally published in *Guggenheim Magazine,* Spring/Summer 1994, p. 7.

The Guggenheim Museum is a masterpiece of spatial flourish that confirms Frank Lloyd Wright's position as America's greatest architect. Didn't he say he was? And he was Wright!

He is the greatest of all time but not of our time. Within the context of now we can't but define his museum as architecture that subsumes the art that is in it—the Emersonian individuality of which dominates its occupants to make of them ironic conformists, and the organic unity of which promotes a harmony via a geometric motival consistency that is ironically as dominating and pretty as that consistency that characterizes Rococo architecture with its rocaille all over!

Hey, today we're into eclectic-culturalism and tense contradiction!

FOR AN ANNIVERSARY OF THE BAUHAUS, 1994

Originally published in *Knoll Celebrates 75 Years of Bauhaus Design, 1919–1994* (New York: The Knoll Group, 1994), p. 93.

May I join in this homage to the Bauhaus in a slightly perverse but a respectful way?

That is, to choose the Fagus Shoe Works in Alfeld, Germany, designed by Walter Gropius and Alfred Meyer as a significant and, to me, beloved icon within the Bauhaus tradition.

A choice perverse in that this building was designed and constructed prior to the founding of the Bauhaus as an institution and a movement—designed, in fact, within the Werkbund movement—that is, as early as 1911–1914.

But still a significant and relevant choice in several ways:

> • this building that exemplifies a seminal work of architecture, which launched what was later to be called the International Style—and is comparable in its originality to what is considered the first building in the Renaissance style, the Foundling Hospital by Brunelleschi in Florence;

> • this building whose eventual irony derives essentially from its technical-industrial vocabulary that was originally adapted from an American genre of factory lofts to accommodate European socialist programs and eventually came to symbolize corporate architecture that was universal and then resort architecture that was world-wide;

• this twentieth-century building whose eventual irony corresponds to that of the fifteenth-century building, which derives from a pagan vocabulary adapted from ancient Roman architecture that came to symbolize the Christian culture of Renaissance Europe.

I love this kind of first building, this quintessential twentieth-century building—based on American vernacular forms (with a dash of Cubism, I admit) employed by sophisticated Central European architects—exemplifying a universal ideal adaptable in many ways within rich and contradictory evolutions.

LEARNING FROM AALTO

Originally published as "Alvar Aalto" in *Arkkitehti,* July-August 1976, pp. 66–67; reprinted in *Progressive Architecture,* April 1977, pp. 54 and 102; and as "Le Palladio du mouvement moderne," *Architecture d'Aujourd'hui,* 191 (May-June 1977), pp. 119–120. Also published in *A View from the Campidoglio* (New York: Harper, 1984), pp. 60–61.

Alvar Aalto's work has meant the most to me of all the work of the Modern masters. It is for me the most moving, the most relevant, the richest source to learn from in terms of its art and technique.

Like all work that lives beyond its time, Aalto's can be interpreted in many ways. Each interpretation is more or less true for its moment because work of such quality has many dimensions and layers of meaning. When I was growing up in architecture in the 1940s and 1950s Aalto's architecture was largely appreciated for its human quality, as it was called, derived from free plans that accommodated exceptions within the original order, and from the use of natural wood and red brick, traditional materials introduced within the simple forms of the industrial vocabulary of Modern architecture. These contradictory elements in Aalto's work connoted—rather paradoxically it seems now—qualities of simplicity and serenity.

Aalto's buildings no longer look simple and serene. Their contradictions now evoke complexity and tension. Aalto himself has become an Andrea Palladio of the Modern movement—a mannerist master, but in a low key. Among the complexities and contradictions I see in his work are its conventional architectural elements organized in unconventional ways, its barely maintained balance between order and disorder, and its effects of plain and fancy, of the modest and the monumental at the same time.

Now that we can survey Aalto's whole oeuvre the conventionality and consistency of his work is very apparent. There is little change in the direction or development of his work over the years in comparison with the varied evolutions in Le Corbusier's work, or even in comparison with those changes between early and late Mies van der Rohe. Moreover, the elements of Aalto's architecture—the windows, hardware, columns, light fixtures, furniture, materials (except for the wood and brick)—are conventional in their forms and associations. They derive from the industrial and Cubist forms and symbols of the Modern style: in a textbook on classic Modern architectural elements, Mies's pure steel sections and travertine slabs and Le Corbusier's idiosyncratic—if now almost universal—forms in *béton brut* would be included, but Aalto's diverse but conventional elements would predominate.

The quality of Aalto's elements comes not from their originality or purity, but from their deviations—sometimes very slight, sometimes gross—in their form and context. And their power comes from the tensions their deviations produce. The handrail in the stairway of the offices for the Turun Sanomat looks conventional, but on second glance you see it as slightly unusual in form and application, and highly special in the refinement of its design. The concrete windows in the Enso-Gutzeit Building resemble those in the rather dry and correct grid of a passé SOM office building, but they are slightly off the norm in their proportions and scale, and highly "incorrect" in their application on the rear facade.

The order of Aalto's architecture is also full of tensions. A comparison again with other Modern masters might clarify my point: Mies is well known for his simple and consistent order which program and human activities serenely conform to; Le Corbusier is known for his classic order with dramatic exceptions and complex juxtapositions involving touches of *terribilità;* Frank Lloyd Wright for his rich but highly motival order. Aalto's order is based on tension rather than serenity or drama or consistency. It derives from exceptions within the order as in the rear facade of the Enso-Gutzeit Building, or in distortions of the original order as in the plan of the high-rise apartments in Bremen, or from an ambiguous order just on the verge of disorder as in the complex plan of the Wolfsburg Cultural Center or as reflected in an architect-friend's complaint to me once: why does Aalto have to use three different light fixtures in one small room?

I think we can learn timely lessons about monumentality from Aalto's architecture because architectural monumentality is used indiscriminately in our time and it wavers between dry purity and boring bombast. Aalto's monumentality is always appropriate in where it is and how it is used, and it is suggested through a tense balance again between sets of contradictions. The auditorium at the Technical Institute at Otaniemi combines collective scale *and* intimate scale, expressionistic forms *and* conventional forms, plain *and* fancy symbolism, and pure order interrupted by inconsistencies planned for the right places.

But Aalto's most endearing characteristic for me, as I struggle to complete this little essay, is that he didn't write about architecture.

A PROTEST CONCERNING THE EXTENSION OF THE SALK CENTER

By Robert Venturi and Denise Scott Brown. Originally published as "Genius Betrayed" in *Architecture,* July 1993, p. 43.

A BACKGROUND

Le Nôtre, in his *French garden,* evolves beyond the finitely ordered Italian Renaissance garden whose central axis is terminated by the sculptured slope of a terraced hill: within the Baroque gardens at Vaux-le-Vicomte and Versailles the central axis remains explicitly open at one end—extending, within its Cartesian order, toward a horizon symbolizing infinity.

Lewis Mumford discussed the significance of Thomas Jefferson's original intention of maintaining open views at *both* ends of the *lawn at the University of Virginia.* According to Mumford, Jefferson was ultimately persuaded by Benjamin Latrobe to insert the Pantheon-library at the northeast end of the central axis and thereby reproduce an essentially traditional-hierarchical order; and then, alas, McKim, Mead and White plugged up the other end less than a century later. Much of the power of Jefferson's second design derived from its spatial and symbolic gesture toward the Shenandoah Valley, from its framed view of the imminent frontier extending to the southwest. But his original design—open at each end—is more significant.

Vincent Scully's interpretation of the *gridiron plan* of the American town is significant too. Here the streets are typically open-ended—there is no ducal palace to terminate an axis—and relationships between streets and between streets and buildings are essentially nonhierarchical: they conform to a democratic ideal. A building in this kind of egalitarian plan derives its importance not from its relative position but from its inherent quality. Our great American cities do not conform to the European urban ideal, where a whole is defined within confining borders and axial terminations, but acknowledge rather an order that is incomplete—fragmental—as it accommodates inherent expansion and progress toward eternal frontiers.

———

We protest not as Kahn groupies or historicist extremists. We are part of a normally dispassionate group of people—critics, architects, and academics—whose sensibilities are outraged, not by the decision to grow, but by the quality of decisions being made concerning the location and character of the addition to the architectural masterwork that is the Salk Center.

THE ISSUE

Louis Kahn designed the Salk Center in La Jolla not as a naive or pompous whole and not without relation to its natural context, but as an eloquent composition that is spatially and symbolically incomplete, with its two richly rhythmical buildings themselves perceptually incomplete and nonhierarchical in their composition as they promote a divine duality and define a powerful axis that is open at each end and that constitutes thereby a significant gesture within an American landscape. The composition of this common space, poised between and open to a vast continent—symbolized by the bosque of trees to the east—and a vast ocean—defined by an infinite horizon to the west—is perceptually, physically, poignantly American as it frames the sea and the land where the old western frontier ends and the new eastern frontier begins. The American continent and the Pacific Ocean, a nation and the world, become poised along the Pacific rim within a global culture whose science, practiced within the architecture, becomes complex and universal, as it heads ever toward its own frontiers.

So the Salk Center complex acknowledges and celebrates an architectural way that spatially and symbolically is quintessentially American. Up to this point, it must be the most significant architectural composition of our century and arguably of all American architecture. It is surely a great expression of our culture and heritage—an American architectural masterpiece, by an American genius, set in the context of the whole of Western civilization— and it is a tragedy that it is being whimsically and imperiously transformed in our time into an ordinary, Baroque bore.

"It's as simple as that."

RECOMMENDATION

Don't speculate on what Kahn intended, when and where. Just relate to what's there—an architectural expression of the American view of space, the world, society. As Esther Kahn succinctly put it: we don't care what the new building looks like—just locate it where it doesn't demolish the genius of the place. Site it nearby, if it must be, but place it off axis and cant it. Learn from Kahn's exquisite, groping sketches of axially planned buildings related nonaxially, as the Greeks did it. Shun symmetry and completeness; honor Lou's abstractions of the infinite sea and the stylized woods representing land, continent, and the human landscape.

"It's as simple as that."

THOUGHTS ABOUT EVOLVING TEACHERS AND STUDENTS

Excerpt from a lecture on Louis Kahn at the University of Pennsylvania, published in *Penn in Ink,* May 1992, p. 6.

The final test of an artist, to put it simply, is: Is he right and is he good? And certainly there is a "right" quality in the heroism of Louis Kahn, as so evident when we review his work from the vantage point of now and consider it in the context of then—as we consider his architecture as reflecting the can-do America of then, in the fifties and sixties, and as characterized by confidence, optimism, know-how—by idealism—when we were on top of the world and before the American economy, social sensibility, and just plain will had succumbed to excesses of military-industrial complexity, decadent capitalism, and John Kenneth Galbraith's *Culture of Contentment:* Kahn's heroic architecture *was* valid for his time—right as well as good.

And from this viewpoint Louis Kahn might be the last relevant Modernist among the great architects of our century—as well as in some ways the first after-Modernist. But it is also right, as I look back explicitly through my own subjective eyes, that *our* emerging approach, that of Denise Scott Brown and myself, was right—that approach of us young architects of that time about to be mature architects of the next time. I was called an anti-hero then, sympathetically, by Vincent Scully—while at the same time our work was labeled ugly and ordinary by Gordon Bunshaft; we took this phrase as a compliment, considering the source, and adopted it. And the bases of our architecture do now appear far more evolutionary than revolutionary, pragmatic than progressive, familiar than original, ornamental than articulated, realist than idealist, vernacular than formal, symbolic as well as formal. And our buildings were elemental in their symbolism and their art;

they looked familiar *and* different, ordinary *and* good, the little houses looked like houses and they even had windows; the fire stations reminded you of something—of fire stations actually, rather than exhibitionist fragments of late Corbu or correct manifestations of Mies exposing their structure out of context—as fire stations of young architects tended to look at that time.[1] *Our* starting points included urban sprawl, commercial strips, and even Main Street, and if Kahn's urban planning acknowledged existing fabric—as opposed to that of Frank Lloyd Wright, the Emersonian individualist, who remade the American city in his own motival image, or that of Le Corbusier, the heroic revolutionary, who demolished the historic city to begin all over again—Kahn's intrusions within the existing fabric could be nevertheless heroic and utopian, as in monumental public parking garages resembling the turrets of medieval fortresses. Perhaps Denise Scott Brown's and my evolving approach to architecture and urbanism that was pragmatic in its social and aesthetic dimensions reflected Nathaniel Hawthorne's somber view that "a hero cannot be a hero unless in an heroic world."

As Kahn's young students we were able to evolve out of him—to learn from his sensibility concerning the condition of his time of then and to attune ours anticipating the quality of our time to come—acknowledging ambiguity and mannerism and pragmatism—to do as Kahn did as he evolved out of Paul Cret, Le Corbusier, Buckminster Fuller, and also out of his own students toward his way.

It is moving to remember his thrilling revelations of the building as not a floating frame but as walls—walls sitting on the ground and with holes in them—and of servant spaces acknowledging hierarchies of space, and of poché in plan; these revelations of then seem ordinary now, but this proves their ultimate force and significance. It is also touching to recall Kahn's saying to Denise Scott Brown "There is truth in Las Vegas" and to recall his conversion to historical analogy as an element of architecture in terms of its process and substance.

---

1. In a later time they might look like an explosion in a Cubist sculpture exhibition: have you looked at Zaha Hadid's Fire Station while envisioning the regular guys who are going to inhabit it and work in it erectly? The heroic and original tradition lives on!

LOUIS KAHN REMEMBERED: NOTES FROM A LECTURE AT THE OPENING OF THE KAHN EXHIBITION IN JAPAN, JANUARY 1993

Here is a short and subjective view of Louis Kahn's work—or rather, three perspectives of his work—as I am reminded of it in the current exhibition designed by Arata Isozaki. I refer to Kahn in the context of his own time, Kahn from the perspective of now, and inevitably Kahn in relation to me as an architect then and now—in short, as I saw Kahn then and see him now.

But I have to add that reconstructing how we saw Kahn and his work then is difficult: the recent past is the hardest time to recapture and perceive when you are focusing on issues of taste and sensibility. For this reason I shall employ the comparative method—contrasting what Kahn was and is, as I see it, with what he was not.

Also, it is important that an underlying assumption, basic to this analysis, is: Kahn was and is a great architect; that is, he was good and right. He was also a great teacher; I speak, I think, as a true student of Kahn—that is, not as a follower but as one who evolved out of him and his work—was liberated by him rather than converted by him.

Some characteristics of Kahn's work, as I see them in the context of then from the perspective of now, and employing comparisons:

- Kahn's architectural vocabulary was UNIVERSAL; it evolved and developed over time but at any one time it was essentially consistent— the same, simultaneously, for example, for a library for a northeastern boarding school in the United States like Phillips Exeter Academy and for a national parliament building in Bangladesh. His vocabulary was rich, but not eclectic—essentially not accommodating to a particular function or to context as ethos of a place.

In this way Kahn's architecture was very much of its time and within the Modern architectural tradition, one of the ideals of which was a universal system applicable in a single unified world whose basis was an order derived from industrial technical forms—very different from our multicultural view today, where ironically elements of universalism are most vividly evident in Pop culture and in fast food imagery promoted via electronic communication and multinational corporations.

• Kahn's architectural vocabulary was essentially one promoting FORM—essentially geometrical, sculptural, abstract—a vocabulary therefore not involving symbol and thereby accommodating again to Modernist tradition. Do you remember Le Corbusier's definition of architecture as "the play, magnificent and just, of pure forms in light?" But Kahn's approach at the same time was not classic Modern because of the quality of MASS characteristic of his form and its deviation from a Modernist emphasis on frame. This approach was most striking in the context of his time, although it paralleled that of the *béton brut* forms of late Le Corbusier.

• And Kahn's vocabulary of mass eschewed ORNAMENT—or at least explicit or applied ornament. What could be called ornament for him derived almost incidentally from functional-structural detail involving texture deriving in turn from materials, joints, etc. It could never be explicitly symbolic, graphic, or lyrical. In the context of the fifties and sixties this was not unconventional, where articulation was substituted for ornament.

• And the expression of Kahn's forms as mass was HEROIC and ORIGINAL—as opposed to ordinary and conventional. Allusions that were populist or vernacular were unthinkable, although Kahn's gentle early houses of the forties and early fifties might exemplify kinds of ordinary-Modernist conventions. Architecture was to be essentially a vehicle for promoting the progressive and attaining the ideal. And again this approach was of its time, when being original was equated with being creative. For example, the Market Street North project in Philadelphia does not exemplify the Corbusian revolutionary idea of the Ville Radieuse with its superblocks without reference to historical or local context, but Kahn's spatial intrusions within the existing fabric of the American gridiron plan were in themselves heroic, as were those castle-like forms of the parking garages.

• The element of BIG SCALE: scale that is heroic predominates within these forms, although it is sensitively balanced by small-scale elements within the composition.

• The EXCLUSION OF SHELTER: the heroic sculptural quality of late-Kahn architecture precluded any expression of architecture as shelter. This is ironical because Kahn's return to archaic basics would seem to encourage an acknowledgment of such an elemental quality of architecture—as is evident in the generic archaic temple.

• STRUCTURAL and GEOMETRIC RHETORIC was prominent in Kahn's work of the fifties as he was fascinated and influenced by Buckminster Fuller's and Anne Tyng's ideas, but this element diminished in the sixties with his later orientation toward sculpture and mass.

• THEORY: the prominent theoretical basis of Kahn's work as he enunciated it in the last part of his career involved equivalents of the HEROIC, ORIGINAL, and UNIVERSAL vocabulary of his form. His emphasis on esoteric metaphysical pronouncements concerning mind, spirit, body, and timeless universal absolutes involved things as they should be rather than as they are, and his contemporary and parallel historical reference focused on the archaic heroics of form. Historical reference I was into too, but I embraced a wider range of historical examples and prototypes that I employed as analogy for analysis. My personal feeling as an artist is one of uneasiness concerning this later aspect of Kahn's stance. I think such fundamental dimensions you embrace not by striving for them explicitly as an artist but by thinking pragmatically about immediate things and achieving them incidentally. It's for others, perhaps, to perceive the sublime and lyricize over it after the job is done. That stuff will take care of itself if you've done a good job of art.

These characteristics of Kahn's forms I have briefly enumerated as I see them in the context of his time and from my perspective now. Here are some other characteristics of Kahn's architecture described as elements that I love and have learned from:

- HIERARCHICAL SPACE: What a glorious revelation the SERVANT SPACE was, with its hierarchical implications and functional acknowledgment of mechanical equipment as implied poché for now. And its implications were stupendous for enriching programmatic-generic space— especially after the naive promotion of mechanical equipment as sculpture deriving from the machine aesthetic—which is currently in as a substitute for ornament.

- The IDEA OF THE ROOM: enclosure is OK, indeed valid and enriching. It is hard to comprehend how original this idea was: after the domination of Modern flowing space, enclosure was shocking.

- The WALL: sitting on the ground rather than as a floating plane on a frame. Believe me, that deserves a Wow!—hard as it is to believe now: it allowed us, Denise Scott Brown and me, to acknowledge Pop-vernacular, for instance!

- HOLES IN WALLS: rather than total interruption of walls—although Kahn was too Modern to stomach the conventional image of the window in his heroic work, he did so in some of his local residential work in Philadelphia. This characteristic in his work evolved out of abolishing the frame wall and was most influential on my work.

- LAYERS: spatial layering *had* been taboo because it promoted redundancy.

- BREAKING THE ORDER: this happened near the end of Kahn's career, but his exceptions were not anguished or mannerist.

It is hard to see from the perspective of today how these elements were shocking in the context of then. And here Lou was sublime in his influence as he liberated young architects and expanded our sensibilities.

It is hard also to reveal that some of these characteristics of Kahn's, described above, represent influences of Denise Scott Brown and myself rather than on Denise Scott Brown and myself—exemplifying a not uncommon case of the son informing the father. Denise has written of this issue elsewhere,[1] and I shall note here that Kahn learned from me concerning the elements of layering, holes in walls, and breaking the order described above; his use of inflection in the case of the pavilions in the Salk Center complex derives also from my critique.

And Kahn's use of HISTORICAL REFERENCE in the fifties and sixties is usually attributed to the influence of his early Beaux-Arts training at the University of Pennsylvania and his impressions from his stay at the American Academy in Rome in the early fifties. But I think it derived more from me when I was close to Kahn in the late fifties and early sixties—during the end, let's not forget, of his fifties geometric-structural period dominated by the ideas of Buckminster Fuller and Anne Tyng. And *my* use of historical analogy as a part of the analytical process of design derived in turn from my Princeton education in the forties as a student of Jean Labatut and Donald Drew Egbert, where Modernism was recognized as a valid movement within the history of Western architecture and not as an end of history. And it is sad to note that historical analogy as analytical method, employed in *Complexity and Contradiction in Architecture* which I was writing in the early sixties, was later misinterpreted (but never by Kahn) as a form of stylistic promotion by later so-called Postmodernists: perhaps if you're good, you're misunderstood!

I have described Kahn's more original than referential, more heroic than ordinary, more formal than symbolic kind of architecture, while Denise Scott Brown and I began in the sixties to look at everyday roadside sprawl more than correctly abstracted ruins and to practice a pragmatism, an anguished realism that included an acknowledged symbolism—itself an approach with a valid tradition where the subject in art can be not gods in Arcadia but bohemians in cafes or Dutch burghers as genre.

---

1. Denise Scott Brown, "A Worm's Eye View of Recent Architectural History," *Architectural Record*, February 1984.

ESSAY DERIVED FROM THE ACCEPTANCE SPEECH, THE MADISON MEDAL, PRINCETON UNIVERSITY

Written 1985.

Chairman Brown, President Bowen, fellow alumni, friends:

I like to consider myself very much a product of the Department of Architecture of Princeton of my time.

And I feel myself to be a son of Princeton—a grateful son—yet at the same time, an independent one, as a son should ultimately be.

I can say conversely that Princeton is a father to me, and if a father's approval is one of our basic needs, you will understand my awe, at this moment, at this sign of Princeton's approval.

Why am I both a grateful and an independent son? Because, to say it simply, my fellow students and I acquired an education at Princeton, not an ideology.

In the forties when we were here, the Princeton school of architecture was considered passé; in the common view it was an architectural backwater—dominated by Jean Labatut who was a graduate of the Ecole des Beaux-Arts.

Harvard was the place.

It embodied the spirit of the time. There, Walter Gropius, fresh from the Bauhaus, confidently instilled the canons of Modern architecture, and Sigfried Giedion, at the same time, interpreted architectural history as justification for Modern architecture—placing Modern architecture at the culmination of history.

Labatut, a convinced Modernist too, brilliantly illuminated principles of Modern design for us students as well, but Modern architecture for him did not represent "the word." It was not a culmination for *all* time, but rather, a vocabulary appropriate for *our* time. He saw Modern architecture as a beginning, not an end—and a beginning interpreted in the context of history.

And history, for Labatut and for Donald Drew Eghbert whom I will come to, was not a way to prove points, but an objective basis for enriching our vision, and an instrument, ultimately, for liberating our work.

Modern architecture was not a revolutionary ideology to be instilled, but a stage in a historical evolution, which, by implication, we artists, through our education, could grow out from. This kind of education was not easy but was very exciting.

I must mention too the significant roles of the chairman of our department, the always supportive Sherley W. Morgan, and the inspiring art historian, Donald Drew Egbert; the latter became a dear and lasting friend to me and a mentor.

This is some of the reason, as I see it, for Princeton's current leadership—why in the last decades she has brought forth more than her share of graduates as innovators and leaders who have significantly influenced the directions of architectural thought and practice today.

In hindsight, *was* the graduate program at Princeton passé—or was it progressive? Was it out of phase with its time—or was it in phase with a broader cycle? Perhaps it was all of these things, or perhaps the question is irrelevant. Perhaps you could say of Princeton's architecture school in my time what was said of Edmund Burke: "He is a wise man, but he is wise too soon."

I imagine you can find similar qualities of complexity and contradiction throughout the structure of Princeton, reminding us of the richness and diversity of its heritage and the spread of its influence.

In this regard I like to recall that the Norman Thomas Library is situated in Malcolm Forbes College—a commemorative duality that links Malcolm S. Forbes, Sr., class of '41, self-proclaimed "capitalist tool," and Norman Thomas, class of '05, six-time presidential candidate of the Socialist party.

How modest I feel at this moment, as well as proud. We artists are known for our egotism, but we are also wracked by doubt. We are quite capable of placing ourselves among the all-time greats and of being haunted at the same time by our bungling stupidity.

This is because we are perfectionists—at this moment I feel ironically aware of all the mistakes I have made in my work. Don't worry, I say to my family and friends here—I shall not enumerate my mistakes on this occasion, comforting as that confession might be—but I *can* assure Princeton, in her current role as our valued client, that my mistakes have been only aesthetic ones and those mistakes are visible mostly to me.

Finally, I think Princeton's fundamental and characteristic grace is in her understanding, in her patience with her sons and daughters in their times of floundering and struggle in the difficult work of being educated and creative.

Thank you Princeton for your education and for continuing to bear with me.

ROBERT VENTURI'S RESPONSE AT THE PRITZKER PRIZE AWARD CEREMONY AT THE PALACIO DE ITURBIDE, MEXICO CITY, MAY 16, 1991

Originally published as "Acceptance," *The Pritzker Architecture Prize* (The Hyatt Foundation, 1991).

My thanks to Jay Pritzker for his most gracious and generous introduction this evening.

My thanks also to President Salinas de Gortari and those officials of the government of Mexico, young and creative, who were our gracious hosts today, and to Ricardo Legorreta for his kindness to me, and from all of us here our gratitude to him for the restoration of this Palacio de Iturbide where we meet tonight, with its exquisite aesthetic, bold and delicate at once.

Frank Lloyd Wright said architects should design from the inside out. But we now accept within our more complex view of things, as we acknowledge context as an important determinant of design, that we design from the inside out *and* the outside in, and—as I said a long time ago—this act can create valid tensions where the wall, the line of change between inside and out, is acknowledged to become a spatial record—in the end, an essential architectural event.

And as a building is designed from the inside out *and* the outside in, so, one can say, is an architect designed in that way—that is, his own development as an artist can work through his development inside—through his intuition, ordered by means of analysis and discipline—but also through his development outside, via the influence of persons and places. As I refer to persons and places I borrow from George Santayana's title of his biographical essays, but I shall include as well, in this description of an architect's development from without, persons, places, *and* institutions.

At this moment I feel a special obligation to acknowledge the need—the need, psychological and material—for support, for appreciation and encouragement—this need, as significant for artists as for children in their development. No matter how sublime your intuition as an artist might be, and how disciplined and acute your own cultivation of that intuition inside, your need for appreciation and recognition from the outside is crucial: as children need loving parents and supportive home and school environments, so do artists need their supporters—trusting patrons and encouraging mentors, the latter sometimes in the form of historical examples of works of artists of the past.

And so, I appropriately and sincerely express at this moment my gratitude to the sponsors of the Pritzker Prize as persons, and to the Hyatt Foundation as institution, for their acknowledgment of good design in architecture and their support, via recognition of architects—and then to the selection committee of the Pritzker Prize that is particularly and signally honoring me today. But I like to acknowledge here as well, as I've said, those persons, places, and institutions who and which, very simply, have meant much to me as a growing artist—and I shall focus on them as well at this moment.

I trust, as I satisfy this need to enumerate particular persons, places, and institutions, that I shall appear not egotistical, but rather the opposite in emphasizing my indebtedness to outside influences; also as I speak I might enlighten younger architects via the example of my particular experiences as these younger architects choose paths of their own as they work.

First—chronologically and perhaps substantively—come my *parents* with whom I lived among beautiful objects, who supplied me with lots of blocks to play with when I was little and good books to read. And with whom I could share their love of architecture. I remember vividly on one of my first trips to New York City—maybe I was 8 years old—my *father's* impulsively instructing the cab driver to pull over and wait as we approached the old Penn Station on 7th Avenue and then conducting me down the gallery that overlooked the great hall based on the Baths of Caracalla. I shall never forget the breath-taking revelation of that monumental civic space bathed in ambient light from the clerestories above. And then my *mother* whose sound but unorthodox positions, socialist and pacifist, worked to prepare me to feel almost all right as an outsider. And again my *father* through whose hard work I was left a modest inheritance that allowed me to be braver and more independent as a young thinking architect.

Princeton University where as an undergraduate in a beautiful environment I walked on air as I could discover multitudes of things within many disciplines hitherto not dreamt of in my philosophy; where *Jean Labatut*'s vivid and creative historical analogies in his drafting room critiques worked to enrich and expand my outlook; where *Donald Drew Egbert,* who later became my closest mentor, described the glories of Modern architecture, but within the context of history, history employed to discover and enlighten, never to justify or promote—history that implicitly acknowledged architectural Modernism as a valid direction for that time, but a Modernism we students could evolve out of—not a Modernism as an end of history, as an ideology: at Princeton I was truly a student, not a kind of seminarian receiving the word that was to be universally disseminated. At the Princeton of my time we students of architecture were encouraged to go beyond.

Fellow students in that college community, especially including my roommate *Everett de Golyer* who revealed to me by his example the attributes of grace, wit, and understanding—and whose widow, my friend Helen de Golyer, it moves me to say, is here tonight.

Rome, as I first saw that city that Sunday in August 1948, as I walked on air—this time in a place rather than an institution—discovering unimagined pedestrian spaces and richness of forms bathed in the "golden air of Rome."

The American Academy in Rome, where as a Fellow within its community, headed by its easy and hospitable hosts, the director and his spouse, *Laurance and Isabel Roberts,* and by means of its location, I might exist every day in architectural heaven, and learn new lessons via *Michelangelo, Borromini, Brasini, hill towns,* and other historical mentors and places, and where I discovered the validity of Mannerism in art for our time, and from whose perspective as an expatriate I could better perceive my own country and the genius of its everyday phenomena, to see the Piazza Navona *and* ultimately Main Street.

Louis Kahn, profound teacher of mine, and ultimately, in some ways, as all teachers become, a student of mine—I trust now I can acknowledge how *my* son informs me through his sensibility as I simultaneously guide him.

Philip Finkelpearl, college friend and best friend, who as dedicated scholar and born teacher appreciated me all along and instructed me in Mannerism as a quality in arts other than architecture and as a dimension of criticism.

Revelations from the supreme architecture of *Frank Furness,* where I learned among other things the vivid lesson that you can change your mind in matters of taste.

Vincent Scully of Yale, friend and respected scholar and critic, who appreciated that first book and our work back when to others in the establishment I was either out or outré.

My students over the years at Penn and Yale, whom I learned from in my role as critic and teacher, and for whom I wrote *Complexity and Contradiction,* somewhat as a subversive version of my course on theories of architecture.

Our office, composed of the most committed and talented group of architects in the world who make our architecture truly collaborative and as good as it is.

Very significantly, *our clients,* of course, especially our understanding house clients in the early days who allowed us to work and therefore to be, including *Peter and Sandy Brant* for whom we designed three houses that were built, and our early institutional clients who were understanding *and* brave, like *Richard Spear* and *Ellen Johnson* at Oberlin College, and *Sydney and Frances Lewis* of Best Products who combined support and grace in their patronage and allowed us to test our ideas about the environment of commercial sprawl.

Princeton again, this time not as incubator for and liberator of an eager artist-student, but via the trustees of that institution as ideal client-patron who have awarded us grand opportunities to work in many ways over many years at another beloved place for me, the Princeton campus.

And *William Bowen and Neil Rudenstine,* as, respectively, recent President and recent Provost of Princeton, who have been the Lorenzo de' Medicis of our office as patrons—full of grace, discerning and appreciative.

Those professional *critics and editors* who understand us rather than exploit us and thereby encourage us; and even those British critics who have amused us over the years with their literate venom—calling the facade of the Sainsbury Wing of the National Gallery "Corinthian rash," or "picturesque mediocre slime," or "another vulgar American piece of Postmodern Mannerist pastiche"—the latter admirable for its rhythmic alliteration.

And those *younger architects and critics* who have learned from us and then gone beyond: what greater satisfaction can we attain than becoming not old fogies in their eyes? I mention the architect *Frederic Schwartz* and the historian and critic *Sylvia Lavin,* who are here tonight.

British architecture, especially within its Classical tradition, where the power and significance of Classical order exists not to be slavishly obeyed and consistently reapplied as manifestation of universality and timelessness, but rather exists to evolve, to distort, as manifestations of its strength, for combining the timeless *and* the timely—as in the inspiring works of Smithson, Jones, Wren, Vanbrugh, Hawksmoor, Adam, Soane, Greek Thomson, Webb, Mackintosh, Lutyens.

Las Vegas, which I learned from via the perspective of Rome and through the eyes of Denise Scott Brown, where we could discover the validity and appreciate the vitality of the commercial strip and of urban sprawl, of the commercial sign whose scale accommodates to the moving car and whose symbolism illuminates an iconography of our time. And where we thereby could acknowledge the elements of symbol and mass culture as vital to architecture, and the genius of the everyday and of the commercial vernacular as inspirational, as the industrial vernacular was inspirational in the early days of Modernism.

Beethoven as conducted by Toscanini, with ease and control—another phrase of Santayana's, qualities he attributed to an able dancer—a Beethoven, the Classicist, not interpreted through hindsight as a Romantic composer, whose expression derives not from the conductor but from the music, and whose tension derives from the balance between the lyrical and the dissonant.

The traditional architecture of *Kyoto* as it reveals the elemental quality of architecture as shelter, as sublime background for the complexity and richness of life and its paraphernalia, which themselves evolve rich varieties of scales and patterns. And *Tokyo,* the city of today, as perhaps a valid manifestation of Deconstructionism, certainly accepting of juxtapositions of diverse cultures and taste cultures (to use Herbert Gans's phrase) of varying scales ambiguously reflecting past urban configurations and boldly promoting present-day tours de force—with *élan, joie de vivre, jeu d'esprit,* with a *panache* that is *incroyable.* (French words seem appropriate for some reason.)

Akio Izutsu, as our hospitable friend and reticent instructor, introducing us to the architecture and civilization of Kyoto in a way that made our first day there the equivalent of that in Rome in its revelations.

And last, you will notice during this loosely chronological description I have used more and more the first person plural, that is, "we"—meaning Denise and I. All my experience representing appreciation, support, and learning from would have been less than half as rich without my partnership with my fellow artist, *Denise Scott Brown.* There would be significantly less dimension within the scope and quality of the work this award is acknowledging today—including dimensions theoretical, philosophical, and perceptive, especially social and urban, pertaining to the vernacular, to mass culture, from decorative to regional design—and in the *quality* of our design where Denise's input, creative and critical, is crucial.

At another level of detail, I could include other friends and clients who have been supportive, but in the interest of not going on and on I shall cease. But also, I trust, this country, *Mexico,* with its layers of architectural splendor and its promise of social and economic progress today, will become a place significant for me in my growth as an architect.

I must end this celebration of an artist's, or of these artists' range of supporters, with my thanks again for this grand token of appreciation, the *Pritzker Prize,* and for these persons and places without which I or we could not have been real artists—artists whose innate sensibility inside has had to be heeded and exercised within a context stimulating and civilized. Hurray for support *and* self-reliance.

Now I trust this biographical enumeration has not turned out egocentric— or folksy—but I have not felt like pontificating about architecture on this occasion, or risking doing that, but rather like expressing gratitude—as an artist who monitors his own intuitions, who trusts and evaluates his own sensibility, hunches, impulses, feelings, and thinks not necessarily the way he is supposed to, on the inside—while acknowledging at the same time the significance of these persons, places, and institutions on the outside.

Bernard Shaw's Eliza Doolittle said: "To be a lady I must be treated like a lady." All I've been saying is the same goes for artists, and thank you for treating me like an artist.

EPISCOPAL ACADEMY FIFTIETH CLASS REUNION STATEMENT

Written 1992.

I have been lucky, happy, and proud as the husband of Denise Scott Brown and father of James Venturi.

I have remained an outsider fortunate in doing work I like and am suited for—and within the intense focus along my difficult path, I have experienced a reasonable balance between extremes of satisfaction and frustration. I have been privileged to work in a professional relationship, intellectual and artistic, with Denise Scott Brown, and as partners we have acquired recognition in our field, favorable and unfavorable. I am ending up not too thin and not too rich, but our life with all its stress has been rich in terms of challenge, travel, friends, and family.

In looking back I realize I also had a rich home life as I grew up beside gifted and original parents, one an emigrant, the other "second generation," who set good examples—ethical, intellectual, and aesthetic—and were loving and supportive.

My nine years at Episcopal were positive, where basic discipline was instilled by a faculty understanding and supportive as a whole—and the discipline I refer to, mental and verbal, nurtured a degree of confidence and ease in my subsequent work as a theoretical writer and practicing architect. But it is sad that I had to be a nerd, as we would now say, in a setting at Episcopal directed toward sports over art.

It was at Princeton that worlds opened up not dreamt of in my philosophy, where I could learn to acknowledge my instincts and follow them as I worked hard at home in that community. At the same time I am sorry I have not kept up many of my Episcopal friendships.

I guess I can summarize my life since Episcopal in the words of a crusty Down East contractor on the coast of Maine who, as a response to my expressing how nice it had been to work with him on a house up there, said that for him "it's been nice—at times."

I write this during a flight on a rickety plane typical of our deregulated airlines, while passengers and attendants simultaneously yak and laugh as at a perpetual house party in a hunky-dory ethos—most passengers dressed as for the beach or in work clothes ironically chic in a time when the work ethic is out—this within weeks of the fiftieth anniversary of Pearl Harbor while Hawaii as real estate is Japanese.

And I write as a lament for our laughing land as laughingstock—while our national economy, social sensibility, creative commitment, and ethical ethos succumb to excesses of military-industrial complexity, decadent capitalism, and rampant bureaucracy that contrast poignantly with qualities of the can-do America of our time at Episcopal, reasonably characterized by degrees of confidence, know-how, direction, production— and a degree of idealism approaching that in our Constitution and Bill of Rights—when we were considerably a land of the free and home of the brave.

LEARNING FROM . . .

TWO NAIFS IN JAPAN

By Robert Venturi and Denise Scott Brown. Previously published in *Architecture and Decorative Arts: Two Naifs in Japan* (Tokyo: Kajima Institute Publishing Co., Ltd., 1991), 8–24, the catalogue for the exhibition "Venturi, Scott Brown and Associates" organized by Knoll International Japan; and in *Louisiana Revy,* 35, no. 3 (June 1995), pp. 4–9, issue serving as catalogue for the exhibition "Japan Today," Louisiana Museum of Modern Art, Denmark.

Until our first trips to Japan and Korea in 1990, our most vivid images of architecture as elemental shelter were the archaic Classical temple or the "Primitive Hut" described by the Abbé Laugier. At another extreme might be a child's drawing of a house, or its representation in the facade of the Vanna Venturi house in Chestnut Hill. Although this building was designed in terms more formal than symbolic, as a Mannerist evolution of Classicism, complex and contradictory in its enclosure and scale, it was also an elemental symbol. The house contained, in the most elemental terms, a large roof to shed rain, a chimney near the center of the roof, walls punctuated by a door opening, a decorative arch-molding over the door to make the entrance explicit, and windows that were conventional holes in the wall filled with conventional window panes. The large, square window with four panes was, from the beginning, an explicit and (hard as it is to believe now) strident symbol, involving conventional and historical reference. The parapeted front and back walls accentuated the facade's essentially representational quality and made the elements within the facade architecturally symbolic and specific.[1] Twenty-five years later, this same elemental quality moved us greatly in the temple architecture of Japan.

We put off going to Japan for many years, despite the fact that we are Modern architects—or perhaps *because* of the ways Modern architects, from Bruno Taut through Wright, Gropius, and others, promoted the classic architecture of Kyoto. Each generation of Western architects has seen in Japan what it wanted to see. The interpretation our generation was exposed to was extra-selective; it corresponded to the minimalist, structuralist, modular purity of early Modern architecture and focused on the villas and shrines of Kyoto. These images of a particular historical Japanese architecture, conveyed through the early Modernists' cameras and the cropping of their photographs, made us think of Japanese architecture as "goody-goody." By editing out the poignant counterpoints of complexity and simplicity, of intricate and plain, our forebears made this architecture seem irrelevant to us. We turned westward rather than eastward. And we were right to do so for another reason; we had enough to learn about our own heritage; Italy and England suited us fine. Also we were aware of the danger of absorbing the forms of the architecture of the East without a knowledge of their symbolism. This is why we acknowledge our naivete as we write here.

So Kyoto could wait. But our first day there contained one of the great revelations of our lives, comparable to that of our first day in Rome (for RV 41 years, 5 months, and 20 days before), our equivalent to "first looking into Chapman's Homer." There was the scale of the Sanmon Gate and the foundations of the Nanzenji Temple, not itsy-bitsy "human scale" but comparable to Italian civic scale in their monumentality—a kind of *terribilità* in wood. Second, there was the juxtaposition of the rich color, pattern, and variety of the sublime kimono upon the pure and apparently simple architectural convention of the temple. For us, both must be included and envisioned within the aesthetic equation. Unlike our purist predecessors, we needed to see the building with the kimonos.

Then there were the objects, the infinite variety of truly precious, not tiresomely precious, dolls, dishes, balls, boxes, boxes-in-boxes, hairpins, statues, chopsticks, chopstick holders, comic books, and idols, made of, among other things, plaster, porcelain, paper, bamboo, and lacquered wood, all skillfully crafted and colored. These items—kitsch or otherwise—on sale in the marketplace outside the temple, play against the severity of the architecture and are perhaps substitutes for the patterned kimonos that once moved among the screens, mats, spaces, structural grids, and overhangs of the buildings. The juxtapositions of extremes in scale are comparable only to those of the architecture of Michelangelo or the Pharaohs. Here, in the joy, vitality, and vigor of its small objects, was a Japanese version of "God in the details."

Then there were the gardens, especially those of the Katsura Villa, which stylize nature and represent and symbolize its diversity with the same infinite genius for multiplicity and miniaturization that we discovered in the markets. Whereas, in the French gardens of Le Nôtre, nature becomes abstracted, in Kyoto the elemental qualities of nature are symbolized; the temple garden, in its variety, unity, and rich combinations, suggests the natural landscape as a whole. And real nature cooperated that first afternoon by supplying the compositionally important raindrops that formed jumping patterns on the ponds, like the patterns of kimonos.

And then the diversity. In the Kyoto temples there was a quite consistent convention of building, but within that were infinite exceptions. The contradictions were stunningly tense in their aesthetic and perceptual effect, and valid and understandable in most dimensions; when they weren't, who would worry, given the context of care? Care—the attention to multitudinous detail in design, from chopstick holders to gilded temple paintings, from foundations to maintenance—created an aura that permeated the whole of the art, the place.

Later, we comprehended an even more profound lesson for us here: that, even more than it was deceptively simple and artfully complex, the Kyoto temple architecture (and that of Nara and the Ise Shrine, we later perceived) was elemental as well as generic. The elemental sheltering quality of traditional Japanese architecture is symbolized by the roof—the hipped roof with large overhangs that is perhaps *the* dominant element of these buildings. Roofs are everywhere. A gate is a roofed shelter as well as an entrance; a garden wall has a little roof to act as coping; roofs are sometimes eloquently redundant, as in the vertical stacks of roofs of a pagoda or in the accommodations to clerestories.

Subsequent visits to Korea and Nikko made the idea of the elemental sheltering roof more vivid. There the complex wooden architecture below the roof is painted in vivid colors and decorated with delicate patterns. Color is kept out of the rain and seen in shadow. The comparatively delicate walls and parapets with fragile finishes, which people live beside and touch, become essentially furniture. This contrast between sheltering roof and furniture below—that which dominates and makes the building a unit, and those elements below at human level which are delicate, intricate, accommodating, "forgiving"—make a classic architecture that we can learn from and cannot forget, an architecture consisting simply of units of shelter, not of sculpture. (Granted, the unitary roofs of silver-colored glazed tiles, especially in villas and temples in Korea, are often seen in groups complexly jammed against each other with astonishing geometric and aesthetic violence.)

We acknowledge, of course, that the elemental sheltering roof derives from a tradition of architecture for a rainy climate. This is one of the reasons for big sloping roofs extended by protective overhangs. And certainly there is a contrary distinguished tradition of the domination of wall over roof, especially in our Western history, from the apse of St. Peter's to the Villa Savoye—and our office follows this tradition in its work; but a somewhat consequent trend toward ignoring architecture as shelter and treating it as sculpture is an unfortunate one. Sculptors make things in the round; their objects have little connection with an inside that must be protected from rain above; their relationship to gravity can be less grave.

Sculpture by its nature can be relatively expensive; even when it is expensive it is cheap by architectural standards. Meandering combinations of *objets* with contrived connections and tour de force construction are other conceits more sculptural than architectural. Their flashed articulations are expensive—and, for an architect, part of being a good artist is to be sensible. So our first visit to Japan, as Decon architecture began to hold sway, reminded us that the essential element of architecture is shelter—even more than space, despite the deification of space in late Modern theory. The unitary historic temple, Eastern or Western, is a basic model that theoreticians and architects cannot afford to forget.

As important as the lessons of historical Kyoto for us have been the lessons of Tokyo today. Learning from Tokyo, for two naive architects, had to do with urban design as well as current architecture. Like children on their first day in a big city, we constantly exclaimed "Look at *that!*"—with an occasional "Now I've seen *everything!*"—as we were driven around, always tired but happy.

Tokyo has its act together—though granted it is a chaotic act. The Japanese love to describe Tokyo as chaotic; the word for chaos in Japanese is adapted from the English. But is not this a convincing chaos or an order that is not yet understood? Or an ambiguity without anguish? Tokyo's chaos derives from the variety of scales, forms, symbols, and rhythms of:

- its buildings, and from its dense juxtapositions of patined village dwellings and global corporate high-rises in the latest architectural styles,

- its macro and micro businesses; some in "pencil" buildings 12 feet wide and 10 stories high, which, from 1950s Modern to the latest Decon outrage, exhibit a genius for the bold and the miniature; others at a multinational scale, set in vast urban renewal landscapes that are more vital and better seamed into the city than those in America,

- its juxtapositions of cultures, where the global organization and the traditional decorative hairpin are accommodated with equal elegance; there is room for not one but many taste systems, and architecture is perhaps freer and more varied than anywhere else in the world,

- its pachinko parlors containing slot machines and outrageous blinking neon chandeliers, packed in and reflected to infinity via mirrored walls and ceilings; these are adjacent to the most sophisticated and refined high-rise office buildings, or to boutiques containing the haute couture of Europe and Japan, in settings designed by Japan's most distinguished architects; these in turn are next to lineups of Coke and other dispensing machines along the sidewalks,

- its small urban shrines, tucked between stores on shopping streets,

- its historical temples sometimes surrounded by gardens, and served by bazaars teeming with thousands of objects, mostly miniatures, irresistible in their craftsmanship, wit, and/or beauty,

- its department stores crammed with high design and luxury items from Europe and Japan,

- the going range of American fast food places.

All of these appear in cockeyed configurations and unimaginable juxtapositions in an urban infrastructure of straight streets and wide avenues lined with trees or regiments of commercial signs; or crooked lanes lined with utility poles draped with myriad wires; or elevated highways routed along and over canals and even over the roofs of small houses whose fenced yards enclose the highway supports.

Then there are the electronically sophisticated signs defining the architecture of the city adorning buildings and lining streets. Tokyo signs are at least as brilliant and varied as those of Fremont Street in Las Vegas. Those in English surpass in wit and joy anything in English-speaking countries: for example, "Oops," "Toy Box," "Bumpies," "Club Kamon," and "Honda Primo." Current Japanese architecture, too, outwits its Western equivalents in its unabashed vitality and joy. Architectural frivolity in the West today is skin deep or laborious; that of this part of the East is sophisticated or naive, like the high-rise held together with hexagonal "screwheads," three feet wide and 18 inches deep, on its curtain walls. There were contemporary buildings that we liked in Tokyo or Kyoto that we could not accept elsewhere. In Tokyo, in their context, they dance a jig at a lively party. In other cities they would seem irresponsible intrusions in a decaying ethos. Pride makes the kitsch OK, and spirit makes the vulgar likable.

There is also the variety and quality of dining. The native cuisine we enjoyed immensely but cannot judge, but some of the best French and Italian meals we've eaten anywhere have been in Tokyo, including an Italian dinner in a black restaurant-cum-staircase—a stunning design by Philippe Starck. Then the taxis, always immaculate, whose roof lanterns, in a variety of forms, symbols, graphics, and colors, identify the over 200 companies they are associated with and reflect the diversity, spirit, and wit of the whole scene.

The layout of Tokyo is constantly referred to as chaotic. It is said that the original plan of the city was designed as a maze to confound attacking armies approaching the grounds of the Shogun's castle, now the site of the imperial palace. This parklike complex, although its buildings are hidden, is one of the few elements that intimates any hierarchy in the formal and symbolic configuration of this enormous city.

If, in the chaos, there are, beneath the surface, rules of order that whisper rather than shout their presence, these possibly derive from the early technology of the city; from the spanning capacity of the light timbers that determined the widths of the rooms of houses, and the breaks and separations mandated for fire protection, and the small-scaled building elements needed for safety from earthquakes. These requirements of the preindustrial era probably determined the fractionated subdivision and property ownership patterns of the traditional city. Upon this destroyed city, after World War II, a new city grew in one decade. It is this city, unified by its 1950s Googie architecture, that is now being renewed and upscaled by the demands of Japan's global economy. The results will be an overlaid pattern of different scales and types of urban configuration, reminiscent somehow of the patterns on a kimono or of the patterned and draped kimonos depicted in a Japanese woodcut.

It is ironic that in Japan, a society known for its discipline, formality, and rules of courtesy, architects are able to do things artistically that they would not be allowed to do elsewhere. The results, for example the recent Pop-Decon constructions in Tokyo, look better there than they would in Europe or America, forming, as they do, part of Tokyo's vivid and unique combination of the exotic and the familiar—and the almost familiar.

Yet, unique as Tokyo is, the architectural ethos we have described could evoke a number of cities in the world, especially prosperous trading cities with international ties, such as Venice, where an eastern-Byzantine flavor combined with "modern" Renaissance and Baroque architecture; or nineteenth-century London, capital of a commercial empire, with an eclectic variety of architectural styles set in a largely medieval configuration of streets.

It is a further irony that the capitals of universal empires—imperial, commercial, or financial—are not prone to universalist vocabularies in architecture, but are responsive to the multiplicity of their domains. The sublime exemplification of this tendency of mercantile empires to favor eclectic architecture is Sir Edwin Lutyens's Viceroy's House in New Delhi. However, as the world becomes smaller, aspects of universality do evolve; today McDonald hamburgers and Toyota cars are almost everywhere. But the combinations of universal elements may still be unique, rendered so by local conditions. In the overall, today's trends may lead to greater diversity rather than to similarity.

Other Asian cities may correspond to Tokyo today in some ways, and perhaps Los Angeles too, but Los Angeles lacks Tokyo's spectacular prosperity, and the American city's pervasive grid and relatively low density significantly change the picture. Is Tokyo Los Angeles condensed, deconstructed, and wittier? Tokyo's careful maintenance of its urban infrastructure and its pervading sense of civic pride may parallel that of western European cities today, but it is outstanding by comparison with any American city. This urban quality is an extension of the Japanese attention to detail, organizational management, pride in workmanship, and superior craftsmanship, whether it involve the craft in the traditional doll, the wrapping of packages, the arrangement of food, the service in a restaurant or aircraft, or the technical and architectural detail of a building.

The Japanese are sometimes criticized for a lack of originality—their traditional art derives from that of Korea and China; many of their contemporary forms are based on Western technical and aesthetic prototypes. We do not have the knowledge to make any particular judgment of this kind, but we think the qualities we have been describing—those of care, skill, and spirit, along with an acceptance of diversity—are as much a part of artistic quality as is originality. And it is the combination of sophistication and naivete, spirit and control, or "discipline and ease" as George Santayana would have put it, that distinguishes this city and its art. It represents, perhaps, an aesthetic ethos that accompanies economic prosperity and high morale. In our reactions, we found ourselves constantly applying French words—*joie de vivre, jeu d'esprit, tour de force, élan, panache, arabesque, pastiche, incroyable*—to these eclectic urban juxtapositions of symbols, forms, scales, civilizations, and patterns. Our own made-up phrase, *valid Deconstructivism,* seemed to define this curious urbanism.

Decon works for cities; it is more natural to cities than to buildings, because cities don't have to keep the rain out or the warmth in (or out) and because cities are not built all at once but incrementally, now that we have no princes but only individuals and committees as builders.

On only his second day in Tokyo, RV found himself saying to an audience of architects, "Love your city, for its spirit and reality which are immediately evident; embrace and don't resist the contradictions and tensions these elements provoke." For us, this urban complex without hierarchy or perceptual order was perhaps the first valid manifestation of architectural, or rather urban, Deconstructivism; one that represented not "the incoherence or arbitrariness of incompetent [art] nor the precious intricacies of picturesqueness or expressionism [but] the richness and ambiguity of modern experience."[2]

What you see in contemporary Tokyo and historical (and contemporary) Kyoto is an accommodation to and a celebration of the realities of our time and its tensions (we forgot to mention the monumental traffic jams); to the plurality of cultures promoted via global communication and flourishing side by side; to the diversity and quantity of overlapping taste cultures (nine symphony orchestras in Tokyo alone)—these complexities and contradictions and the resultant ambiguities lead to a richness of effect and a spirit that are the fate, and should be the glory, of the art of our time. In our art today, it should not matter if you don't like it all, if this detail isn't quite right, isn't quite to your taste: such tensions between what you like and dislike should, in the end, heighten your tolerance *and* your sensibility, and will allow the city to be "chaotic" in its formal configuration, disciplined in the elements and maintenance of its infrastructure, overwhelming in the prominence of its detail, *and* to read as a capital of global business organizations.

Ultimately the remnants of those feudal street layouts, the value of the land and consequent inhibiting effects on the consolidation of land parcels, and the spirited growth of the era create real tension and evolve artful urbanism. We learn here from the combination of elemental reality in architecture and from the spirit in its craft.

---

1. See R. Venturi's interpretation of this house as a symbol in his Gropius Lecture, Harvard, 1982, published in *Architectural Record,* June 1982, pp. 114–119.
2. Robert Venturi, *Complexity and Contradiction in Architecture* (New York: Museum of Modern Art, 1966; second edition 1977), p. 16.

"VENTURI SHOPS"

Previously published in *Louisiana Revy,* 35, no. 3 (June 1995), Louisiana Museum of Modern Art, Denmark.

Denise Scott Brown and I have written of our initial responses as American architects to Japanese art and culture, historical and contemporary—adding thereby our own perspective and interpretations to those of Western artists and architects of the past who explicitly acknowledged influences in their writings or made them apparent via their work. We explained how we had delayed going to Japan partly because we were put off by interpretations of various architects of this century who emphasized aesthetic-minimalist simplicity and explicitly excluded complexity and contradiction as they described the sublimely pure compositions of temples and shrines of Kyoto and the Katsura Detached Palace and excluded everything else by means of a mental-aesthetic blackout and photographic cropping.

We shall never forget our astonishment on that first day in Kyoto—February 28, 1990, which we shall forever celebrate—when we perceived the pure shrines of Kyoto within their impure context, not only in their immediate setting, that of the garden symbolizing the natural world as a complex whole—not to mention, it is safe to assume and easy to visualize, that context constituted by figures in colorful, patterned kimonos moving within the spaces—but also in their extended setting which includes the market place. We embraced within our perspective the markets teeming with aesthetic and technical complexity and acknowledging dimensions sensuous and lyrical in terms of color, pattern, and scale. So Kyoto as an exemplification of Japanese art and architecture became a matter of shrines in gardens *and* markets in streets cum figures in kimonos visualized all over—of simple shrines made sublime by the juxtaposition of complex context.

And we could also see that the pure order of the generic shrines teemed with variations and exceptions. This perspective of Kyoto with wide-angle lens, this inclusive view, exalts simplicity *and* complexity and embraces thereby harmony and dissonance in a whole that is rich and tense in its range of contradictory dimensions. And this interpretation of architecture and urbanism of then enlightens our response to the architecture and urbanism of now so we can love and understand Tokyo today as well as Kyoto eternally.[1]

Now for the objects that make up the market. These objects fascinate us because they exhibit at once skill, pride, and wit. These are rare and precious elements in our time and that's why we adore them: in our country you might find combinations of any two but seldom all of these three qualities at once. In the end we are fascinated by the element of care. In Japan God *and* workers are in the details.

We are not normally collectors, not having the stomach, time, or pocketbook for collecting. Most of the collected objects illustrated here are manifestations of the celebrated Japanese custom of giving gifts—and the generosity manifest in this custom has for us been characterized by our friend Akio Izutsu, who enjoys our childlike delight in ranges of objects, sophisticated and Pop, crafted and kitsch, and who showers us with gifts in Tokyo and on our travels in Japan. The sources for most of these objects are what Akio Izutsu calls Venturi shops, so many of which he and we have immensely enjoyed browsing in. Denise Scott Brown and I do *some* shopping of our own in Japan, so the word shops in the title of this book can be read as a verb *or* a noun.

It is important to note three things as you review the illustrations accompanying this essay: 1. A few of these objects, it has been noted, although designed and marketed in Japan, were made in Taiwan, Hong Kong, or China. 2. Their range spans from almost outright schmaltz to those elements involving high art and/or containing religious content. 3. There is not a categorization among these kinds of elements in terms of how they were collected or how they have been arranged in the accompanying illustrations. The random juxtapositions do not imply any lack of respect for the symbolic-cultural content these objects contain, but they do work, we hope, to demonstrate the richness within their range.

I hope you will enjoy this range as well as the skill, pride, wit—and care— these objects exemplify for our time.

---

1. It is important to mention the revelations in Yoshinobu Ashihara's *The Hidden Order* (Tokyo: Kodansha International, 1989), which significantly informed our view of Tokyo.

66
Miscellaneous objects from Japanese
markets
Photo credit: Matt Wargo

67
Miscellaneous objects from Japanese
markets
Photo credit: Matt Wargo

68
Miscellaneous objects from Japanese
markets
Photo credit: Matt Wargo

LAS VEGAS AFTER ITS CLASSIC AGE

By Robert Venturi and Denise Scott Brown; published in *Neon, Artcetera* (Nevada State Council on the Arts), Winter 1995–96.

Revisiting Las Vegas by invitation of the BBC a quarter century after our original trips to research the Strip was fascinating for us. A comparison of Las Vegas in 1994 with what fifteen Yale students, Steven Izenour, and we found in 1968 and documented in *Learning from Las Vegas* in 1972 demonstrates a vivid and significant evolution, urban and architectural—perhaps comparable to returning to Florence a century after the quattrocento?

Our restudy owes a debt of gratitude to the spirit and understanding of Bernadette O'Brien, who interviewed us and who, with her crew, produced the program on Las Vegas aired in January 1995 on the BBC's *The Late Show.*

LEARNING FROM LAS VEGAS

The subject of the original study was the commercial strip, an element of the automobile-oriented sprawl found at the edge of most American downtowns. The Las Vegas Strip was its archetypal and therefore most instructive example. Although in many ways like the classic commercial strip, it was not the prototype but the phenomenon at its most pure, rising from the open desert without historic underlays. It was also emblematic in its time of all urban sprawl—as we wrote in 1968, Las Vegas was to the strip what Rome was to the piazza.

The Strip of the middle 1960s was configured to accommodate perception from cars moving at about 35 mph rather than the 4 mph of the urban pedestrian, and to provide parking space for stationary cars. Its basic urban form contained:

- large signs immediately on and perpendicular to the road, with big-scale ornament and graphics (high readers) designed to be perceived at relatively high speeds across broad spaces,

- vast parking lots along the road behind the signs,

- gaudy, flashing building facades set parallel to the road, beyond the parking lots,

- relatively simple generic buildings behind the facades.

Architecturally and urbanistically, *Learning from Las Vegas*:

- revealed the Strip as a landscape of symbol in space rather than form in space—its two-dimensional signs, not buildings, providing identity in the amorphous sprawl (Tom Wolfe wrote, "Las Vegas is the only town in the world whose skyline is made up of neither buildings, like New York, nor trees, like Wilbraham, Massachusetts, but signs"[1]),

- discussed the forgotten symbolism of architectural form—forgotten because current Modern design, then and now, denied architecture's symbolic content and emphasized its abstract form; and of course good taste dictated you don't like signs, especially big, commercial ones,

- reminded our readers of the rich tradition of iconography in ancient Egyptian temples and pylons, Classical Greek pediments, Roman arches, Early Christian basilicas, and the Gothic facade of Reims cathedral—a three-dimensional theological billboard if you read it as a medieval Christian,

• considered signage, for example, the distinguished electrographic neon work of Vaughan Cannon's Young Electric Sign Company, as vernacular art of the twentieth century. When midcentury commercial signs and billboards are treasured icons of American folk art, will this fragile Las Vegas heritage be restored as a second Williamsburg?

• defined and distinguished between the "duck"—the building as articulated sculpture—and the "decorated shed"—the building as generic shelter whose planar surfaces are decorated.

Another subject within this study was taste and American taste cultures as defined by Herbert Gans.[2] In an era when architects had the answers, then, forever, and universally for *tout le monde,* we recommended taking a nonjudgmental approach to taste and accommodating to pluralism and relativity. Las Vegas, the pop-cultural landscape par excellence, promoted "bad" taste that was vital.

Though it's difficult for architects to believe, this study emanated as well from the social planning movement of the 1960s and the admonitions to architects by Gans, Jane Jacobs, and others to be more open to values other than their own and less quick to apply personal norms to societal problems—to be part, as we used to say, of the solution rather than the problem. People "voted with their feet" by going to Las Vegas; architects, the social planners suggested, should hold their disdain for its visual environment long enough, at least, to discover why people liked it. Our study was part of a broader attempt to find ways to place our architectural talents at the service of our social ideals.

RELEARNING FROM LAS VEGAS

The Strip changed over 25 years, not only through the addition of new elements, but by the elimination or modification of some elements and by change in context that altered the significance of other elements.

Urbanization
The Las Vegas Strip has been officially renamed Las Vegas Boulevard. This signifies its urbanization. Through the development of its surroundings, the

Strip has become a conventional urban element. A proliferation of streets parallel and perpendicular to the Strip has produced superblocks, whose density derives from the building of larger and ever larger hotels and the replacing of parking lots with parking structures. The Strip is no longer a linear settlement in the desert, it is a boulevard in an urban setting; sprawl has become edge city. Traffic jams and busy pedestrian sidewalks attest to this evolution. Up front, sidewalks have been landscaped and parking lots have become front yards, their asphalt surfaces converted to Romantic gardens planned to draw pedestrians from the Boulevard to the hotel porte-cochère.

From Signs to Scenes, Electrographics to Electronics, Decorated Sheds to Ducks

The Strip has seen a considerable reduction in the number and size of its signs and a parallel evolution from signography to scenography, or from the decorated shed to the duck. Vivid examples of the trend toward scenography include the MGM architectural lion's head, the Luxor Hotel pyramid, the Excalibur castle, and, most vividly, the Mirage Lake cum volcano and the Treasure Island Caribbean town. In their front yards, where parking lots once predominated, the Mirage and Treasure Island offer dramatic performances—the latter with real actors and sound effects—to be experienced essentially by pedestrians on the Boulevard. These hotels promote a vivid, duck-oriented scenography and demote signage and neon lighting. The flamboyant neon of the Golden Nugget Hotel on Fremont Street has been removed, and on the Strip neon is being replaced by LED or its incandescent equivalents. The moving pixels permit changing imagery and graphics for a multicultural ethos in an information age.

Gentrification

The move from signs to scenography reflects an evolution from Vaughan Cannon to Walt Disney. The Disneyfied Boulevard provides a three-dimensional, theater-like experience for the pedestrian, with evocative imagery for role playing—a wicked pirate in a Caribbean theme park or a degenerate gladiator in a Pompeian mall. This is a total departure from the car-oriented iconography of the Cannonized Strip.

The change involves a kind of gentrification. The imagery is now not so much of wickedness or vulgarity made safe and decorative, but rather of a family place, wholesome in its immediate references, if bizarre in its ultimate effects. This promotes expanded markets and bigger profits, but will its wholesome scenography end up as "blandly homogenized good taste . . . boring as only paradise can be"?[3]

Mall and Edge City
Twenty-five years ago Las Vegas consisted of downtown with a Main Street (Fremont Street) and the Strip in the desert. Today downtown is still pretty much downtown, but the Strip—oops, the Boulevard—with its urban-scenographic accessories, has become in some ways the equivalent of the shopping mall that accommodates the pedestrian in safe and explicitly artificial environments.

Beyond, at the outer limits of Las Vegas's residential sprawl, is developing an "edge city" where casino-hotels sit on a highway rather than a strip. The new Sam's Town, for instance, appropriately for its era, combines iconographic signage and ducklike scenography with parking beyond—a combination of the old and the new in an evolving context.

FROM LAS VEGAS TO LAS VEGAS

We can summarize Las Vegas's development over time as from:

the Strip to the Boulevard

urban sprawl to urban density

parking lot to front yard

asphalt plain to Romantic garden

the decorated shed to the duck

electric to electronic

neon to pixel

electrographic to scenographic

signs to scenes

iconography to scenography

Vaughan Cannon to Walt Disney

pop culture to gentrification

pop taste to "good" taste

perception of the driver to perception of the walker

strip to mall

mall to edge city

folk art, vivid, vulgar, and vital, to unconvincing irony.

In *Learning from Las Vegas* we described our personal paths, geographic and cultural, that went "from Rome to Las Vegas." Would an analysis of our recent journey, from Las Vegas Strip to Las Vegas Boulevard, prove as instructive as the first for architecture?

---

1. Tom Wolfe, "Las Vegas (What?) Las Vegas (Can't Hear You! Too Noisy) Las Vegas!!!!," *The Kandy-Kolored Tangerine-Flake Streamline Baby* (New York: Farrar, Straus and Giroux, 1965).
2. Herbert J. Gans, *Popular Culture and High Culture: An Analysis and Evaluation of Taste* (New York: Basic Books, 1974).
3. Steven Izenour and David A. Dashiell III, "Relearning from Las Vegas," *Architecture,* October 1990, pp. 46–51.

AT WORK

SOME AGONIZED THOUGHTS ABOUT MAINTENANCE AND PRESERVATION CONCERNING HUMBLE BUILDINGS OF THE RECENT PAST

Focusing on Our First Built Project—Only Some Thirty Years Old!

Written 1993.

I write about our North Penn Visiting Nurses Association Building. Over the years it has generally not been appreciated. It was poorly maintained and then there was the offensive addition in back—I'm afraid the original director, whose name I forget, did not like her building very much. The building was recently purchased by a CPA firm. They have further renovated it without respect for the original quality of its design—although the head of this firm, when the artistic significance of his building was revealed to him by a noble local architect, expressed sympathy and understanding concerning the situation.

I love this, my first built building, and I feel it has genuine artistic and historical significance—despite its modest size—involving elements that now seem everyday, because of their subsequent influence on architecture of our time, but were original then. I refer to the use of ornament, abstract and symbolic, in the redundant juxtaposed ornament over the entrance opening, as well as the hierarchical scale of this opening in relation to the scale of the windows and to the molded borders around the windows in front: at the time a dear architect-friend put his arm over my shoulder and said "Bob, you never decoratively border windows," and ten years later he did it himself. But especially new was the overall shape of the building with its particular angles that makes of it a fragment as well as a whole as it inflects, by means of its angled shape, toward the parking court—thereby making the parking lot a positive element in the composition as a whole.

This latter quality of a building that *occupies* outside space but also *molds* outside space was especially original for its time when orthodox Modern principles of architecture held sway: then you designed "from the inside out," never the other way around. It is interesting to note that the National Gallery extension on the Mall in Washington by my friend I. M. Pei, which contains similar angular forms, was preceded by our little building—as was the inflected form of the pavilions that distinguish Louis Kahn's justly renowned Salk Center in La Jolla.

I have just read of Philip Johnson's Four Seasons Restaurant's being placed on the National Register of Historic Buildings: if I may say so, this little work, whose cost was a fraction of that grand work, is more significant in terms of its originality and quality.

Architecture is the most fragile of the media.

GUILD HOUSE, TWENTY-FIVE YEARS LATER

Written in 1995 for the submission to the Twenty-Five Year Award of the American Institute of Architects.

Ordinary *and* Extraordinary

How thrilling *and* sad it was to hear someone say, driving by the Guild House recently, "You wonder now what all the fuss was about."

The design of Guild House seemed extraordinary in its time because it looked ordinary. As housing for the elderly sponsored by the Friends Neighborhood Guild, it sits at home in its context—a conventional urban neighborhood in north Philadelphia combining typical row houses and occasional industrial buildings of the second half of the last century all in brick.

Its design was extraordinary because:

A Building on a Street; Not a Slab or a Tower in a Superblock

It was not a monumental slab or a pure tower as a point in landscaped space as idealized superblock—but a generic building directing space on a lot along a street pragmatically working within the existing urban fabric.

The Reasons for Its Irregular Shape

As an irregular non-slab—whose front was different from its back!—it could embrace exterior space in front and maximize the area of apartment units facing the view of the Philadelphia skyline toward the south and the number of corner rooms in the units.

Not RC but Brick

Its exterior surfaces were not made of exposed reinforced concrete that would work to one-up the old brick neighborhood; its analogous brick surfaces helped make the building at home in its context and promote urban unity.

Windows Rather Than an Absence of Walls

And there were windows on its facade—the bête noire of Modernism—not only holes in walls rather than absences of walls, but conventional windows that were symbolically explicit—not only double-hung but bisected by mullions: they not only were windows but they looked like and reminded you of windows. (This almost square four-paned window has since become, of course, a motif in architecture all over.)

Hierarchy of Scales

And the same kind of window appeared in different sizes and this promoted hierarchy of scale and diminished the modular consistency that reigned in architecture at the time.

Ornamental Pattern and Hierarchy

The most extraordinary element for the time was the ornamental pattern on the facades—and the most difficult for me to handle, not so much because of what critics would say but because of what I was thinking as a result of my upbringing: would this aesthetic gesture be equated with crime by Adolf Loos and his Minimalist cohorts looking down from Modernist heaven? But the pattern deriving from a white brick area at the base and a stripe near the top had an aesthetic justification—again to reinforce the element of hierarchy— creating base, middle, and attic in the manner of the facades of Italian palazzi. I must admit I enjoyed the contradictory juxtaposition of this tripartite decorative order upon the six-story functional order expressed literally via the layers of windows on the facade. These thin stripes might look pathetic now when stripes are all over.

Hierarchy Encore

Another hierarchical element of the facade is its central portion, expressing again a base, a middle, and a top via the entrance, the series of balconies, and the arched window (!) of the community room acting as termination—again as counteractions to the modular consistency, vertical as well as horizontal, of Modernist facades of the time. Again, today this architectural effect you can find in the facades of many multi-storied buildings—as well as the arched window.

The Facade as Plane

The wing walls at the balconies flanking the arched window say the facade is a plane along the street as well as a surface of a form.

Realistic Sculpture and Duality

This kind of generic architecture requires iconographic flourish—that manifest in the sculpture above the arched window in the form of a television antenna as objet trouvé; because the client was Quaker there could be no Madonna on top. And then there is the duality derived from the position of the column at the entrance—this column in granite, itself structural *and* decorative, and uniquely big in a time when the thinner the better prevailed.

Inside, the corridors are nicely not long and contain decorative tile friezes designed by elementary school students of the neighborhood. Many of the rooms have windows facing two ways.

Non-Coercive Architecture

But most important perhaps, the place works as a background for living that is not coercive—where, for instance, the American occupants were not forced into a kind of imported architectural enclave for Continental Socialist proletarians of the twenties that American architects ironically imposed in the fifties and sixties. I love the photograph of the "ordinary" occupant whose furniture is at home and whose lace curtains could look OK in our laid-back architecture.

P.S.

Oh, and the chain link fence enclosing the two front yards was then ordinary and therefore extraordinary in its context rather than chic, but its posts rhythmically evolve in plan as they approach the center of the composition. Like the architecture of the whole, the composition of the fence promotes an aesthetic tension between the ordinary and extraordinary all at once.

P.P.S.

It is nice that this building has been influential, or rather that subsequent architecture has evolved in parallel ways, although not all of the manifestations can one call positive.

THOUGHTS ON FIRE STATION NO. 4
TWENTY-FIVE YEARS LATER

Written 1992.

We worked hard to make Fire Station No. 4 in Columbus, Indiana, as well as the later Dixwell Fire Station in New Haven, Connecticut, look like a fire station. We consciously and explicitly made this inherently civic but modest building not heroic and original: we made it ordinary, conventional, familiar, in terms of its formal and symbolic image—conforming to your generic idea about how a fire station looked—representing perhaps how a child would think of it. It is hard to realize now how outrageous this approach was at the time—the sensibility of the recent past is always the hardest to resurrect—because everything was heroic and original in the then late Modern period in architecture. The material for a fire station by a great architect at this time would probably have to be *béton brut* concrete, at home in southern France but hard to attain technically and maintain over time in the USA; its form would have to be, no matter what, unfamiliar; its scale would have to be monumental more than civic; its relation to its setting, especially that of a small town, would look to be one of bold contrast frequently implying contempt—the houses around it probably looking meek and the firemen sitting in front of it or baking pies inside it feeling silly, or at least uncomfortable.

Our approach in urban terms was pragmatic; we started with what we had in urban America and decided that what was there was varied and not all bad. It was hard to be not heroic, not to ride contemptuously down Main Street on a white steed, but rather, motor in and decide it was almost all right.

Also we did not disdain commercial graphics (signs) or even decorative pattern or even symmetry if it was functional. Our buildings even began to include windows—that looked familiar and were not desperately disguised within spandrels as parts of horizontal or vertical stripes on the facade or as pure absence of wall altogether.

So we used conventional elements in this building type at once functional—it is a garage for trucks plus a barracks—and symbolic—it is a distinguished civic building type but minor within the hierarchy of civic building types: i.e., it is not a city hall, much less a disguised esoteric pavilion for a garden! And we weren't afraid of brick, and colored brick whose pattern aesthetically affected the perception of the final form of the building via two-dimensional modulation rather than sculptural articulation.

We followed an old tradition in Western art that admits appropriateness, that represents the ordinary and makes it extraordinary by artful modifications and modulations in scale, use, and proportion, that promotes tense art over pompous art. Beethoven did this in his third movement rondos that are peasant tunes adapted. In architecture and urbanism let's sometimes start with what we have and evolve from there rather than start all over again, heroic and original.

SPEECH FOR THE CONFERENCE "INTERIORS FOR HISTORIC BUILDINGS"

This talk was delivered December 7, 1988, at the request of Lee H. Nelson, FAIA. The conference was sponsored by the National Park Service, American Society of Interior Designers, General Services Administration, Pennsylvania History and Museum Commission, Rhode Island History and Preservation Commission, Historic Preservation Education Commission, Historic Preservation Education Foundation, New York State Parks, Recreation and Historic Preservation, and Georgia Institute of Technology.

———

I am apprehensive about giving this talk because I usually like to know what I am talking about. This is because I'm going to talk about process more than substance.

I can talk here only as an architect. My firm and I have been doing some work involving restoration and rehabilitation of some distinguished buildings, and I am an individual who has long had an interest in historical architecture and a reliance on it for the lessons it can teach. But I am not an art historian, and, very significantly, I have none of the specific and complex kinds of training that your fields—those represented in this audience—demand.

But I shall get on with it—trusting that as an outsider I can steer a course among the extremes of banality, naivete, and the outrageous.

This I shall try to do by focusing on an issue that concerns me as a practicing architect, an issue that applies to architecture as a whole, but also to the fields of restoration and rehabilitation.

My perspective is that of the architect, in this context, who works to "effect change responsive to the historical environment," to quote David De Long's elegant definition—who is to match his knowledge and experience concerning program, engineering, and code compliance with his sensibility concerning the historic and aesthetic fabric of an existing building.

Now we all know at least two distinctive characteristics of this process in architecture: (1) it is extremely complex, despite De Long's short definition, and (2) it involves many specialists—working together.

I wrote a book a long time ago called *Complexity and Contradiction in Architecture* where I analyzed the effect of modern experience on architectural form—the modern experience that involved complexity and contradiction as I defined it and that promoted, in the end, richness over simplicity and tension over unity—that is, promoted a mannerist approach to the art that acknowledged ambiguity as an essential aspect of meaning. I was little aware then of the effect the complexity and contradiction of the modern experience would have on the process of architecture as well as on the form of architecture.

And this has derived from the need for many specialists working together, each with his or her own focus within the complex whole at hand, and it involves two kinds of specialists: consultants and bureaucrats—those that work on the basis of professional or technical competence in their field, and those that work within government agencies to ensure compliance with codes.

And the challenges posed by this phenomenon are compounded as you combine the dimensions of restoration and preservation and architectural determinants.

Along with the formal and aesthetic complexities and contradictions in architecture deriving from the modern experience has evolved a particular attitude of our time that is psychological—that of an abhorrence of risk. This is perhaps a manifestation in our evolution from the Me Generation to the Why-Me? Generation. This tendency to Cover Your Ass has paralleled the enormous increase in our time in our field of governmental regulation via expanded Codes and proliferating Design Review Boards (although it has been said that the growth of this kind of bureaucracy has been a matter also of filling a vacuum—that caused by the decrease in federal and state funding for planning and housing agencies in the last decade).

These tendencies have encouraged a legalistic approach to our work as well—cover yourself to avoid legal risks—so that lawyers as well as consultants and bureaucrats enter the process in a new and significant way. A number of not-so-large architectural offices now have a lawyer on their staff. Next might be in-house insurance agents.

And this spirit of minimizing risk and maximizing regulations extends now to the aesthetics of architecture—this evident in the proliferation of local Design Review Boards and urban design regulations. In this instance, all we can say is: thank God similar boards and regulations didn't exist in the old days in the cities of Medieval and Renaissance Italy, or even in the Oak Park of Frank Lloyd Wright's day. But worse perhaps than the effect of our urban design do-gooders is the effect on the First Amendment—worse than the stultifying rigidity of many of the regulations are the discretionary powers of the Design Review Boards which tend to promote an arbitrary form of rule by Man rather than rule by Law.

But let me inject immediately and emphatically: I *am* for acknowledging the valid manifestations of complexity and contradiction in the design process today—as I have been in the aesthetic dimension of architecture. And unequivocally I *am* for professional responsibility and governmental regulation in regard to user safety, fire safety, the accommodation of the disabled—as I support social and ecological imperatives. These regulations in sensible forms are essential to any complex, modern, civilized community and we should comply with them positively and enthusiastically.

Moreover, beyond these specific responsibilities there lies the positive challenge of achieving the sophistication and richness that comes from facing complex issues and exploiting the opportunities that specialization affords.

What we should resist is focusing on our own area of responsibility at the expense of the whole—of upholding our special territory from the "onslaught" of other specialists—disregarding a sensibility toward the whole and an understanding of the give-and-take in the creative process.

We should understand in our varying roles as specialists, professional or bureaucratic, that we work within a greater context. In this way our work can become essentially creative and not strategic. Strategy is an enemy of spirit and a promoter of drudgery.

———

Here are examples from my current experience and that of our office of some fanatical specialization or some bureaucratic meddling that has encouraged strategic planning at the expense of creativity:

A plaza is mandated in the local urban design code for the front of a building we are designing in a city in the Northwest—required apparently for aesthetic amenity. And this plaza has to include in 23 percent of its total area a form of landscape greenery.

Does this mean the Palazzo Rucellai, sans piazza, in Florence, or the Piazza San Marco, sans a blade of grass, in Venice would both have to go back to the drawing boards?

In the same city the facade of our building must include in the area of its facade at street level 18 percent for glass fenestration for the amenity of pedestrians—here, with considerable strain on the interior program of the building and in partial contradiction to seismic code requirements of that city.

What if such a code had existed in seventeenth- or eighteenth-century London with its consequent effect on the rusticated bases of the churches of Wren, Hawksmoor, and Archer? You need a natural variety in a city as it evolves via a mediation of outside and inside requirements: you can't legislate amenity—much less art! Neither ideology on one hand nor simplistic regulations on the other will do in the pragmatic *and* idealistic accommodation necessary for the working of a city and the beauty of it.

How about stairways?

Almost any monumental stair today has to have not just appropriate handrails at its edges but a series of handrails as well, a maximum of every 8 feet or so, across its width. These recall a maze in a stockyard containing cattle or an entrance to a subway in Manhattan. Think how this requirement would affect the steps around the Parthenon.

Also, the spacing of the vertical struts of the railings of most stairs today has to be so close as to resemble the grilles over the windows in a ward for violent patients. This is, I think, so babies won't get their heads stuck in the railings.

The curators in a museum we are designing are recommending for the surface of the walls of the picture galleries a value based totally on a scientific standard of light reflection without regard for the symbolic content of the architecture and for the element of association inherent in the design of a context for historical exhibits.

For another museum we have been negotiating for many months to accommodate a city agency that feels our bricks on the rear facades will not absorb dirt quick enough: how's that for sophistication via patina?

Or take Nantucket and its notorious guardians—the Historical Review Board—with its curious view of what makes that beautiful town precious. The question concerning Nantucket is: do you admire it for its unity or for its diversity?

If you ask is Nantucket beautiful and lively because of its consistency or inconsistency, I vote for the latter.

Much of the architectural aesthetic of this historic town is based on sets of rules—on vocabularies of orderly Georgian and Greek Revival proportions, details, and symbols. But its essential quality derives from the variety that works within these bounds and often from transgressing the rules not through ignorance, but sometimes from playfulness, and always from a profound yet easy understanding of the whole on one hand, and circumstantial requirements on the other—creating in the end the vitality and tension that make that place a joy to be in.

It is said that the current requirements mandated for the handicapped for housing in New York City add 5–8 percent to the construction cost of apartment buildings. Meanwhile, 3,000 families, many with children, remain in squalid hotels at an average cost of $1,300 per month. So much for looking at the whole picture.

And what an ultimate irony: this concern for a risk-free environment in our everyday existence while we live all of us as never before in history under a threat of instant and total annihilation—in a time of an unprecedented buildup of nuclear arsenals and a threat of nuclear holocaust. And yet how many of us work for disarmament and peace while fiddling and regulating while Rome might burn?

———

Finally, let us be tolerant in our art and in our ways: let us be not purists, but sensible in both meanings of that word—in our working together for the good of the whole.

In these cantankerous ramblings of an old architect—ramblings involving presumptuous suggestions—in the end I am simply making a plea for facing the issues in working together, and enhancing the claims of creativity over strategy: in other words, let's try for less agony and more ecstasy in the way we work.

I must end on a truly positive note concerning the three projects we are working on now with Short and Ford and Connie Greiff of Heritage Studies; and Robert Neiley in Boston; and George Thomas of The Clio Group and Marianna Thomas. None of the frustrations enumerated above applies to working with them: but rather mutual understanding and exciting and constructive dialogue enrich the process.

And when I work on preservation projects with Nick Gianopulos of Keast and Hood, I afford him the highest compliment that a fellow worker can make: when Nick says no, you can't do that, I believe him utterly.

THE PRESERVATION GAME AT PENN:
AN EMOTIONAL RESPONSE

Written 1993.

Oh, for some sensibility and sophistication concerning the complexities of urbanism—for creative balances among historical continuity and evolutionary growth, historical reference and daily utility, quaintness of the picturesque and genius of the everyday—in the end, oh, for accommodation to vital activity essential to an urban setting that is not a historical tableau, that is never complete. This pragmatic plea applies with only rare exceptions—such as those of an iconic complex like the Piazza San Marco or a symbolically vivid College Hall at the University of Pennsylvania. Let us achieve authentic quality by enhancing reality rather than embalming sentiment.

And, oh, for some courage to face realities of now as well as glories of then—and not with naive and sullen piety but with just plain vigor! How about the high road over the easy way—the road that acknowledges the creative richness of complexity over the extremist ideology of simplicity. Oh, for some sophistication to understand the complexities of urban dynamics—because when the good goes simplistic it becomes tyrannical, and when the good goes tyrannical it goes bad. And when the good goes bad, beware.

This outburst is occasioned by the continuing disturbance in parts of the community of the University of Pennsylvania concerning our design for the new laboratory building for the Institute for Advanced Science and Technology, which is to replace Smith Hall in the science precinct of the campus and modify the architectural context of the Furness Library across the street. This opposition promotes a kind of sanctification of Smith Hall—proclaimed for its supposed historical and aesthetic significance while it is really as memorable as a pair of old socks from J. C. Penney, projecting neither the suavity or validity of a truly generic example of architecture nor the force of an original masterpiece. The only thing amazing about this undistinguished academic building is its identicalness to what was originally a commercial dental supply building up the street by the same architects—and its retardataire banality as a post-Ruskinian, post-Furnessian, post-Richardsonian, German neo-Classical turd whose style is c. 1830—although it was designed c. 1890! So it is a retardataire bore with a manufactured history—the historically significant things that are claimed to have happened inside are largely disputed by objective historians; if you try hard enough you can find that something important happened in any old row house in West Philly—how about the first Italo-Polish marriage celebrated on Regent Street in the ethnic history of our area? Why not fight to save the Dunes Hotel and sign in Las Vegas—whose significance, historical and aesthetic, surpasses that of Smith Hall by a long shot!

As for the inviolability of Smith Walk as a sacred route corresponding in historical, aesthetic, and symbolic significance to the Pan-Athenaic Way—this walk is realistically to be enhanced in the new site plan as part of the new building design by means of its adjusted focus on the apse of the Furness building rather than, as currently, on an indeterminate point of that facade. This slight adjustment improves safety at the pedestrian crossing midblock on 34th Street. But the most significant issue here involves the relation of the adjusted Smith Walk to the campus as a whole. The new design is crucial within the master plan as it promotes identity and continuity for this now-major pedestrian circulation route at Penn and connects Locust Walk at the western end of the campus with significant activity that is anticipated at the eastern end of the campus as it is developed. This enhanced element within the campus requires activity along its route more than sanctity. Smith Walk is now stupid as it approaches Furness: Smith Walk via our scheme will sing as it approaches Furness—and all of this happens without touching the axial position of the statue of Provost Smith.

I feel confident and far from arrogant in making these claims: I am an architect who has dedicated his life to acknowledging spatial, symbolic, and historical context in my roles as writer and practitioner. It was I who initiated, in my M.F.A. thesis at Princeton of 1950, the idea of context in architectural planning and employed the word for the first time—the word as it is applied universally in our era—this at a time when history was bunk as urban setting, and orthodox Modernism was "in" with a confidence, if not a vengeance, that is hard for aesthetic and historical naifs to recall or comprehend in our time. This thesis (whose design component was a new chapel for the Episcopal Academy) was based on the tenets of Gestalt psychology that context is the perceptual basis of meaning and that change in context effects change in meaning.

Upon the second tenet of this thesis rests our justification for the positive influence of the IAST building as background—as background, spatial, formal, and symbolic—within the complex of buildings in this part of the Penn campus, especially for the Furness Building.

The new building through its facades promotes a rhythmic composition that creates a background appropriate for the exquisite fanfare that is the essence of Furness. And the new building through its spatial manifestations at this end of Smith Walk promotes a composition that enhances diversity and tension among forms—and, by achieving dynamism for an evolving place, thereby eschews aesthetic correctness and dry rectitude. Along with this go our justifications for accommodation to functional and social dimensions of the architecture that in turn enhance vitality in this science precinct and the academic community it is in.

Remember, pious preservationists, architecture isn't sculpture—you design from the inside out as well as the outside in. And it's old doesn't mean it's good, and it's new doesn't mean it's bad. Good can happen.

Let us beware of sanctimonious naifs—devious members of preservation squads—ideological fanatics promoting architectural necrophilia—evangelical historians whose pious airs are matched by bad manners—all too authentic bureaucrats and goody-goody community nerds—unprofessional architects (proclaiming our perspective cheats and our design stinks)—and uncultured academics benumbed by tenure with time for making trouble rather than sense, while in the end making of preservation a perversity and preventing history in the name of preserving it. Remember: each Renaissance masterpiece you revere within a city like Florence replaced a Gothic or Romanesque structure; do you think the site of the Strozzi Palace is a former parking lot? (Granted: Robert Venturi isn't Benedetto da Maiano, but the complaining architects aren't VSBA.) Replacement rather than expansion as a function of urban growth is new to American naifs but it represents a dominant tradition within our cultural heritage. How about substituting reality, vitality, and tension for ideology, perfection, and deadness!

And how about those scientists whose interests and whose work you disdain—those scientists of now who are committed to vital work rather than pretentious mischief, who acknowledge reality, evidence creativity, and make history, who need now effectively to concentrate within a special and supportive setting and communicate within an immediate academic community?

Let us design from the inside out as well as the outside in! Let us accommodate the immediate and vital needs of the workers at Penn and thereby accommodate community as well as sentiment. Let us not set a stage for a sculptural tableau. Let us work within an evolving community—not a historical district but a growing campus: let not nostalgia subsume presence. And let us remember John Summerson: preservation "in its best form [is] a mark of civilization . . . [that] illustrates in a concrete way our power to embrace human achievement wherever and whenever it has reached an honourable level. . . . The subject [of preservation] is, however, subtle and delicate, susceptible of fatuity, hypocrisy, sentimentality of the ugliest sort and downright obstructionism. In its worst form preservation may be a resentful fumbling, a refusal to understand the living shape of things or to give things shape."[1]

---

1. From *Heavenly Mansions* (New York: W. W. Norton, 1963).

A SERIES OF RESPONSES FOR *VIA*, THE JOURNAL OF THE SCHOOL OF FINE ARTS, UNIVERSITY OF PENNSYLVANIA

Responses as opinions concerning the following places, written for *Via*, no. 12: "Simultaneous Cities," edited by Ralph Muldrow and Patrick McDonough, to be published in January 1996.

Seaside: It was very nice when we saw it in the winter but I hope it is OK with the cars in the summer.

Chicago: An exquisite and beloved museum of architecture that includes Sullivan *and* Richardson *and* the Chicago School *and* Wright *and* Mies *and* Tigerman: is it to be America's Florence?

Broadacre City: Formal and cultural consistency imposed via motifs by an oppressive genius for a single class in the name of individualism and democracy. Buildings, cars, and probably the andirons and the women's dresses were to be unified—in a design that was, ironically, as universal, culturally and formally, as was the Ville Radieuse!—boring irrelevance, unless you call it a modern version of the English Romantic park with pavilions or a precedent for Levittown.

Philadelphia: Unity *and* variety, consistency *and* inconsistency, order *and* disorder, harmony *and* dissonance, egalitarianism *and* hierarchy: this prototypical gridiron plan can contain individualistic architecture galore—as it promotes an egalitarian system where hierarchy among buildings derives from their inherent quality rather than from their special location—the glorious prototypical city therefore as open-ended, never complete, a constant fragment of itself.

Reston, VA: Lawns promoting lawns.

Ville Radieuse: A good idea, just so the parks among the slabs don't become parking lots, the building forms don't exclude shopping below, and the high-rise apartment system—created originally for the continental socialist proletariat and ultimately subsumed by the middle class—is not imposed via an American architectural elite as public housing on a culturally antagonistic American underclass.

Tokyo: The city of now—not inflicting universal consistency but accommodating multiculturalism—juxtaposing the remnant village, the global complex and mega-electronic iconography—the old and the new—with *verve, esprit, joie de vivre, élan.*

Las Vegas: The city of signs spewing the vital if vulgar iconography of now—*terribilità* verging on *orribilità.*

L.A.: The city of the auto.

Florence: Human scale and ultimate refinement as you walk within it—while dodging the cars and the Vespas.

Rome: The eternal city—not for its ever-consistent forms but for its ever-consistent relevance.

Rose Valley: Gentle coming together of nature and art in a gentle social environment.

Levittown: Broadacre City for the masses, who have modified it over time via house decorations, lawn sculpture, and converted garages.

Washington, DC: An original city plan that juxtaposes a nonhierarchical, egalitarian, open-ended grid plan on a system of hierarchical diagonal Baroque avenues, axially terminated by important buildings. It currently contains parvenu architecture par excellence, despite or because of aesthetic control by the Washington Fine Arts Commission.

Parc de la Villette: A late twentieth-century version of a late eighteenth-century *jardin anglais, avec follies* galore.

Ravenna: Home of what might become a late twentieth-century architectural prototype—that is, the Early Christian basilica whose interior surfaces glitter with mosaic iconography—iconography that in its historical context is ornamental, universal, and eternal, and presages the glittering outdoor electric-sign surfaces with ornament and information of our time that are multicultural and ever-changing.

PERSONAL APPROACHES AND POSITIONS TOWARD CONTEMPORARY ARCHITECTURAL PRACTICE

By Robert Venturi and Denise Scott Brown. Written in 1992 for the *Harvard Architectural Review* but never published.

There is "not one universal culture." —Isaiah Berlin

One way to describe our view of where architecture is today is simply to observe that the "Gentle Manifesto" in *Complexity and Contradiction in Architecture* and the position expressed in *Learning from Las Vegas* have been embraced within mainstream architecture and theory in the last few years, but embraced in a way that is somewhat perverse and ignores warnings accompanying the original messages—granted that authors and theoreticians of much architecture today would deny any influence, perverse or positive, derived from these sources, or any parallel, ironic or otherwise, between their approach today and ours of the mid-sixties and early seventies.

We record some more specific responses to current directions in architecture in the series of oppositions that follow. Each pairing suggests our position today by contrast with what we are *not*. Some respond to current directions (Hype-Modern and Deco-Modern) and others to earlier directions (Late Modern or Postmodern).

Our approach to practice in the 1990s acknowledges, in general, multicultural contexts that are global, and dynamic evolutions—social, political, and economic—that our architecture must accommodate. As practicing architects we regret the lack of social dimension in our national overall ethos and

Federal policy, and therefore in our national architecture and within our own practice.

In essence our position—responsive and intuitive—encourages rich varieties of architecture that are generic and responsive to context, formal and symbolic; our position discourages trendy architectural rhetoric that takes a naive and ironic guise of universal order.

It encourages architecture as elemental shelter and background for living and discourages architecture as articulated sculpture left out in the rain, and as scenery for acting.

Oppositions: Approaches and Positions
Deriving from Response and Intuition in Some Barely Detectable Order

generic architecture in context	vs	universal architecture as rhetoric
Sever Hall	vs	the Wexler Center
dynamic evolution accommodated in our time	vs	hype revolution promoted for our time
generic architecture accommodating dynamic evolution	vs	heroic architecture tilting at windmills
the generic building fitting like a mitten, accommodating flexibly over time	vs	the signature building fitting like a glove tailored to perfection, inflexible, indeed eternal
pragmatic accommodation	vs	idealistic imposition
discovering the familiar	vs	stalking the exotic
ordinary becomes extraordinary	vs	extraordinary becomes ordinary
everyday vernacular	vs	playground of the gods

commercial vernacular and signs	vs	industrial vernacular and machine aesthetic
architecture for everyday sensibility	vs	architecture as one–upmanship
children *and* sophisticates like it	vs	elitist–esoteric
mass culture too	vs	high culture sole
Scarlatti *and* U2	vs	Scarlatti
incidental originality	vs	overt originality
vernacular, familiar	vs	outlandish
be good	vs	be original
ordinary and conventional	vs	heroic and original
anti–hero as hero	vs	hero as hero
avant–garde as incidental	vs	avant–garde as goal
real avant–garde	vs	rear avant–garde
authentic avant–garde	vs	establishment avant–garde
épater the avant–garde	vs	*épater* the bourgeoisie
aesthetic tension	vs	aesthetic bombast
deep satisfaction from focusing on realities	vs	cheap thrills from wowing journalists
solutions to real problems	vs	submission to ideal forms

architecture for the world we live and work in	vs	architecture as arcane diagrams and colored models that look good on the pages of a publication
ceci tuera cela	vs	*cela deviendra ceci*
second glance architecture	vs	wow! architecture
aesthetic based on artistic intuition	vs	aesthetic based on ideological promotion
try to make sense	vs	try to make an impression
architecture	vs	ideology
architecture defined as firmness + commodity + delight	vs	architecture derived from literary criticism, semiotics, philosophical theory, psychology, strange ideas about perception, etc.
theory as support for architecture	vs	theory as substitute for architecture
architecture as the subject of theory	vs	architecture as the victim of theory
architecture	vs	arconcepture
frozen music	vs	frozen theory
architecture as high-faluting craft	vs	architecture as arty theory
generic order that accommodates exceptions	vs	universal order that's pure and simple

generic order accommodating everyday	vs	universal order promoting trends
variety deriving from circumstance	vs	variety for its own sake
contradiction as valid response	vs	contradiction as picturesque hype
unusual angles as exceptions	vs	unusual angles as motifs
art found in the limitations of order	vs	hype generated by exploitation of disorder
accommodating variety	vs	exploiting variety
order modulated by circumstance	vs	circumstance swept under the rug
some dissonance creates tension	vs	all dissonance creates boredom
contradiction as exception	vs	contradiction as the rule
the "difficult whole"	vs	the scene of an explosion in an industrial park
a floor is a floor is a floor	vs	a floor is a ramp
complexity and contradiction	vs	expressionism and picturesqueness
mannerist architecture	vs	ubiquitous contradiction, gratuitous ambiguity
richness and ambiguity	vs	unity and clarity
urban chaos as affecting	vs	architectural chaos as affected
frozen music	vs	frenzied music

realist complexity	vs	minimalist simplicity
"messy vitality"	vs	goody-goody urbanism
surface ornamentation	vs	sculptural articulation
decorated shelter	vs	structural expressionism
lyrical and/or ugly	vs	expressive
adapt hype sensibility conditioned by TV commercials and loud rock	vs	adopt it
applied ornamental pattern	vs	structural and functional exhibitionism
"decorate construction"	vs	"construct decoration"
the decorated shed	vs	colored structural industrial sculpture
pastiche	vs	disguised pastiche
function and structure as function and structure	vs	function and structure as decoration and abstraction
Deco	vs	Decon
meaning from symbols	vs	expression from form
representation	vs	abstraction
diverse symbolism	vs	symbolism of the old factory
cultural pluralism	vs	unity *über alles*

orders	vs	order
relativity and diversity of taste cultures	vs	good taste
cultural and social diversity	vs	universal order
global architectures	vs	global architecture
contextual accommodation	vs	universal imposition
intimations of local context	vs	dogma of universality
architecture that both accommodates to place as context and enhances place as context	vs	architecture as carpetbagger
accommodation to context via analogy *and/or* contrast	vs	accommodation to context only via analogy, goody-goody historicism
the building as shelter	vs	the building as pavilions articulating a village
the town is buildings	vs	the town is a building (megastructure)
the town is buildings	vs	the building is a town (Decon)
electronic technology	vs	engineering technology
electronic iconography	vs	engineering expressionism
ARCHITECTURE AS ELEMENTAL SHELTER AND BACKGROUND FOR LIVING	vs	ARCHITECTURE AS ARTICULATED SCULPTURE (LEFT OUT IN THE RAIN) AND SCENERY FOR ACTING

LETTER SENT TO SEVERAL ARCHITECT SELECTION COMMITTEES CONCERNING COMPETITIONS, DRAFTED BY MEMBERS OF THE OFFICE OF VENTURI, SCOTT BROWN AND ASSOCIATES

Written 1984.

Chairman, Architect Selection Committee:

Thank you for your kind letter advising us of our selection for your project short list. We are very sorry we have to politely decline to pursue your project. However, we do want to explain carefully to you and at some length why we feel we cannot participate.

There has been a growing realization among clients over the last decade that their role in creating new buildings is as important as that of the architect. The client's role is not only to provide the money and be the final arbiter of what is provided—that has always been understood—but also to participate actively in program and design decisions. This realization is confirmed by our own experience. When we have worked with a client who is both a sympathetic supporter and collaborator as well as a demanding taskmaster, we have done our most satisfying work. This is true whether the measure is some standard of aesthetic excellence, the usefulness of the facility to its users, or the efficiency of the delivery process. Conversely where we have worked without a user-client, as sometimes happens, or with a client who is less than vitally interested in the project, we have been less satisfied with our performance.

Unfortunately, the competition process does not allow for real collaboration; it specifically and precisely precludes it. Little wonder that the few buildings which have eventuated from this process have not generally been well received either by the critical community or by the users.

It is sometimes suggested in response to the observation set out above, with which few seem to disagree, that the competition process should be used not to select a design, but to select a designer, thereby discarding the product while retaining the architect. This ingenuous suggestion has several logical flaws, fatal ones we believe: the most serious is that it does not take into account human nature. One is in effect proposing to a designer that he or she throw out the product of weeks—often months—of the most intense labor and start over with a clean slate. But the architectural baggage so painfully acquired is not so easily discarded, and the stage is set for an unsuccessful relationship concluding with an unsatisfactory project. This because the architect arrives at an answer before the client has formulated the questions. Parenthetically, it should not be thought that the creation of a building is a linear process—programming, design, documentation, construction. Design informs program as much as program informs design. Eliminate that interaction and the question may never catch up with the answer.

There is yet another fundamental problem with the competition process—one which is both economic and human. It requires extraordinary commitment to arrive at and to present a solution to a design problem. We have yet to see any stipend offered, even in a limited competition, which bears a reasonable relationship to the cost of competing. For a project of this scale, a typical stipend would be in the range of $10,000 to $20,000. The cost of preparing the competition entry—if done thoroughly enough to stand a chance of succeeding—will substantially exceed $40,000. The difference will come, in varying proportions, out of the pockets of the architect and of his paying clients. This can hardly be thought fair, even if architects, in their eagerness, agree to it. The paying clients, who have shown their trust in the architect by selecting him directly, don't get to vote on the issue. And suppose all of the competitors were fully compensated for their work—most projects are not so richly supported that money can be wasted on the selection process without affecting the performance or quality of the completed facility. The human cost of this process is not cheap either. We invest our very souls in the work we do—as do our colleagues. Ours is a profession and an art in which one becomes accustomed to disappointment. But you always die a little bit when the product of your labor is rejected and your dream remains unbuilt.

We, of all people, fully understand the burning desire of a client to see the finished product before committing to buy it. We buy ready-made suits for that very reason. But designed buildings are not tailored suits and we think there is a degree of abdication of responsibility in succumbing to this desire. To create a design the architect has had to go through a process of self-education and development. We are often surprised by the designs we create. This, as is well understood, is within the nature of art. The client should be surprised too. But if the client has not been through the design development process, he/she may reject what surprises him/her and abrogate innovation.

This should not be taken to mean we are opposed to all competitions. We have entered some and won some—although the winning has only once resulted in a completed building. Open competitions have had the well-advertised benefit of exhibiting new talent, and they are usually harmless enough since few competition winners are ever built. But the current growing enthusiasm for the limited competition we clearly see as pernicious—adverse to the best interests of the client and the architect. And because we have come to see the issue in this light we feel compelled to decline to participate. As sometimes acknowledged leaders in our profession we cannot evade that responsibility.

We do regret missing the wonderful opportunity your project presents.

ANSWER TO CHARLES K. HOYT, EDITOR, *ARCHITECTURAL RECORD*, REGARDING COMPETITIONS

A response to a question Hoyt posed to several architecture firms regarding their attitude toward competitions. Written 1992.

Would you retain a doctor who prescribes cures before examining the patient and performing tests?

Don't potential clients realize architects who spend all that time and money getting a job have to take it out of doing a job? Good architects spend all their fees on making the design better and their performance smoother; they shouldn't have money left for hype marketing.

Professionals presenting designs without a contract with the client (and that means without contact with the client) produce products, not art. Architecture derives from collaboration between client and professional: good architecture derives from collaboration with users, not from wowing of users.

A good salesman is a bad artist.

Project managers are often a legitimate necessity because of the complexity of process in our time but are often in the end a competitor more than a facilitator: it is in their interest to make the architect look bad so they look good. The worst thing is they diminish communication and trust between architect and client, and therefore the architect's professional role is diminished and the architecture suffers.

THE OVERWHELMING OF THE ARCHITECT: WHAT IT TAKES TO BE AN ARCHITECT IN THE NINETIES: A MODEST TIRADE MAINLY FOR MYSELF

The Architect as Businessman, Salesman, Lawyer, Psychiatrist, Actor, Consultant-Referee, Pragmatist and Idealist and Masochist— and Then a Professional and a Designer

This essay was presented by the author at the annual Convention of the American Institute of Architects in Washington, DC, in May 1991. The ideas have been expressed by him in other fora since then.

––––––––

1. Commercial marketing skills and entrepreneurial-scholarly commitment dedicated to preparing an encyclopedic tome promoting at once an extraordinary philosophy of art and an organizational chart worthy of a Harvard M.B.A.—this is called a proposal, which is a response to an R.F.P. that is much longer than Thomas Jefferson's Declaration of Independence and has been composed by committees of bureaucrats justifying their existence and lawyers justifying their fees—while at the same time rehearsing your performance and that of your staff as dramatis personae in a production called a job interview, meanwhile diverting your energy from, and consuming time for, the work in your office you and your staff are committed to—that is, for design for the clients who have previously favored you with commissions.

2. If you are unlucky enough to make the so-called short list (consisting of many competing firms) you employ an ad man's skills in reducing the verbosity of the above-mentioned tome to succinct sound bites syncopated with series of spectacular slides of your buildings photographed at cockeyed angles with weird lighting effects that rival the pizzazz of a TV commercial to impress a Kafka-esque selection committee that knows what it likes when it comes to architecture; but, above all, you exude the charisma of a matinee idol, preferably a summa cum laude graduate of a leading drama school who

can handle these interviews as the show biz auditions they are; and it wouldn't hurt to have been a science major to promote the right chemistry—while flaunting dubiously professionally ethical preliminary sketches and snazzy models that parallel in their method cures prescribed by a doctor before examining the patient—what V. S. Naipaul calls knowing the answers before one knows the problem—thus encouraging superficiality and promoting ideology, not art. I'm so tired of having to be clever rather than good to get the work and stay in business. In the end more creativity can go into getting the job than doing it—and perhaps more energy as you become the eternally traveling salesman succumbing to becks and calls—victim of vagabondage; it's hard to be a creator and a promoter. And then there is the agony of rejection which happens most of the time at the end of this harrowing process.

3. And yet, to misquote Oscar Wilde: the only thing worse than not getting the job is getting the job—somehow—via pleasing a dominant individual on the committee or being mediocre enough to accommodate a consensus of the committee: you have to seem charming but not flip, great but not threatening. Then you employ the legal skills of a Philadelphia lawyer to counter the ever-unique inch-thick contract the client's lawyers propose along with a macho business ethic for negotiating fees that hopefully can accommodate God in the details and support the staff of huge proportions architectural offices currently require to accommodate J.D. and P.R., and to counter the clients' lawyers' negotiating lower architect's fees that in the end assure either lower design standards or eventual bankruptcy while sapping the architect's energy and taking the joy out of the job: work hard and pay the price. And as an educator, you often have to bring the client committee around to an anticipated cost-per-square-foot budget conforming to construction costs beyond those of a minimalist fifties loft building rather than those for the signature building of the decade the committee simultaneously expects.

4. Machiavellian strategizing to establish the architect's professional role as trusted agent of the client while the project manager intrudes within this elemental relationship by "protecting" the client from the architect and making himself look good at the expense of the architect—is it that the

architect works to make the architecture look good while the project manager works to make himself look good? Meanwhile the conscientious architect risks alienating the client while being realistic about promoting the client's interests.

5. Psychiatric genius in preventing building committees from generating architectural camels—this by promoting empathy and collaboration between client and architect because architects' best ideas should come from simpatico clients.

6. The resilience of a referee in a boxing ring mediating among myriads of petulant consultants each demanding perfection for his part of the design at the expense of the whole—each with a board nailed over his ass—these consultants, as sanctified specialists, promoting with airs of superiority an approach you yourself originated some years ago. Oh, for the rare consultant whom, when he says no, you can believe.

7. Placating design review boards perversely promoting naive ideals concerning architectural unity—do-gooders bathed in piety promoting deadening architectural harmony or goody-goody urban design; or historical commissions promoting historicism while piously preventing history from being made in their time (thank God there were no hysterical commissions in medieval and Renaissance Italy). Or government agencies justifying their bureaucratic existence by implementing codes that all too often verify the law as an ass, sir. No longer does form follow function: form follows regulation: perhaps as bad as a corrupt bureaucracy is a zealous bureaucracy.

8. Administering the construction while resisting the temptation to do the construction manager's job within the architect's fee, becoming a remedial expert supervising rectification of bad workmanship rather than implementation of good workmanship—while keeping at bay the contractors' Seattle claims consultant with your Philadelphia lawyer by your side, answering hundreds of superfluous questions whose purpose is to build a record and writing letters to cover *your* ass, while paying mounting insurance premiums as protection from contractors who measure their skill in terms of the number and magnitude of their claims.

9. Auditing additional services that become the perverse resultant of the above hoops you are put through, so that the project architect becomes an accountant.

10. And near the end, fortitude in the face of uncultured architectural critics, promoting their ideology and cleverness at your expense by relishing spectacle over subtlety, whose debasement of your completed building works to promote their status as sophisticated theorists rather than ambitious journalists.

11. But the ultimate tragedy can be the architects' mistakes in design—of omission and commission—that come from not having the time or peace of mind to engage God in the details, to assess the design as it evolves when artists must be not defensive but creative and critical—mistakes in that architectural kind of design that cannot be ultimately revised during rehearsals or edited in proof sheets till the last minute or modified till the end with a dab of paint—these mistakes in concrete, literally and figuratively, that haunt architects ever after despite the reasonable excuse that they were burned-out valid paranoids consumed in strategizing rather than creating who could steal only bits of time for design—if they were unlucky enough to get the job in the first place: the agony is replacing the ecstasy.

But things are almost bearable when a client loves the building in the end and appreciates your commitment—the client who is discerning *and* appreciative—and the building in your own eyes is almost all right—as you live off of Benjamin Franklin's maxim: "Beauty is not in being perfect, beauty is in knowing how to make the design so the imperfections are unimportant."

LETTER TO FRIENDS ABOUT TO VISIT THE SAINSBURY WING

Dear Jim & Sue (pseudonyms),

I trust things have been arranged with John Hunter for the visit to the Sainsbury Wing; if any problems, please let my office know and they can reach me here in Geneva.

This is to inform you of certain things in the design we are not responsible for and that exist because of sad relations with our client.

1. The shop off the lobby looks like a Scandinavian kindergarten & was designed by a shop "specialist."

2. Same for restaurant on mezzanine: a restaurant *spécialiste* cum *muraliste.*

3. The wall above the "lifts" at top of grand stair should have bold lettering delicately carved in the masonry but no politically or diplomatically correct combination of words could be agreed upon.

4. There should be a great window at the end of the central gallery toward Pall Mall to disentomb the effect: the curators wanted the wall for a big picture which you can't read from a distance.

5. The ground-floor lobby is plain boring—sans the color it needs at that point because the lord wanted it that way: thank God we won the Revolutionary War.

6. The front arcade will be dirty because the client on the advice of their project manager saved 100£ by removing a hose bib from the design.

7. The place is cluttered with furniture like the inside of a fubsy pub.

8. Some of the workmanship stinks because the client restrained us while supervising the contractor: the client's project manager accused us in a letter of "excessive diligence" in carrying out our work.

9. Other mistakes are our fault so I won't point them out. I think you will enjoy John.

Bon voyage from us both,

Bob V.   Geneva Aug. 25, 1993

P.S. I forgot to mention the FURNITURE that they didn't let us design—they wanted a "British designer"—who turned out not to sustain the tradition embracing Chippendale, Adam, Hepplewhite, Sheraton, and Morris.

P.P.S. A year later: I hear they've hung (hanged) a painting atop the big staircase, which is like a coloratura singing an aria on the Brooklyn Bridge.

P.P.P.S. I see from recent photos they've placed a phone booth smack in front of the entrance.

THE HALL AND THE AVENUE

Thoughts Concerning the Architectural and Urban Design of the Philadelphia Orchestra Hall of Several Years Ago from the Perspective of Now, and Then Via Multiple Addenda Further Descriptions of Agonizing Evolutions of Designs of the Facade—Positive and Negative

By Robert Venturi and Denise Scott Brown. Written 1993 through 1995.

Things are looking up for Philadelphia's Avenue of the Arts and proposed Orchestra Hall. In fact, with a supportive mayor and important donations the prospects for these projects seem more hopeful than in some years. Nevertheless, an eerie aura surrounds the issue of the design of the Hall and there are rumblings in the community that the buildings projected for the Avenue in general don't measure up to *les Grands Projets* of Paris.

For these reasons and as a way of ensuring the continuity of the process of design, we architects need to call attention to the formal and stylistic content of the Orchestra Hall design and to recall the acoustical determinants, urban challenges, and economic and code constraints that originally and significantly guided the design—as well as to discuss issues deriving from the recent call for *grands projets* on the Avenue of the Arts: only Ben Franklin could do justice to this latter subject but I will try.

At the beginning of our work on this project we advised our client that the established construction budget would restrict the design of the building to the equivalent of blue jeans, rather than permit the white tie and tails the word "gala" would evoke; we added that we did not mind designing beautiful jeans—just so jeans would not have to look like tails.

The challenge to meet the limited budget yet achieve aesthetic quality intensified as we became aware of the unusually complex and expensive acoustical requirements defined by the consultant and approved by the client—which evoked acoustical quality comparable to haute couture. For instance, acoustical flexibility is to be attained via voluminous reverberation chambers and moving parts whose heaving tonnage is to make the Hall's structural engineering comparable to that of a drawbridge rather than a building. Uniquely expensive and equally invisible are measures appropriate for isolating the structure from the vibration of subway trains below Broad Street. And complex life-safety and egress codes had to be acknowledged from the start. Requirements such as these intensified during the design process, resulting, for instance, in minimizing the stonework and surface ornament on the Hall's exterior—which elements are crucial to this design based on surface detail seen close up rather than on hype sculptural form that looks good from a distance or as a model. It appears necessary now to justify and reaffirm the inherent character of the design—reminding the Orchestra community of crucial determinants that influenced it.

We architects worked from the beginning to make a virtue of necessity, avoiding flamboyant forms and symbols, dramatic architectural gestures, un-necessary sculptural or structural articulations, exotic materials, hyperorna-mentation, and expressive references to advanced technology. Rather we hoped to derive quality in the design of the Hall by establishing tense bal-ances among necessary elements that are generic and conventional—em-ploying materials and ornament that admit precedent and acknowledging architecture as primarily the art of enclosure: an art of generic essence, not of sculptural haute couture. Down with cheap tails!

This stance evolves its aesthetic from its economic reality and starts out for real to end up on budget. It eschews trying to be what you aren't, then ending up with compromised fantasy. Yet it represents a creative and posi-tive approach to design, one with distinguished precedent in architecture where a generic building rather than a "signature" building may be implic-itly rather than dramatically functional. We have sought to define a generic hall that takes its precedent from earlier concert halls—along with other distinguished prototypes of generic architecture as rich and varied in their range as the Classical temple, basilican church, Italian Renaissance palazzo, American college hall, Philadelphia row house, and industrial mill building. Here is to be a building not representing an expensive dramatic gesture, original but pretentious, but a generic design distinguished by its conventional quality. And thereby it is not so different from our beloved Academy of Music. The new building's simple all-enclosing form is made of plain materials inside and out employed with imagination, and familiar elements such as windows that create compelling rhythms on the facade and frame imageful activity inside. Patterns of conventional and modest materials ornament its exterior surfaces and project civic scales, monumental and intimate from its modest form.

Inside, too, the two buildings are similar. Although the old is a generic theater known as an opera house, the new a generic chamber known as a concert hall, both welcome attendees through a sequence of auspicious lobbies and foyers and both use surface ornament and sensitive lighting to create special settings for artful performances and gala events. Unfortunately these qualities cannot be comprehended from the architectural model in the Academy lobby, which portrays the interior of the Hall, for instance, as the day after an explosion in a coal mine.

So what you have for this first design stage is not an image of tails with a budget for jeans, not a minimalist sculptural *objet* or a journalistic gesture that's to look good in the newspaper, but a preliminary design—a preliminary design, I emphasize—for a building that will work well and look good in reality as it is subject to development and refinement in the next stages of design.

———

In addition to the realities of budget and the demands of acoustics, the design of the Orchestra Hall must acknowledge the qualities of setting. This civic building must sit appropriately in its urban setting—on Broad Street in Philadelphia. And Philadelphia ain't Paris: the current rumblings in the air for the support of *grands projets* worthy of our Avenue of the Arts must be acknowledged and answered because our Avenue of the Arts is not *un Boulevard des Arts* where *grands projets* derive grandeur from *grandes places* they dominate or grand axes they terminate. Philadelphia needs great projects that are authentic for the city's own cultural context and at home within its own urban order—that is, in the grid and on the street.

One glory of our city as an urban whole is its gridiron plan—with its tense and vivid juxtaposition of consistency in its planning dimension and chaos in its architectural dimension. The plan established by William Penn represents that of the prototypical American city, where urban quality and architectural hierarchy derive not from the special location of, but from the inherent nature of, individual buildings—as they sit in the grid and on the streets. On South Broad Street, for instance, the relatively small buildings of the University of the Arts and the Academy of Music sit cheek-by-jowl with their much bigger commercial and office tower neighbors, but they express their relative civic importance through the quality of their architectural scale and the significance of their symbolism.

The American gridiron city accommodates both unity and diversity by juxtaposing diverse architecture on a unified plan. We have no height lines imposed for buildings along a Champs-Elysées. Buildings on a street can vary in height, but also in size, material, function, and symbolism: the Union League is opposite a skyscraper on South Broad; the Pennsylvania Academy of the Fine Arts is there with the boys on North Broad; the Academy of Music is not at the end of a Boulevard de l'Opéra; and theoretically our mayor's house could sit across the street from a deli. Our buildings derive their hierarchical standing not from their ordained position but from their inherent character: our urbanism is egalitarian as well as diverse. And our cities are never complete—they are constantly a fragment of themselves. No civic monuments terminate axes—metaphorically our streets extend to infinity—to an eternal frontier of endless opportunity. Viva the fragment city!

There *are* exceptions. Broad and Market streets, for instance, suggest hierarchy through their central locations and exceptional widths. There are some diagonals, including the admittedly Parisian Benjamin Franklin Parkway and the regional avenues to Lancaster, Baltimore, and Frankford, etc. And City Hall, the Art Museum, and Girard College do acquire grandeur from their locations at the ends of axes. But these beloved, vivid exceptions prove the rule—*et ça suffit.*[1]

In urban architecture context is all. We love Paris for what it is, but we love Philadelphia for what *it* is, and we must not Parisify Philadelphia. *Grands projets* make heroic gestures in heroic places: we need new Pennsylvania Academies made pragmatically for regular places—lively city buildings that are at once generic and unique, that direct space and enhance the quality of a street. Although it has a special designation, the Avenue of the Arts is, appropriately for Philadelphia, a street, a gala street, but a street, a Main Street, and City Hall is the *grand projet* at its head. Philadelphia Orchestra Hall should be a proud citizen of Broad Street and the Avenue of the Arts; it must not try to achieve grandeur through denying its precious context.

There are some recently erected complexes in Philadelphia that attain their grandeur by denying the street or by turning their backs on it, thereby deadening their streets and dulling them commercially. Let us remember that the street is the soul of the gridiron city.

Surely many Philadelphians adore Paris, but to import Paris as ideology would be to debase its essence. So up with multiculturalism and down with cultural colonialism—and the accumulation of *parvenus projets* exemplifying a retardataire avant-garde! So *vive la différence* and remember the difference. Don't copy Paris: enhance Philadelphia. *A bas Philadelphie,* long live Philadelphia!

And, finally, Philadelphia is not Sydney where the famous opera house as sculptural symbol is designed to be seen from across a bay. Nor is it Los Angeles: *our* building sits not off the street but on it. My esteemed colleague, Frank Gehry, has designed Disney Hall appropriately for *its* context, as hype-heroic gesture par excellence; it is designed to be seen *in* a space, *from* a distance, and in a suburban-urban kind of setting. It is a freestanding sculptural element that dominates a park while our building is an architectural element that directs space—along a street and off a sidewalk. His building as a sculptural gesture looks good from a distance; our building via the quality of its detail looks good up close—and at eye level. We love Los Angeles as the city of the automobile but let us remain the city of brothers, not angels.

Another characteristic of our hall for the Philadelphia Orchestra is its accommodation to the element of light. The forms of the halls in Sydney and

Los Angeles are designed essentially to look good during the day—their surfaces articulated via the reflection of sunlight and resultant shades, shadows, and highlights—accommodating to a formal-sculptural aesthetic in the tradition reaching back to the Parthenon. But our hall is designed as 24-hour architecture—as Jean Labatut called it—to look good specifically at night as well as by day as the surfaces emanate light at night as well as reflect it by day. This makes for an architecture that accommodates iconography as well as form via the symbolic shapes of interiorly lit openings and the symbolic messages of electronic signage.

ADDENDUM I: *LES GRANDS PROJETS:* OMINOUS RUMBLINGS: A FOOTNOTE ON CULTURAL COLONIALISM

Under the aegis of the Foundation for Architecture and the Alliance Française, a delegation of French critics, architects, planners, politicians, and economists will hold a public forum in Philadelphia this fall to explore "how Philadelphia can learn from the Parisian experience" and "publicly share their views of how Paris uses design to create outstanding buildings and generate excitement through design."

A sponsor of the forum, Philadelphia architect David Slovic, complains in *The Philadelphia Inquirer* of April 11, 1993, about the disappointing design of the Avenue of the Arts' proposed new buildings. "They seem lifeless, lacking in scale, grandeur and inventiveness. . . ." The article, in which this author discusses a "Parisian lesson we might very well profitably adapt," is accompanied by a cartoon where a provincial William Penn on City Hall salutes a suave Eiffel Tower across the sea. He also quotes the *Inquirer* architecture critic Tom Hine saying "We don't need 'ho-hum' design for the Avenue of the Arts, we need a *Grand Projet.*" This same critic advocates "a series of new buildings with the quality and caliber of . . . the Pennsylvania Academy of Fine Arts . . . or City Hall itself." These he describes as "instant landmarks." Doesn't he know that each of these buildings was despised in its time? And more recently, even Louis Kahn proposed the demolition—except for the tower—of City Hall.

A case is made by Mr. Slovic for the Pompidou Center, which he describes as a "bold design" containing "carefully thought out otherness." But that building is arguably one of the most retardataire of this century. And in Philadelphia, it might translate as Pompousdou. Architectural critical analysis is tricky and perhaps this critic should moderate his certainties about buildings not yet constructed.

As architects and urban planners we must acknowledge that cultural institutions and performance facilities can contribute significantly to economic and social vitality within our cities, and that we must plan them accordingly. But let us, as we promote this activity and accommodate its architecture, acknowledge that American culture, Pop and otherwise, is pervasive worldwide, that Le Corbusier admired American cities, that American models influenced the architects who originated Modern architecture in Europe, and that, profoundly misused, these models provide the dominant image of the Centre Pompidou. We are provincials no longer. (In fact, the shoe is on the other foot: the French are now concerned by the importation into France of too much American culture.) Let us not reimport what we once exported or impose some remote and impossible Baroque aesthetic utopia on our front yard. Down with cultural inferiority complexes! Let us design architecture for the real context, cultural and urbanistic, of pragmatic Philadelphia.

And, finally, it should be acknowledged that a European form of government-in-the-arts can become a mixed blessing in terms of freedom of expression—despite marvelous examples of *grands projets* in the Paris of the Second Empire. And, in particular, Philadelphia proponents of this Parisian approach should assess social imbalances that can attend and cost burdens that can accrue as you formulate kinds of urban planning that are monumental in our time.

Note: As a Philadelphia architect whose firm is privileged to be designing a governmental building for a distinguished city in France, I frequently go there, not as an importer but as an artist—not to teach the French about my distinguished culture, but to accommodate them within their distinguished culture. Up with valid multiculturalism, but down with cultural imperialism—and cultural colonialism!

By the way, Mr. Slovic, wait till you discover Tokyo, the city of now—
and wow!

**ADDENDUM II: RANDOM REACTIONS AFTER THE PUBLIC FORUM IN
PHILADELPHIA ON *LES GRANDS PROJETS* OF PARIS ON NOVEMBER 10, 1993,
AND AFTER READING ELEANOR SMITH MORRIS**

Merci à Louis XV for the Place de la Concorde, but it's not so easy to attain
royal patronage in our time and the results wouldn't be so good: *pourquoi?*—
because the inherent complexity of our time eschews the beauty of imposed unity.

In Philadelphia one Place de la Concorde (Logan Square) is fine, two *ser-
ont trop*.

If not in French, the adjective grand in English, or American, makes one
uneasy: do not *projets* that are *grands* border on pretentious in the context of
notre epoch?

Our city, like any American city today, can hardly support its maintenance
budget—or that of its museum! Plus we Americans have had grand military
budgets competing with tiny urban budgets.

Grand axes can mean grand taxes.

Is this yen for *esprit* a ruse for getting different architects for the proposed
Broad Street projects? If so, it's a dangerous game; empowering an aesthetic
elite to promote "design excellence"—especially a self-proclaimed, sophisticated, avant-garde, modernist elite—can end in aesthetically correct banality and/or pretension. Might it be argued that the governmental elite of
France promoted a hyped-up version of a Modernism 70 years old?

Concerning spirit, we must risk generosity of spirit over grandiosity of
spirit!

Remember, critical evaluation in architecture is tricky: what's good today
can stink tomorrow and vice versa.

Juxtaposing Parisian urban forms on Philadelphia is questionable—but so is equating a political process of Paris with a political process for Philadelphia. Paris is a national capital—Philadelphia isn't even a state capital. Paris's funding source is a national treasury that can sustain a grand policy promoting tourist-oriented culture—yet Paris, like Philadelphia, suffers from problems involving governmental debt and social crisis. In this context, can *grands projets* border on "let them eat cake"?

Think twice about "cultural capital[s] . . . promoting cultural magnets" via *grand projets* and remember London, which exemplifies "piece-meal incremental adjustments that respected tradition rather than . . . grand schemes in the French manner" and ends up *the* tourist capital of Europe—and don't forget good old pragmatism as you think big about cities in our time.[2]

And *les Grands Projets, je regret,* don't turn me on; their "new modernity" is warmed-over Modernity—like leftovers sprinkled with spice; I don't learn from them, they bore me. *Sont-ils grands, mais pas supérieurs?*

Why are these *projets* almost always photographed from above rather than at eye level? It is because they're grand sculpture rather than civic architecture: civic architecture in a city combines big scale *and* little scale to be seen and enjoyed at eye level!

I'm tired of architecture that looks good from above, from a distance, as a model in a board room, on a screen at a conference, in a newspaper.

Are *grands projets* often boring yet bizarre intrusions? Perhaps Paris is exciting *malgré les Projets.* The Paris we love is the city of unity par excellence—*the* great city of the world where exquisite unity derives historically from unified culture and, in relation to architectural patronage, from autocratic process—from governmental process dependent on royal, imperial (cum Baron Haussmann), and presidential patronage, the latter involving Valéry Giscard d'Estaing and François Mitterand.

But in terms of form and process this kind of urban unity is not for now—not for American cities whose consistent grid plans accommodate inconsistent building plans—embracing hype-commercial signage and plural-ethnic symbolism, and whose political traditions eschew "government in the arts." This kind of urban unity is not for a global context that can enhance multi-culturalism. And not for Tokyo, the city of now, whose *joie de vivre* derives from vestigial village streets, minute shrines in gardens, global corporate headquarters within a high-tech infrastructure all mixed up—where mess is more.

What if I were to say there's nothing wrong with the Champs-Elysées that a few billboards won't cure? Is that so different from saying how about *grands projets* for South Broad Street?

ADDENDUM III: FURTHER REFLECTIONS ON WHAT THE PHILADELPHIA ORCHESTRA HALL ISN'T AS WELL AS IS

The Philadelphia Orchestra Hall:

- is a generic symphony hall appropriately expressive of its purposes in its architectural form and symbols, and not a pompous-heroic, abstract expressionist decoration, contoured and distorted into a hype-sculptural gesture,

- confirms the quality and enhances the vitality of the urban street it sits on: it does not contradict the integrity of the street. In its particular context, it directs rather than occupies space,

- is a building with details and looks best seen close up from the street, not a piece of abstract sculpture that looks best seen like an architectural model from a distance,

- is a hall—a room spatially and symbolically—with unashamed reference to the historical precedent of the hall as setting and enclosure for orchestra and audience together,

- defines the spectacle as music-in-a-room, not orchestra-on-a-stage,

- is an architectural work of art that must act as background for another art, that of musical performance. It must not compete with that other form of art. It should not be a heroic and original architectural spectacle,

- employs appliqué ornament, in league with lighting and symbolism, to enrich spaces inside and forms outside. Remember Pugin: It's all right to decorate construction but not to construct decoration,

- although designed as a setting for gala and civic assemblies, must not be intrusive. You must not be tired of it a decade from now,

- is not a machine for listening in. Viva acoustical technology, but viva also architectural artistry that does not simplistically symbolize technology,

- is not architectural sculpture looking good by day but iconographic architecture emanating light as well as reflecting it.

ADDENDUM IV: THE HALL AND THE AVENUE

I never dreamed I would have to write another addendum for the defense of our design for the Philadelphia Orchestra Hall. Originally we had to respond to the critics for whom it was not fancy enough—who wanted it cheap *and* fancy—then to local architects for whom it was not pompous enough—who wanted a *grand projet parisien*. And now we have to justify it to an essentially new client group for whom it is commercial and vulgar or whatever—one of these critics wants the design to be inspired by McKim, Mead and White's Post Office on 8th Avenue approached by a grand flight of steps! (Some of the other suggestions have been based on principles of design inappropriate for this project but ironically derived from past work and theories originally introduced by Robert Venturi and Denise Scott Brown!)

The design has kept evolving even though the work was officially put on hold at the end of the schematic design phase in 1989, because architects can't stop thinking. But the process of refinement has proceeded also because a significant part of the urban context has changed—that is, its explicit setting is no longer drab South Broad Street but bold Avenue of the Arts whose life is to thrive and glitter at night. Also the new client committee has permitted a less stringent budget for the architecture of the front facade, so the original plain but elegant aesthetic of a Philadelphia Friends Meeting House with iconography can evolve into that of a hype but civic hall appropriate for an Avenue of the Arts.

I have explained in earlier addenda how this Orchestra Hall is different from typical halls of our time—it consists not of a sculptural Minimalist architectural form designed to be seen from a distance in a park or across a plaza or a bay but rather a series of surfaces that correspond to and reinforce the edges of the streets they are on, that you don't see therefore as a whole from afar and that do contain interesting detail to be perceived close up in a street and obliquely from down a street. And, most important, its forms are not articulated, like all architecture since the Parthenon and before, to reflect sunlight and thereby derive its image via the perception of highlights, shades, and shadows—by day. It represents an architecture whose surfaces are specifically designed to emit as well as reflect light—perhaps like a lantern—an architecture designed for day *and* night—its surfaces illuminating rather than illuminated.

This kind of architecture—in a dense city grid, not at the edge of downtown like the Dallas hall or in a plaza as in Lincoln Center or across a bay like Sydney—and this particular example of architecture, must acknowledge the architectural density within its street setting by day and the light intensity and electronic glitter it is in or will be in and must contribute to at night. If the Avenue of the Arts is to succeed it must be a place filled with light and glitter. If it is to be not the drab, ominous, dangerous place center city represents currently at night, our Hall must contribute to this gala aura of activity and vitality. And if a source for this kind of architecture is commercial, so be it—don't forget, the original source of the establishment Modern architecture of today was vernacular-industrial factory buildings; a CEO reading this document today is most likely sitting in a Modern-style office building whose architecture is glamorized-industrial in terms of its source. So vernacular-commercial elements made appropriate by their enhancement via art and detail have an OK precedent.

And, as the art of the commercial vernacular informs us, we work within a transition from electric to electronic technology and imagery—and, as the Europeans of the early part of this century went to America to be inspired by its industrial vernacular, we Americans now go to Japan to be inspired by its electronic iconography manifest in commercial signs.

But as important as the aesthetic exaltation of electronic glitter are the symbolic and iconographic dimensions this civic architecture for night must acknowledge. Again, unlike the hall at the edge of town or in the suburbs, this architecture's essence derives less from its abstract and/or structural form and more from its various kinds of reference. Its major symbolic element is its rhythmic complex of windows on the Avenue of the Arts that combine, vividly at night but also by day, to suggest an abstracted silhouette of a Classical facade with columns, capitals, and pediment—a modern version of the emblem of civic architecture. This two-dimensional configuration works also as a logo, an elemental image that is memorable and that you carry away with you—but an image that is stretched in its proportions horizontally so it reads effectively obliquely as you approach it along the street. Significant and enriching also is the ambiguity of this imagery, especially in daylight, so it isn't perceived as a Postmodern historicist gesture.

This aesthetically ambiguous imagery is reinforced by the quality of the skeleton frame that the facade is now composed of: this frame is different from its conventional Modernist counterparts in that its configuration does not conform to the consistent rhythm of the modular aesthetic nor are its members, vertical and horizontal, identical in size—and this makes for the complex contrapuntal rhythms that promote the ambiguity of the image of the civic temple facade. And its infill material is not totally of glass—some of its infill beyond the diagonal members that connote Classical pediment at night consists of spandrel glass, as do the interstices between "columns." The "capitals" of the "columns" are suggested via polychromatic enameled and stained glass panels within the frame. These elements together create a glittery effect by day and reinforce a symbolic effect at night. Spandrel glass is considered "commercial" today but tomorrow will be as respectable as Mies van der Rohe's "industrial" elements of today.

The use of bright primary colors as an element of the aluminum frame surfaces of this facade is significant—following a rich and dominant tradition that embraces the facades of Classical Greek temples and in Philadelphia the facades of the Art Museum with its terra-cotta ornament and the Pennsylvania Academy of the Fine Arts with its varied combinations of white and red masonry and tile. Also significant is the combination of Modern abstraction and iconographic reference within the uneven modular system of the frame facade, with its colored rectangular accents as capitals by day and night, as it combines a kind of Mondrian composition—but with a significant difference—a non-abstract reference! The salmon red of the frame surfaces is relatively dark in value so as to read as black at night by not reflecting ambient light of the street. We trust children will like the polychromy of this facade as I did that of the Art Museum growing up in Philadelphia.

Another purpose of the glass wall by day (or glass windows by night!) is simply that of creating old-fashioned Modern transparency: you can see activity inside the lobby from the outside, and that contributes to the vitality of the street outside. Also you are aware thereby of the rich layers and levels of space that are part of the architectural composition of the lobby inside.

Below the great windows another kind of iconographic element projects across the facade—a floating staff of musical notes in stainless steel that constitutes a frieze. The tradition of symbols on civic and religious buildings is manifest in the temples of Egypt and Rome and in all forms of Classical architecture—the facade of the Paris Opera is teeming with tens of statues, bas-reliefs, medallions, busts, and graphics. Two favorite and characteristic buildings of Philadelphia are the City Hall topped by its huge statue and the PSFS building topped by commercial-size graphics. Our graphic ornamentation is very big to acknowledge the world importance of the Orchestra, the civic scale of the Avenue of the Arts, the hype sensibility of our era, and its particular setting.

At the lowest level of the front facade, at eye and sidewalk level, is another element employed to create interest via glitter and detail and to accommodate another level of communication—that of changing specific information. There are kinds of media possible now and probable in the near future that can, via backlighting and/or via LED pixel-related imagery, produce sparkle and information about the Orchestra and its active recording activities and/or programs and news concerning other institutions on the Avenue. (It should be noted that the informational signage in this part of the design might be paid for and maintained by recording companies who have contracts with the Orchestra.) This lower frieze at eye level should extend around the corner to adorn the otherwise plain façade of Spruce Street. By the way, remember how boring it can be walking by a vast cultural building too proud to be interesting!

I'm afraid the critics of now are not aware of what's coming and who's coming to this part of center city Philadelphia. Here is a façade that can be at home in its context and enhance its context as an Avenue of the Arts for all kinds of people that make up our city and will make up the Orchestra's audience and supporters—that can be civically dignified and of our time by using the methods of our time in artful ways. Remember, even the grandiose Boulevard de l'Opéra in Paris is teeming with cafes and shops along the sidewalk that enliven it and combine with its monumental-civic-cultural dimension as urban foreground to *l'Opéra*. So must our Avenue of the Arts in Philadelphia become also Main Street and embrace cultural *and* commercial activity.

And then there is safety: where there are not brightly lit shop windows or cafes at sidewalk level on the Avenue there must be other elements that create light and interest and therefore safety as well as amenity at night.

Hooray for an appropriate, 24-hour architecture exploiting iconography within a dense urban fabric.

---

1. An urge to Parisify Philadelphia about forty years ago parallels that of today when they made a *grand projet* out of Independence Hall by abrogating its Anglo-American urban context within the gently scaled fabric of the city and effected thereby its architectural humiliation as a pathetic termination of a Baroque axis that was to be called Independence Mall.
2. Eleanor Smith Morris, "Heritage and Culture: A Capital for the New Europe," in *Building a New Heritage,* ed. G. J. Ashworth and P. J. Larkham (London: Routledge, 1994).

TOWARD A SCENOGRAPHIC ARCHITECTURE FOR TODAY: GENERIC FORM WITH ORDINARY-EXTRAORDINARY SIGNS: A DESCRIPTION OF THE DESIGN OF THE KIRIFURI RESORT PROJECT IN NIKKO

By Robert Venturi and Denise Scott Brown. Previously published in *Sekai,* February 1995, pp. 290–300 (in Japanese).

I. LEARNING FROM TOKYO AND KYOTO AND NIKKO

We have explained in "Two Naifs in Japan" how we came to embrace a grand ethos of Japanese art, architecture, and planning, loving and learning from the Zen temples and shrines of Kyoto *and* the Buddhist shrines and temples of Nikko; the sublimely simple temples of Kyoto *and* the kimonos within them *and* the markets beyond them; and also from the complex order of modern Tokyo where village shrine and global corporate headquarters meet and electronic commercial graphics create an iconography comparable in splendor to that of religious mosaics of Ravenna. Our perspective includes the wonder of the everyday, now, as well as the wonder of the art of the past.

By our own decision, and possibly by our good luck, we visited Japan late in our careers but at a point when we were, perhaps, most ready to learn its complex lessons. We had been put off by the historical Modern architects who depicted the truly sublime architecture of Kyoto as preciously simple and essentially exclusive. We shall never forget our astonishment on our first day in Kyoto—February 28, 1990, which we shall forever celebrate—when we saw the pure shrines of Kyoto in their impure settings; immediately, the garden symbolizing the natural world as a complex whole, and beyond, the marketplace and city, whose aesthetic and technical complexity includes sensuous and lyrical dimensions etched in their colors, patterns, and scales. In the mind's eye and from traditional woodcuts, we could also envision a human context, overlaid on temple, garden, and market, of moving figures in colorful, patterned kimonos. So Kyoto as an exemplification of Japanese art and architecture became a matter of shrines in gardens *and* markets in streets with figures in kimonos all over—of simple shrines made sublime by the juxtaposition of complex context. But the pure order of the shrines teemed also with variations and exceptions, so that the whole, suspended at the fine line between order and dissolution, becomes a rich and tense drama of contradictory dimensions.

This inclusive view of Kyoto, a perspective with a wide-angle lens, exalts simplicity *and* complexity and embraces harmony *and* dissonance. It is this interpretation of traditional Japanese architecture and urbanism that enlightens our response to the architecture and urbanism of now; we can love and understand modern Tokyo *and* eternal Kyoto.[1]

In sum, by visiting Kyoto we came to understand the temples, not as a Bruno Taut, Walter Gropius, or Mies van der Rohe would see them but as a part—a supreme part but a part—of a complex whole relevant indeed to our present needs and interests as architects. The Modernist interpretations of Taut and Gropius were explicit, those of Mies implicit in his work. There was also the wonderful retort of Frank Lloyd Wright to my young architect friend on a liner traveling to Paris: "Young man, you are going in the wrong direction." But it was not only the goody-goody stance of Modern architects that turned us away from Japan; we felt, too, that we had enough to learn from our own culture, historical and artistic; and as we too traveled in the wrong direction to Italy, France, and Britain, we were right, though Wright was right too.

It was easier for Wright (and Gropius, Taut, and Mies) to get it right; their interest in historical Japanese art was largely formal and they could derive what were essentially abstractions from their cropped and edited views of temple interiors and exteriors. What we derive from what we have seen and how we employ it is more difficult and fraught with danger. We abstract too, but not from the formal-spatial dimension of historical Kyoto—rather from its symbolism, representational and iconographic, and from sources beyond the Katsura detached villa and others loved by the Moderns; from a wide range of taste cultures and architectural sources, historical and current.

What we have done with what we have learned is original, in the context of recent and current history, but traditional when we remember scenographic Baroque architecture—exterior and interior—and iconographic architecture of ancient Egypt and the Early Christian period. The reference, as opposed to the method, of our architecture suggests genre traditions in painting—seventeenth-century Dutch painting, nineteenth-century schools of Realist painting, early twentieth-century Constructivist architecture with supergraphics, twentieth-century American commercial art and roadside architecture, and especially midcentury Pop Art, with its adaptation of ordinary and conventional elements made aesthetic through transpositions of scale and context.

The experience of Japan accelerated thought processes developing in our minds in the late 1980s while we completed two museum projects and surveyed the fitful flurries of schools and labels in architecture around us. Tokyo, Kyoto, and Nikko helped us find our ground in the quicksand architecture of today. The Kirifuri project is an example of how we learned from Japan, but all our work from the 1990s should be seen as under this influence.

II. DESIGNING FOR KIRIFURI

In designing the Kirifuri Resort we have aimed for a scenographic architecture where generic forms are adorned with signs and the conventionally ordinary is made aesthetically extraordinary. We hope our interpretations will appear more fresh than naive as the work of strangers who are inspired by the Japan of now.

Project Program
The program for the Kirifuri project has four major elements.

The bridge: Vehicular and pedestrian. To cross a ravine near the entrance to the site and act as an imageful sign.

The hotel: To accommodate living facilities and rooms of Western and traditional Japanese design. Facilities include a public bath with hot-spring spa; public lobby containing check-in, commercial, and conference facilities;

two dining spaces, one with bar-cafe and Karaoke, the other with public and private spaces, Western and traditional; interior tennis courts; day care for children; administration; kitchen and services; employees' room; and interior below-grade parking.

The athletic building: To contain a large, indoor swimming pool, locker-dressing room facilities, lounge, gallery with commercial space, wet and dry dining spaces, and numerous spa facilities.

A natural landscape: A forest and clearing to be seen as a setting for the buildings but also as an important ecological heritage to be supported and enjoyed from trails and outlooks.

The site was divided into three zones, with the athletic building in Zone A and the hotel in Zone B; Zone C was to be maintained as a natural habitat.

General Design Approach

Our approach to the challenge of creating an architecture of well-being at Kirifuri was to submerge ourselves in the site and the problem, engage in thoughtful analysis, and draw on aesthetic intuition. At the outset of the project the design team, working in collaboration with the client, the Ministry of Posts and Telecommunications, explored the Kirifuri plateau in sparkling sunshine and serene mist, visited existing resorts in the region, revisited the national park and the great historical complex of shrines in Nikko, and held extended discussion meetings with members of the architectural team and others. The ultimate goal was a design that works well in its use, maintains its natural setting and historical context, and can be enjoyed by the many different people who come to it.

At the outset we enunciated the following objectives:

Natural context: To acknowledge the crucial significance and supreme beauty of the site. To create patterns and processes natural to the ecological systems of this particular landscape. To promote respect for and enjoyment of nature.

Diversity and rich unity: To create within the landscape a unity that is varied and rich. To include diverse elements—formal and symbolic, natural and cultural—that work symbiotically to create an ethos both universal and of Japan today. To reflect the genius of Japan and contribute to the vitality of its culture, by designing juxtaposed elements, some harmonious and others dissonant, that respond to values and lifestyles of work and leisure, tourism and nature, and to a heritage, cultural and religious.

Symbiotic dualities: To acknowledge grandeur and process in nature and complexities and contradictions in design, by accommodating the often contrasting requirements of:

families	and/or	groups or tours
individual	and/or	communal
young	and/or	old
happy adults	and/or	happy children
	———	
relaxation	and/or	athletics
laissez-faire	and/or	routine
restful	and/or	active
leisure	and/or	sweat
unwind	and/or	rejuvenate
passive recreation	and/or	active recreation
spa	and/or	athletics
strolling	and/or	hiking

serene	and/or	show-off
mind	and/or	body

---

high season	and/or	low season
short stay	and/or	long stay

---

analogous with nature	and/or	contrasting with nature
natural landscape	and/or	architecture
nature natural	and/or	nature modulated
present	and/or	future
indoors	and/or	outdoors
beautiful sun	and/or	serene mist

---

private	and/or	public
local community	and/or	national communities
local ethos	and/or	universal ethos

---

modesty	and/or	grandeur
symbolic	and/or	formal

old	and/or	new
traditional reference	and/or	original images
convention	and/or	innovation
rustic	and/or	modern
craft	and/or	technology
natural materials	and/or	synthetic materials
wood and copper	and/or	plastic, concrete, steel

Our aim was to balance these wide-ranging, contrasting, rich, and ultimately symbiotic dualities, in ways that are tense, sensitive, and original.

Ecology and environment: To view the natural landscape, with its dynamic topography and rich misty forest, as both background and stimulus for the design of the complex. To see the ecological-environmental characteristics of Kirifuri as determinants of its built forms; to design strategies to ensure that the values of this place will be sustained and enhanced. To derive land use and design guidelines for landscape and architecture from patterns and processes inherent in the landscape; to use advanced biotechnical methods creatively to handle runoff pondage, paving, and other significant elements. To demonstrate the significance and quality of ecological systems in Kirifuri via carefully engineered trails.

Culture and history: To acknowledge the cultural as well as the natural context, the landscape—local and universal, historical and communal—that includes Nikko as a functioning community and as a renowned religious, historical, and architectural place.

Architecture and planning: To design workable and likable buildings that function well and look good, as a whole and in detail. To orient buildings for sun and view. To employ advanced technological equipment to promote comfort and permit sophisticated forms of communication.

Our approach was mainly to clarify existing values concerning the architecture of leisure and well-being and, in the end, as perceptive artists, to accommodate these values and on occasion direct them.

We hoped to create a place to be used and perceived in a variety of ways; that pleases many people, including children, helping them relax, and/or think and/or sweat and/or show off—a place that promotes art not ideology, where the unity is not too obvious and valid contradiction is accommodated, where the whole can be rich and include range and tolerance among all the zones. We wanted to learn from Kirifuri, love it, and enhance it.

III. THE DESIGN

The Bridge
The bridge spans the ravine at the approach to the hotel. Because it is perpendicular to the toll road and conspicuous from it, this structure is designed as a sign to identify the complex and enrich its image.

Its form juxtaposes a reinforced concrete structure, derived from contemporary engineering technology, with a decorative plane on each face that symbolizes a traditional Japanese bridge. The planes, whose arcs embrace the span of the structural bridge, are composed of corrugated aluminum whose color is recessive within its natural setting.

The Athletic Building
This building is apparent from the road and works as another sign identifying the complex. Although the large, glazed surfaces and geometric patterns of its essentially generic form stand out against the site's undulating fields and leafy forest, the building is also recessive in and analogous to its context, through its neutral colors that are like those of nature in summer and winter. The delicate articulations and distortions in plan and section that accommodate the contours of the site, the variations and plays of scale, and the simply proportioned windows that look modest and familiar, soften the building's form and modulate its geometry, as does the sometimes undulating concrete base that subtends delicate curves at the top of its retaining

wall. Standing on this wall, two-dimensional representations of trees made up of a concrete lattice ornamented with colored aluminum "blossoms" create architectural layering along the main facade and enhance the building's organic dimension. At the gable ends, representations of traditional Japanese roof rafters tie the building to the site and to its history.

Inside, the building's pools, baths, promenades, restaurants, and an enclosed garden work together spatially and visually. Although areas where occupants are dry are separated from those where they are wet, spatial, visual, and social links and connections are maintained and are a major theme of the interior. Interdependence is supported architecturally by means of the "flowing" space that inheres in the building's complex cross section. This helps promote a communal feeling, exploits the variety of activities, enhances their effect, and helps to project a sense of theater.

The building section—like that of a basilica—produces hierarchies of space. A big central area contains communal pools, and small lateral spaces are for individual uses. The central space is not consistent within the overall order: to accommodate to the natural site it "goes down hill" in section and "sidles to the left" in plan.

The interior structure admits shafts of ambient natural light through clerestory windows during the day. The light is modulated by lacelike space frames that span the major space. These are composed of standard steel elements that are connected to form truss configurations. Attached to them are decorative planar forms suggestive of leaves that in combination with the space frame convey the sense of a forest clearing and refer to the forest that is famous in Nikko. Looking south the surfaces of the "leaves" are bright green to suggest summer; looking north they are warm yellow to suggest autumn. During the day the "leaves" modulate natural light to create an aura: at night they reflect artificial light and sparkle.

The Hotel Complex and the Village Street

The hotel is designed to be perceived as a series of modest buildings set recessively against the texture of the wooded site. In form, the whole is complex and small-scale; symbolically, it suggests a rural village, particularly at its approach which evokes a village street.

It is significant that you arrive by car within, not at the edge of, the complex. Beyond the entrance lies a second pedestrian "street" that is the hotel lobby. Off this linear space are restaurants, a cafe, conference rooms, and commercial areas; along it are decorative and symbolic two-dimensional representations of historical, traditional, contemporary, ordinary and conventional village elements—depicted by colorful, abstracted and stylized signs and murals placed perpendicularly to the axis of the "street."

The scenography of the "village street" reflects the traditions and celebrates the spirit of Japanese urban and village life, making the hotel lobby a lively and gala place for adults and children. Its ornamental and symbolic elements include:

Subjects:	old and new street views, street elements and details, rural and urban public telephones post boxes barber poles signs banners vending machines electric and telephone lines and transformers false flower bunches on poles lanterns
Depicted through:	photographs, oil painting reproductions, reproductions of historical prints, neon tubes, black-and-white and in color
Depicted on:	panels and signs perpendicular to street
Material:	electronic graphics on laminate protected vinyl

Scale: varieties, but all larger than real

Outside, the architectural forms of the hotel subtly suggest traditional rural architecture via their proportions. Symbolically, ornamental elements appliquéd to the buildings suggest traditional roof forms and overhangs when perceived from eye level in perspective. Appliqué patterns on some wall surfaces suggest exposed wood frame construction.

The Landscape

The landscape architects and ecological planners, Andropogon Associates, have described their design as follows:

> The environment of the site was studied closely to discover what kind of place it is and how its natural environment works. This study showed a wild place of high ridges and precipitous valleys covered with rich vegetation, but in this precise location not a pristine forest, for the trees have been cut down several times in the past. The intent of the design is to preserve and enhance the vigorous young woodland that is now growing back so that the buildings will eventually be set entirely within a mature native forest, much as a traditional village might once have been.
>
> The site features are designed to dramatize the beauty of this natural landscape. The approach to the hotel is across a bridge spanning a ravine, curving and rising to fit the contours of the hillside and supported by a single central column to avoid damage to the wooded slopes. A series of glimpsed views to valley and mountain unfold along the winding drive, culminating in the arrival at the "village street" that is the hotel entrance. The hotel is connected to the athletic building on the lower part of the site with a covered walk that takes a direct and dramatic route, stepping down a long ridge and leaping back across the ravine on a high footbridge. A more leisurely and accessible path also connects the buildings, while other informal trails allow visitors to experience the many different aspects of the forest, from the hidden rocky stream bed to high places with magnificent views. A unique feature of the construction process is the hundreds of native

trees and shrubs that were dug from the site and stored for replanting later. All new plantings will represent plant communities of the Nikko region.

The Complex as a Whole

Each building of the complex is generic in its expression. Upon its elemental form are juxtaposed symbolic gestures, some with subtle allusion, others with dramatic flair. This architecture thereby combines the generic and the dramatic.

The athletic building in Zone A and the hotel complex in Zone B, although different from each other, contain similar external elements and materials. These consistencies promote a sense of unity within the complex.

The landscape design maintains the natural quality of the place and contains and offsets its architecture.

IV. THE SYMBOLIC ELEMENT

We have hoped to express in Kirifuri's architecture-for-recreation the vigor and wit that are a part of Japanese public life today, and at the same time design the hotel and athletic building to be marketable to and loved by the public.

The explicit inclusion of symbolism is intended to broaden the resort's appeal to the public and to enhance its architecture by expanding its range and increasing its dimensions.

All architecture includes an element of symbolism in its composition and evokes expressions and meanings that derive from reference or association. These qualities enrich the character of the architecture as a whole. Architecture almost inevitably employs some elements that are conventional, familiar, or historical and that make for implicit or explicit symbolism; even Modern architecture, whose aesthetic was based on the expression of function and structure, derived its vocabularies from industrial vernacular architecture of the early twentieth century and structural engineering of the late nineteenth century. These sources provided by implication the symbols of a dawning age of new technology, universal in its application and universally beneficent.

It is perhaps significant that the Imperial Hotel designed for Japan at the beginning of the century substantiated via its name a purist aesthetic appropriate for its time, but that a hotel designed at the end of the century symbolizes a village street—the form and symbolism of which exploit and celebrate the vitality and variety—and joy—of the Japanese urban scene, which is unsurpassed in the world in our time.

The architecture of the Kirifuri complex employs symbolism in two ways: first via spatial and formal elements that are suggestive even if abstracted—as in the wings of the hotel that suggest a village recessive in the woods; in the applied trellis elements that, seen obliquely, suggest the traditional roofs of historical Japanese architecture; and in the decorative patterns on the end elevations of the village pavilions that depict fragments of Mondrian compositions and suggest timber frame construction.

A second way of employing symbolism is seen in the hotel lobby's "village street" and in the athletic building's abstracted decorative "leaves." This symbolism is literal and realistic. It refers to elements that are not heroic or original but natural or ordinary. The "ordinary" aesthetic is based on that of Pop Art, where old and familiar elements are depicted via new media, at a different scale, and in a new context. New meaning is thereby acquired and aesthetic tension achieved.

The symbolic qualities derive as well from the joining of cultures—traditional-craft and contemporary-hype—where village ethos and global ethos, high and low cultures, and local and universal cultures are juxtaposed within the Japanese urbanism of our time. Symbolic and representational elements of today's cultural mix, when combined in the tense manner of Pop Art, can look both familiar and unfamiliar.

Another artistic precedent for Kirifuri's symbolism is Dutch genre painting of the seventeenth century. R. H. Fuchs describes the discovery and glorification of the everyday experience in Holland and the replacement of the heroic idealizations of aristocratic art with realistic illustrations of the daily life of middle-class society in the Dutch Republic.[2] Fuchs discusses the celebration of generic order over high tradition through the representation of indigenous and vernacular culture in paintings by Pieter de Hooch, Jan Steen, Franz Hals, Jacob van Ruisdel, and Jan Vermeer. Their cluttered combinations of realism and symbolism, metaphor and representation, parallel later realism using vernacular sources in the work of Van Gogh and the French Impressionists.

A most relevant precedent is the distinguished Japanese print tradition of depicting everyday life in a stylized and aesthetic manner.

The signs in the symbolic street combine historic-traditional and contemporary-conventional references that are essentially familiar. The symbols are portrayed mostly as large, two-dimensional signs, perpendicular to or parallel with the street. They are often appended to columns. On spaces along the street that are enclosed, depictions of street elements or scenes are applied as realistic and colorful panels with electronic graphics on laminate protected vinyl. Dynamic juxtapositions among all these elements achieve an effect of rich clutter.

The "street" is covered by a glass roof and terminates at each end with a glass wall, so it appears to extend under the sky and into nature. There are representations of roof overhangs at its edges. As "street" meets woods, another juxtaposition traditional within Japanese architecture is acknowledged, where the serene and controlled shrine meets the rich and cluttered market.

The use of symbolism in architectural design inevitably involves difficulty and must be done with care. The effects of symbolism, stylization, and abstraction must subtly enhance, not distract from, the whole. Aesthetic courage must be balanced by aesthetic restraint.

Foreign architects could view as exotic what to local observers is banal; yet foreigners might see new wonders in familiar elements—endeavoring to make art in an era of hype and celebrate in the meeting of street and woods the vitality of the ordinary and everyday.

The degree of sophistication we are working toward can, we hope, be achieved with the help of a committee representing the client, local architects, historians, and anthropologists. Their advice on subject matter, aesthetic manner, representation, symbolism, stylization, and abstraction will support the aim of producing architecture that is sophisticated *and* naive, serious *and* playful, that adults *and* children will like, now *and* over time.

V. WORKING IN JAPAN

To work within Japan's rich tradition and beautiful environment, in association with the eminent firm of Marunouchi Architects of Tokyo and its distinguished and experienced staff, has been a privilege and honor for Venturi, Scott Brown and Associates.

Lately we have pondered the difficulties of being an architect in our time— not those that emerge naturally from being creative, not the agony that must accompany the ecstasy, but those that derive perversely from inefficiency, irrationality, lack of trust or sensibility, and greed—where we architects must become lawyers, accountants, salespeople, and psychiatrists, as we struggle to achieve the professional and artistic goals we have dedicated our lives to.

In Japan we have been able to be truly architects in our relations with our client, associate architects, and all those at work on the project, including the community bureaus. Our contract, for instance, was speedily negotiated and was considerably less than two inches thick. More important, our client, the Ministry of Posts and Telecommunications, was an oxymoron: a bureaucracy that was not Kafkaesque, that understood what it wanted with adequate precision and did not change its mind beyond a tolerable norm. Toshio Nonomura, who is in charge for the client, was demanding *and* appreciative; above all, trusting his architects as they recommended an unconventional design. This trust is essential to achieving quality in art and makes for a responsible professional relationship, but it requires patience, sophistication, and, in the end, courage to go along with an evolving process where the architect learns from the client and the client from the architect. In short, we have worked within a rational, communicative process of a type we have found to be rare in our country and others. This understanding and support came partly, perhaps, from the Ministry's long experience in building.

Understanding, supportive, *and* efficient have been our associate architects and their engineers. This has been a true collaboration of minds and talents based on mutual respect. Marunouchi Architects' main responsibility has been technical and managerial, but their contribution to the design, via principal architects Yoshitaka Taguchi and Susumu Yamagiwa, has been crucial.

This has been a particularly happy example of a new form of designing and documenting projects whose emergence relates to global practices evolving in architecture today. It was reasonably common in the past to separate the design of a project from its documentation for construction. This happened frequently within large commercial firms. But over the last decade, there has developed a separation of the two types of architectural practice; design "boutiques" have sprung up in America and Europe that work with production firms in the city or country of the project. Between them, the design and production firms evolve methods of making the interface between design and execution. The "boutique" may be named the design architect of record, though how much of its design appears in the final building may vary considerably with individual firms and projects.

We have not in the past worked in this manner because we have produced in our own office the working drawings for all buildings, including major foreign works (but excepting laboratory buildings, where specialist firms design and document the interior labs, while we site the building and design and document its exterior and sometimes its public spaces).

Our experience in Japan has heartened us to the possibilities of the separation between design and production and given us confidence that this can be a practical method of working, if enough effort is made on all sides and if the production firm is a good counterpart to the design firm. Luckily, at Kirifuri, these requisites have been met and the fee has been sufficient to permit the interface to be a responsible one. Robert Venturi has traveled to Japan to date twelve times for this project. Members of Andropogon, staff members of VSBA, and members of Marunouchi have made trips in both directions. This has enabled us to attain the level of cooperation we deem required.

The allocation of work between the firms is one normal for this type of collaboration. Venturi, Scott Brown and Associates were responsible for the preschematic and schematic design phases and spent a majority of the time allocated to these phases. Part way through design development a handover was instituted, as construction documents, bidding, and construction administration were to be the prime responsibility of Marunouchi Architects. Divergent from the norm, perhaps, was the amount of information we were able to gain from numerous meetings and discussions with Marunouchi in early phases. In design development, as we sought advice on Japanese construction practices, there was an unusual and exciting exchange of ideas that included chief researchers at the technical center of manufacturing companies. Part of the collaboration was through sketches generated by VSBA and faxed to Marunouchi. Frequent visits were made in both directions to review the development of documents. Information from these sources influenced decisions about materials, finishes, and assembly and permitted timely adjustments to take care of Japanese methods of documentation and construction. We have had the satisfaction of seeing our ideas well understood and faithfully translated into Japanese working drawings. The whole has felt like a seamless process. Marunouchi along with their engineering consultants and we have felt like one office.

Last but foremost, there has been Akio Izutsu, friend and mentor, whose crucial guidance introduced us to the variety of Japanese culture, historic, recent, and current, and helped us understand Japanese procedures. His and his staff's graciousness as our travel guides and hosts, his profound knowledge, his tolerance and patience with our naivete, made our times with him among the richest and most artistically rewarding in our experience.

The understanding, support, and trust shown us in Japan are particularly moving given the difficult, indeed dangerous, road our design has taken. At the beginning of the process, when our evolving iconographic approach became evident, Toshio Nonomura said: "We must be sure we don't end up with a Madame Butterfly," at once giving us a good metaphor and showing his awareness of the dangers of our approach *and* his understanding of it. Near the end of the process, responding to our concern that the project's scenographic iconography might attract criticism because it is different from the dominant current architecture in the abstract-formal tradition, Akio Izutsu said: "But I admire the human dimension in what you have done." For us, it was a quiet way of saying the most important thing.

---

1. The revelations of Yoshinobu Ashihara's *The Hidden Order* (Tokyo: Kodansha International, 1989) have significantly informed our views expressed here.
2. R. H. Fuchs, *Dutch Painting* (London: Thames and Hudson, 1978).

69

Kirifuri Resort in Nikko, Japan, for the
Ministry of Posts and Telecommunications,
in association with Marunouchi Architects & Engineers, 1992

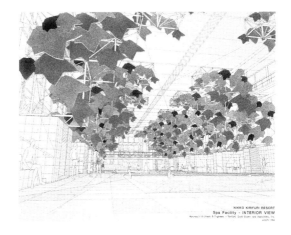

70

Kirifuri Resort in Nikko, Japan, for the
Ministry of Posts and Telecommunications,
in association with Marunouchi Architects & Engineers, 1992

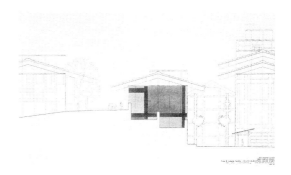

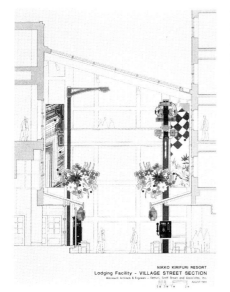

71

Kirifuri Resort in Nikko, Japan, for the
Ministry of Posts and Telecommunications,
in association with Marunouchi Architects & Engineers, 1992

IMAGERY VIA LIGHTING AND ELECTRONICS FOR LOKER COMMONS, MEMORIAL HALL, HARVARD UNIVERSITY

Written 1995.

Something that is hard to do in architecture is to create aura, aura *and* sparkle, in space inside a building—as opposed to ambient light inside a building that derives from reflection from architectural surfaces.

This kind of light in space is to be an essential element in the design of the basement in Harvard's Memorial Hall. The building itself represents America's supreme example of Ruskinian Gothic, in which our team of architects and consultants are restoring the Great Hall with its hammer beam trusses and stained glass windows—the latter itself supremely exemplyfing nineteenth-century craft and contributing aura via the penetration of exterior light through colored glass. This ground-floor space is to revert to its original use as a great dining hall—to be limited in our era to freshmen. It is to become an institutional space par excellence.

The part of the interior I focus on here is the basement, which is to be renovated to become Loker Commons—the central meeting place for the whole academic community, a flexible space to lounge and eat in and for communication of all sorts—a non-institutional kind of place for hanging out in. The design of this Commons incorporates little architectural imagery because its architectural quality is to derive not essentially from light reflecting off surfaces and articulating details but from light sources themselves that create sparkle and accents within a recessive aura.

The architectural surfaces and the furniture are to be neutral in hue and dark in value, so that the small amount of ambient light derived from ceiling fixtures will tend not to be reflected off surfaces but to focus on people to make them accents.

An exception occurs at the series of old-fashioned bulletin boards for varieties of tacked-on notices whose surfaces, spotlit from above, reflect light as they also articulate circulation through the space. Another exception occurs in a parallel zone behind the bulletin boards, where during the day an existing row of small high windows admits ambient light into a series of peripheral niches that contain booths accommodating those who enjoy being on the periphery. The other side of the room is lined with food counters and constitutes a parallel zone which is brightly lit from above.

But the essential effect in this interior derives from sparkling interplay between two kinds of light sources—the first, a row of parallel colored fluorescent tubes arranged on the ceiling to decoratively articulate major circulation; the other, two electronic sources—an LED board as a frieze with moving images along and above the food counter, which you incidentally look at, and an LED board as a screen that terminates the circulation route, which you specifically look at.

These electronic elements promoting flexible imagery—graphic, narrative, abstract, and/or symbolic—work as sources of ornament that appeal to the hype sensibility of our time and as sources of information, dynamically complex and multicultural. And their setting as a meeting place incidentally adapted from a conventional basement—not arty-architectural but generically flexible—can further adapt to a kind of grunge aesthetic for this generation. Here architecture becomes non-architecture.

Can it be said that the sparkle of pixels in the Loker Commons downstairs corresponds to the glory of *vitraux* in the dining hall upstairs—where twentieth-century electronic technology meets nineteenth-century historicist craft—where informational iconography meets traditional iconography?

In the basement of Memorial Hall contemporary electronics succeeds revivalist craft.

Addendum: signs are wonderful but troublesome elements because unlike abstract ornament they require an ingredient of content and, ironically, while our information age projects lots of graphic imagery, it is still hard to organize multiculturally correct content. However, we think this dimension/medium can be enriching and valid and—via changing electronic signage—essential to the ethos of this place. Let us recall the civic-cultural graphic tradition within architecture—Classical and Medieval—which has enriched architectural settings in the past and which, in its Victorian-Romantic manifestation, is an essential part of the distinguished architectural setting upstairs.

P.S.: I have recently been informed by Martin Meyerson of the development of the electro-mechanical computer during World War II by Howard Aiken in the basement of Memorial Hall—so are we extending evolutionary information technology in this place?

WHITEHALL FERRY TERMINAL—*PLUS ÇA CHANGE . . . ENCORE*—A SOMEWHAT INTEMPERATE RESPONSE TO CURRENT CRITICISM OF THE WHITEHALL FERRY DESIGN

Written 1993 through 1995.

The outrageous element of the design of the Whitehall Ferry Terminal in the minds of many critics is that it is based not on "advanced" structural expressionism but on old-fashioned imagery.

We cannot resist the temptation to remind today's clamorous critics of the criticism directed toward the Eiffel Tower before it was erected in 1889. The famous letter quoted below (with even then its touch of anti-Americanism) was published as a protest by a "Committee of Three Hundred" (one for each proposed meter of the tower) against what was to become perhaps *the* symbol of their city. Among the signatories were Gounod, Massenet, Dumas, Prudhomme, Meissonier, and Garnier.

> Dear Sir and Compatriot:
>
> We come, writers, painters, sculptors, architects, passionate lovers of the beauty, until now intact, of Paris, to protest with all our force, with all our indignation, in the name of unappreciated French taste, in the name of menaced French art and history, against the erection, in the very heart of our capital, of the useless and monstrous Eiffel Tower, which public hostility, often endowed with good sense and a spirit of justice, has already baptized the "tower of Babel."
>
> Without falling into an excess of chauvinism, we have the right to proclaim aloud that Paris is a city without rival in the world. Beside

its streets, its spacious boulevards, along its admirable quays, amidst its magnificent promenades, rise up the most noble monuments that human genius has created. The soul of France, creator of masterpieces, radiates from this august flowering of stone. Italy, Germany, Flanders, so justly proud of their artistic heritage, possess nothing comparable to ours, and from all the corners of the universe, Paris attracts curiosity and admiration. Are we going to let all this be profaned? Is Paris going to be associated with the grotesque, mercantile imaginings of a constructor of machines to be irreparably defaced and dishonored? For the Eiffel Tower, which American commercialism itself would not want, is, without any doubt, the dishonor of Paris. Everyone knows it, everyone says it, everyone is deeply afflicted by it, and we are only a feeble echo of universal opinion, so legitimately alarmed. And lastly, when foreigners come to visit our Exposition, they will cry, astonished: "What! Is this horror what the French have found to give us an idea of their much-vaunted taste?" And they will have reason to ridicule us, because the Paris of Gothic sublimity, the Paris of Jean Goujon, of Germain Pilon, of Puget, of Rude, of Barye, etc., will have become the Paris of Monsieur Eiffel.

It suffices to understand what we put forth, to imagine, for an instant, a ridiculously tall tower dominating Paris, like a gigantic black factory chimney, overpowering with its barbaric mass Notre-Dame, Sainte-Chapelle, the Tour Saint-Jacques, the Louvre, the dome of the Invalides, the Arc de Triomphe, all our humiliated monuments, all our belittled architecture, which will be obliterated in this stupefying dream. And for twenty years we will see spreading out over the entire city, still vibrating with the genius of so many centuries, we will see, spreading like a blot of ink, the odious shadow of the odious column of tin.[1]

A century ago the outré element for the cultural elite was a timely *structural* expression that they considered tasteless in a civic monument within the historical context of Paris. A century later the outrage for cultural elites (those of Manhattan and Staten Island) is a timely *symbolic* image that they consider retardataire or vulgar for a civic monument juxtaposed against the modern skyline of Manhattan.

What an irony: today's retardataire establishment, calling itself avant-garde, advocates a structural expressionism that exploits engineering forms glorious a century ago, promoting an imagery that is acrobatic and a rhetoric that is archaic. Everyone else in our post-industrial age knows the Industrial Revolution is dead, and we proclaim therefore: no more antique decorative fragments ironically appropriated from the Eiffel Tower aesthetic attached to our buildings for the late twentieth century!

Is the Whitehall Ferry Terminal design in its ultimate symbolic significance in New York Harbor the equivalent of the Eiffel Tower in the city of Paris, as we designers have tried to make it? Who can say at this time? But it is true that good architecture is rarely liked universally in the beginning; the challenge is to have the right people hate it. In over 30 years of architectural practice many of our designs have been ridiculed or ignored at first, while 15 years later everyone is doing them; granted, somewhat misinterpreted.

It is significant that the clock is a sign, a representation of a clock—not a real mechanical clock but an electronic depiction of a clock as its "hands" move across its face via the medium of LED pixels that sparkle day and night.

It is significant that this clock is a civic and symbolic ornament—this connoted via its great size which promotes civic scale and its essential obsolescence which promotes its symbolic quality. In the old days the presence of the inevitable clock as part of the exterior architectural design of the railroad terminal at least was decorative *and* functional, as many approaching passengers did not own watches to assure them or alarm them as the case might be. Today a clock in such a context is hardly functional because virtually everyone wears a watch.

And in its shape, the clock both reflects (from Manhattan's standpoint) and generates (from Staten Island's standpoint) the form of the barrel vault that floats behind it. And the vault represents a gesture toward the past when architecture of the urban infrastructure was truly civic in its scale and symbolism.

And the Jumbotron inside this vault represents technology of *today*—and contributes an iconographic dimension that complements the spatial dimension within the waiting hall.

But it is important to emphasize the formal as well as the symbolic significance of the clock—of the circular form that vividly works as a contrast to the rectangular forms—those of the famous skyscrapers that create the famous skyline behind the clock and constitute its context from the water. By this bold contrast the essential quality of the skyline is made vivid and the ferry terminal itself is enhanced as an important, if relatively smaller, element. Here the element of architectural scale works as well—where the clock, smaller in size but bigger in scale, as its image works against its background, creates a proper significance for this civic building in its context within the city as a whole.

So why is this clock as a sign considered banal or oppressive by vocal opponents on Staten Island when it so aptly complements the Manhattan skyline formally and symbolically and compliments the Borough of Staten Island— looking good *in* Manhattan and *from* Staten Island while working vividly as a sign readable from afar and as a symbol whose hype twentieth-century images can correspond to that bold nineteenth-century imagery characteristic of the Statue of Liberty across the bay?

ADDENDUM

The project described above represents the winning design of an invited competition sponsored by the Economic Development Corporation of New York City. After public condemnation of the design by representatives of Staten Island and after the election of 1993, the city government required the clock's removal from the design—and soon after severely reduced the budget. Since the latter requirement predestined the former requirement, it was easier for us to swallow the former.

The second design, besides eliminating the old clock and acknowledging the new budget, accommodates as well expanded complex program requirements for existing underground circulation and above-grade pedestrian and bus circulation and an entirely new requirement, that of a car-on-ferry system. The section of the building is lowered and simplified to accommodate the lower budget, except for an upsweep toward the north to frame the immediate view of Lower Manhattan from the inside, and the south facade toward the water can be equated admittedly with an electronic billboard. But the wavy curves of the parapeted profile of this facade prevent it from looking like a billboard and work also to contrast it with the rectangle-dominated composition of its urban "backdrop"—as an electronic LED signboard whose moving and changing images include content—ornamental and informational—and whose really modern technology permits bold perception from afar across a bay.

This second design has met with mixed reactions. Can it be the fate of civic architecture, if its design is truly of its time, not to materialize in its time but to materialize only after its time? Can it be that the really good that's new can be appreciated only by the authentically naive or sophisticated—which is not the vociferous market for civic art and architecture in our time?[2]

In the end a Whitehall Ferry Terminal design requires support deriving not from community consensus or political pressure but from understanding and bravery—hard to acquire for a civic architecture that is neither banal nor pretentious. Or else there is always the ultimate accumulated compromise that consensus promotes and no one likes in the end.

---

1. Recounted in Norma Evenson, *Paris: A Century of Change, 1878–1978* (New Haven: Yale University Press, 1979), p. 32.
2. Of the four other civic projects we have been awarded in Manhattan, one was canceled as a result of community pressure (the Westway project), two we were edged out of, and one fizzled out.

THOUGHTS ON THE ARCHITECTURE OF THE SCIENTIFIC WORKPLACE: COMMUNITY, CHANGE, AND CONTINUITY

Delivered at the conference "The Architecture of Science," Harvard University, May 1994. To be published in *The Architecture of Science,* edited by Peter Galison and Emily Thompson (Cambridge: MIT Press).

I should first warn you: I come to this subject of relationships of architecture and science as a practicing architect; and my generalizations are really pragmatic responses to everyday experience; and, at that, to everyday experience squeezed into the life of the fin-de-siècle architect—a life that allows little time for generalizing. I shall try here to use plain words to make sense out of pragmatic responses-as-generalizations-within-a-context-of-chaos—and plain words and making sense is unusual, some of you may know, for architects of our time who measure the profundity of their theory in terms of the obscurity of their verbiage.

But, if I go from the particular to the general in my everyday thinking, I shall attempt in this discussion to go from the general to the particular and focus at the end on some work of ours, and mesh thereby, I trust, with what my esteemed friend and former client, Arnie Levine, will say.

THE RESEARCH LABORATORY

As an architect I shall tend to talk about the lab building as architecture more than about science in architecture. The most important thing, in my opinion, about the architecture of the Research Laboratory is that it is *generic*—and I shall focus here on the relevance of generic architecture for such a building type in particular, but also on its relevance in general for architecture for our time. And my discussion of a kind of generic architecture will concentrate on three of its characteristics:

- the element of *flexibility*—spatial and mechanical—that is promoted inside,

- the imageries of *setting and place* that are accommodated inside,

- the elements of *symbolism and ornament*—permanent and/or changing—that enhance imagery on the outside.

But before elaborating on these three elements of flexibility that characterize generic architecture as I am defining it, I should briefly refer to historic tradition that distinguishes generic architecture, a wide-ranging tradition that embraces:

1. The *New England mill:* where you find space as loft—and other industrial-factory kinds of buildings of the last century that flexibly accommodate changing functions and systems inside. (The Fagus Shoe Works by Walter Gropius, arguably based on American industrial vernacular architectural precedent and arguably considered the seminal building of the Modernist International Style, is significantly generic in terms of its aesthetic-symbolic reference as well as its functional program.)

2. The *Italian palazzo:* where you find chambers en suite surrounding a cortile—starting as a dynastic residence and evolving into a civic building—as a diplomatic headquarters, museum, etc.

3. The *Early American college building:* housing classrooms and dormitory that evolved into college or university administration headquarters—spatial and symbolic, highly symbolic—as at Harvard, Princeton, Brown, Dartmouth, William and Mary.

All of these generic prototypes contain adaptable/flexible spaces that evolve over time. This tradition includes as well:

4. The *conventional laboratory building:* whose spatial and mechanical flexibility is particularly significant today for accommodating dynamic

change inside, change that involves processes and technologies—the conventional lab building whose tradition can embrace Thomas Edison's various sheds and lofts originally in New Jersey and Cope and Stewardson's turn-of-the-century Medical School Buildings at Penn whose academic dimension is symbolized in their stylistic Jacobean exteriors.

5. And there is the particular relevance of the *generic loft building for the architecture of today in general*—where dynamic functions change over time at a quick pace and when architectural essence is becoming no longer spatial but inconographic. This point I shall come back to.

———

Flexibility—for today: where no longer does form follow function: that's not ambiguous enough. It is rather that:

- form accommodates function*s*—functions that are inherently changing—as they are complex and contradictory,

- functions that are accommodated rather than expressed—this is more and more relevant in science buildings in particular and in architecture in general—for change that is more characteristically revolutionary than evolutionary and that is dynamically wide in its range—spatial, programmatic, perceptual, technical, iconographic—where in our time functional ambiguity rather than functional clarity can accommodate the potential for "things not dreamt of in your philosophy,"

- functions that engage spatial and mechanical systems inside—and symbolic and ornamental dimensions outside,

- where generally the work space is at the edges near the windows for enjoying the amenity of natural light and the view—and the mechanical space is in the center and at the top for maximum access,

• where the scale of the architecture is physically generous—to create an aura of generosity as well as accommodate the dynamics of flexibility.

———

Setting and place—counterpoints:

for concentration: *setting,*
for communication: *place,*

setting—as lab—along windows,
place—as eddy—off corridor,

setting—as working labs located along the edge to connect with natural light from windows,
place—as niche, window seat, eddy—off the circulation route, possibly exploiting natural light as an attraction at one end of the corridor and an amenity,

setting—as background for work and focus—alone or with a group of colleagues,
place—as opportunity for meeting—meeting that is incidental rather than explicit (academics are perverse: if your architecture explicitly pronounces a place for interaction, they might not use it—a certain ambiguity concerning the function and nature of the space is perhaps essential here),

setting—as more or less local,
place—as signification of a whole (or perhaps a suggestion of a whole)—of a community, an academic community within a campus—so you function alone *and* in a community,

setting—a probably messy space—for the clutter of creative action, analytical, intuitive, physical,
place—a mostly orderly space—for re-creation, so to speak,

setting—within the consistent structural order—the generic order—of the loft, accommodating variety within order—spatial, perceptual, functional, mechanical,
place—as an exception to the rule of the consistent order of structural bays—accommodating a special space,

setting—accommodating change and dynamics in the lab—wow, look at this!
place—accommodating a permanent ambience where you anticipate the comfort of the familiar—but where there *can* be the surprise of the unfamiliar—like "Wow! John, of all people, said something brilliantly relevant this morning as we chatted!"

setting—neutral, recessive architecturally—to diminish distraction—artists' studios are in lofts not essentially because artists are poor but because they feel they can't create a masterpiece in someone else's masterpiece—a setting for inspiration *and* perspiration—artists and scientists are not priests performing rituals,
place—imageful architecturally—to create amenity and identity,

setting—for table-distance work focus,
place—for long-distance eye focus with a view.

A technical irony regarding the significance of Place for now: imageful Place that is local might be more essential than ever in our era of electronic communication to and from all over—in our era of *networking*.

An aesthetic irony is that accommodation to Place in this architectural context promotes a rhythmic exception within generic order and creates thereby aesthetic tension.

———

Symbolism that engages iconography and ornament on the exterior:

Symbolism as the attendant flourish within generic architecture that eloquently breaks the consistent order—that consistent rhythmic order—on the outside (and some places inside), thereby creating aesthetic tension.

Symbolism involving ornament, sign, iconography on the outside.

Traditionally evident—as in the cupola of Nassau Hall at Princeton, the *portone* with *stemma* of the Italian palazzo, the sign atop the mill, the hieroglyphics all over the temple in Egypt.

The difference between outside and inside—at least in the lab building, and especially for the academic lab building—is very relevant, where architectural consistency and neutrality of the workplace inside is counterbalanced by explicit symbolic content on the outside that acknowledges the significance of the community, of the institution as a whole.

Another role of exterior symbolism and ornament in the generic academic lab building is to acknowledge and accommodate the architectural context of the campus—and enhance it. And it is true that exterior symbolism on our lab buildings has so far derived more from accommodating particular architectural context than from general scientific sources.

The significance today of *iconography* for a generic architecture as a whole—and the significance of electronic technology as the medium for iconography—I shall touch on below.

What the generic laboratory academic building is not: it is not an architectural vehicle for sculptural articulation that makes for expressionistic architecture that is heroic and original—that constricts flexibility and promotes distraction.

SCIENCE AND TECHNOLOGY AND THE EXPRESSION OF TECHNOLOGY

This subject others are focusing on in this conference: I shall mention some issues briefly as I see them:

Expressing function stinks, as it inhibits change and encourages conformity—accommodating functions is what works.

Modernism employed industrial engineering imagery as an architectural aesthetic, sometimes called the machine aesthetic, along with a Minimalist-Cubist-abstract aesthetic—this, it can be said, via an adaptation of the vernacular vocabulary of the industrial loft—essentially the American generic loft of the turn of the century—and this exemplified a wonderful/valid historical-architectural evolution—or revolution—formally acknowledged in this country when Dean Hudnut invited Walter Gropius to Harvard.

The Neo-Modernist movement in the architecture of today involves a revival of engineering expressionism more explicitly ornamental than before—involves in the end an ironical architectural vocabulary based on industrial imagery as industrial rocaille—an imagery that is now around 100 years old and in our admittedly postindustrial age is no more current or relevant than—or no less historical than—that imagery of the Classical orders of the Renaissance that is 500 years old. Everyone must agree that the Industrial Revolution is dead but few architects acknowledge that electronic technology is what can be fundamentally relevant for architecture today—which, combined with generic order, can enhance, can indeed signify, an iconographic dimension—an iconographic dimension that is for now, unlike the spatial-structural dimension that was for then—an iconographic dimension nevertheless with a vivid tradition behind it.

So industrial and engineering-structural imagery of space is incidental for now while an ornamental-symbolic imagery of appliqué is valid for now.

And perhaps historical precedents for a generic-iconographic architecture that is for now are the Egyptian pylon with its hieroglyphics, the American roadside architecture adorned with commercial signs, Sant'Appollinare Nuovo in Ravenna whose evangelical murals ornament a generic basilica inside, a Constructivist project, a Sullivan bank, or an electronic-architectonic feature of Tokyo: let function, structure, and space take care of themselves efficiently and without fanfare—this for scientific workplaces in academic communities and for architecture as a whole. Perhaps the conventional scientific laboratory within this definition is the prototype for a valid and vivid architecture for now as a whole.

———

The scientific laboratory buildings by our office that are represented here illustrate variously qualities of the generic loft whose interior flexibility accommodates programmatic, spatial, and mechanical evolution over time and whose exterior ornamentation within the consistent rhythmic composition of the loft accommodates symbolic dimensions appropriate for a communal academic building. Exceptions to these forms of order deriving from incidental interactive spaces enrich the composition of the whole inside and out.

The design of most of our science laboratories represents work we have done in association with Payette and Associates of Boston, who are most significantly responsible for the major interior spatial-mechanical-programmatic elements of the architecture. And it is Jim Collins of that firm whom we have had the pleasure and honor of working with in the last decade.

FROM INVENTION TO CONVENTION IN ARCHITECTURE

Originally delivered as the Thomas Cubitt Lecture before the Royal Society for the Encouragement of Arts, Manufactures and Commerce, April 8, 1987; then published in the RSA Journal, *January 1988, pp. 89–103.*

I *am* an architect, I *was* a theoretician—when I was young and had little work. I had to talk and write then to keep busy, although not to keep out of trouble; writing about complexity, contradiction, ambiguity, decoration, symbolism, Mannerism, and even, in the late hours of pure Modernism, writing about Lutyens as well as Las Vegas got me into trouble.

But busy old architects do not theorize and probably should not—there is always the danger of lapsing into ideology—or they should theorize only as an accompaniment to their work. Yet I was explicitly requested by the Board of the Cubitt Trust to philosophize, not just to show our current work, and the Trustees of the National Gallery will not allow me to show the design of the Sainsbury Wing until next week, and also I appropriately promised the RIBA that my first lecture-presentation of that project would be before that body—and yet for this to be a good talk I must deal with what is on my mind now, which is our current work, especially the National Gallery extension.

A way out of this dilemma is to continue speculating archly on this subject of architects' talking versus architects' showing, until it is time to conclude with "Any questions?" But I shall try to instill some substance here by discussing what is currently on my mind, and the minds of my associates, in a general way—admitting that this will correspond to what is on the drawing boards in our office in a particular way—and this is the phenomenon of the popular art museum in the center of town. It is a phenomenon widely acknowledged today; the art museum as the archetypal building type of our time, as the cathedral of today, is almost a cliché. But Sylvia Lavin in the November 1986 issue of *Interiors* has described the phenomenon profoundly and succinctly. She writes:

> For every age there is a building type that sits on the apex of an architectural hierarchy and most completely expresses the aspirations and desperations of its time. In the Renaissance, cultural values were embodied in sacred architecture, while Le Corbusier's explorations of various forms of housing reveal the social upheavals of the early twentieth century. As western civilization has become increasingly complex it has become more difficult to pinpoint where our values lie, yet the museum is perhaps the building type that best reveals our cultural agenda. Certainly the war between the Modernists and the PostModernists is, in significant part, being fought on the battleground of museums. More important, in this age of general comfort, if not affluence, where social inequities are often expressed in sophisticated and subtle terms that are at home in the world of art, the museum has taken on a highly charged significance. Not only does the character of the contemporary museum come close to the core of recent shifts in architectural theory and ideology, but defining it as an institution now involves confronting a wide range of social and political phenomena.[1]

I shall categorize, as I see them, some architectural implications of our archetypal museum—of the popular art museum in the center of town— which involve sometimes dilemmas, always challenges—with some reference to the four museum projects in our office that are in the design stage now. I shall end with an approach to the facade as a manifestation of urban context and as an example of evolving Classicism. This latter will become a justification of an aspect of our National Gallery design in particular and an apologia for our work in general, which is what you might expect from any talking architect, in the end.

The popular art museum in the center of town is not only a repository for the conservation and display of works of art, it is an explicitly didactic institution, involving educational components—places for instruction via lectures, cinema, television, computers, as well as books. It includes perhaps an artist's studio. It accommodates a big staff beyond that of the traditional curators and conservators to administer the new programs. It has a shop and a restaurant with kitchen. It is often a place for entertainment (especially in America)—a presumably beautiful and monumental environment for openings and other ceremonies. The ratio of space for art versus support space in the nineteenth-century museum was something like 9 to 1; today it is more like 1 to 2—that is, only one-third of the total space might be for displaying art.

The art museum today has expanded its market—it is no longer a place for a cultural elite; where attendance at the National Gallery was a little over half a million visitors per year in the mid-nineteenth century, its attendance is now over three million per year—spanning wide ranges of taste, cultures, and nationalities—accommodated of course by active educational programs.

Many art museums in the United States are moving downtown. The site for the new building we are designing for the Laguna Gloria Art Museum is in the center of town: it is moving from an idyllic but remote suburb of Austin, Texas. Our Seattle Art Museum is moving from a kind of elitist park at the edge of town to a dense urban site in the central business district, essentially to attract a wider range of people, to increase the museum's attendance and enhance its influence. By this juxtaposition of art and commerce it will perhaps also promote an immediacy between fine art and everyday life that has been lost in the modern experience. The creation of the image of the museum building in a dense urban setting is, of course, a significant architectural challenge.

Part of the challenge lies in the need to reassess the nature of art exhibition today. Whereas in the past collections were relatively static, today they are relatively changeable, owing to increased purchasing programs, the ever-increasing supply of new work available to museums that exhibit contemporary art, and the advent of the temporary and traveling exhibition where new art is displayed or old art is combined in new ways according to a theme. This requires various degrees of flexibility in spatial configuration and lighting and promotes various approaches to the architectural setting for art, including spaces that are symbolically neutral or historical or modern-mechanistic, that are contained or flowing in character.

rooms of the Pitti Palace, where Pietro da Cortona's mural on the ceiling and his easel painting on the wall are found in the same gallery. The other extreme is the early Museum of Modern Art, where neutral and flexible spaces encourage changing exhibits and provide a background that is not analogous with the historical imagery of the painting. Here, natural light is usually eliminated and the background is designed as a stage set to be manipulated by the curator and changed at frequent intervals. The walls are usually white.

Our approach lies between these two extremes. It allows some flexibility and yet suggests an abstraction, an elemental expression, of the setting that the artists anticipated when painting the pictures. A positive, associative context, we think, renders the paintings real and memorable for viewers, whereas an anonymous, early-MoMA context tends to make the art resemble reproductions in a book. However, we feel the gallery setting should not replicate the chapels or palace rooms in which historical paintings were originally hung but should recall instead the substantial architectural character and the air of permanence of these spaces.

Concerning the galleries as rooms:

In palaces, paintings were displayed in rectangular rooms and lit by windows. Nineteenth-century galleries were based on these palace rooms but windows were replaced by roof monitors. In the twentieth century, galleries tend to be designed as flowing space or space that can be temporarily defined, and the technical requirements of lighting are expressed as positive architectural elements.

In the National Gallery extension, to suit the character of its Renaissance collection, but also in our other art museum designs, we have returned to the earlier tradition. Galleries that are rooms defined by familiar, traditional walls, floors, ceilings, doors, and windows are more appropriate, we feel, for exhibiting paintings than are galleries where the forms and symbols are original, mechanistic, and modern.

A further question of architectural scale lies in the design of gallery spaces in relation to the size of the paintings, the scale of their images, and the number of people looking at them. In the Early Renaissance collection of the National Gallery extension, for instance, we have relatively small paintings with intricate images. They were created for small chapels or the relatively small rooms of quattrocento palaces and burghers' houses, and were seen originally by perhaps several dozen people a day. These paintings, as artistic icons, are now seen by thousands of people per day—the over three million visitors a year to the National Gallery correspond to about one-third of the whole population of the Italian peninsula in the fifteenth century. The galleries themselves must accommodate, then, small objects and large crowds. The rooms must be large enough to take the crowds but small enough not to overwhelm the paintings. Doors between galleries must be relatively wide but the axial vistas, seen through room openings, must not be too long or Baroquely grand to respect the scale of the early Renaissance paintings. I think part of the secret here is (like God for Mies van der Rohe) in the details. Architectural detail in the galleries must be small in scale and highly refined to relate to the scale and intimacy of many of the paintings.

In lighting the galleries we must accommodate other sets of contradictory requirements, this time of architecture and science: each gallery space should be an elemental room, yet, at the same time, it must admit light in a way that does not harm the paintings.

In our current work we have tried for:

- Natural daylight in the galleries but no direct sunlight or ultraviolet rays on the paintings.

- Illumination (a mixture of natural and artificial light) at the lower wall surface where the paintings hang, but no halo of bright light at the top of the wall.

- No overt, mechanical expression of the means of admitting and controlling natural or artificial light.

- Daylight that is recognizable as daylight—and therefore no horizontal daylight systems of skylights, but rather clerestories with recognizable windows in them, and, of course, appropriately protected to control the amount of daylight. Also night or late winter afternoon lighting that does not try to replicate natural light.

• An image of window as symbol. An art museum can have few windows—this is because of the need for wall space inside to hang the paintings and for protection against excessive daylight to conserve the paintings. Security is also an issue. But an occasional opportunity to look out while in galleries is desirable for two reasons: a window in this context is what makes a gallery a room, a room for art rather than a tomb for art; it makes of the gallery a true place—by making the gallery familiar and by giving the viewers the chance occasionally to be reminded of where they are, to see the real world and identify with it while within the magical world of art; this makes the magic more magical through the comparison. This we have accomplished through spatial layering, where the window is in an inner wall set back from the exterior wall which has its own window: so you see the inner symbolic window juxtaposed on an outer "true" window, and thus the immediate window of the gallery is shielded from direct rays of the sun.

Now for the exterior of the popular art museum in the center of town.

Seen from outside, a building without windows almost inevitably looks stark and hostile—associated with forts or jails; yet a popular museum must look open and inviting. Thus the quality of the entrance is important and the ornamentation of the exterior walls significant. Wilkins did well in the National Gallery with his central open portico, which is inviting, and his walls decorated with rhythmic pilasters, varied moldings, and those niches that are a symbolic form of window.

Then there is the question of presence. The art museum in the center of town is a building of high civic importance, but it is smaller than the buildings around it. This is especially true in the United States, where the low museums are often framed by high-rise office buildings. Also the location of the art museum may not be special in the hierarchical plan of the city— it may not, for instance, be a focus at the end of an axial boulevard. As an institution in the thick of things, it is along a street. This is the case with the Whitney and Guggenheim museums and the Museum of Modern Art in New York City and with our museum in Seattle.

How do these important institutional buildings surrounded by less important but bigger private buildings achieve presence? Again, through architectural scale—by being small buildings with big scale. But again, the big scale must be juxtaposed with little scale—the big scale for presence, the little scale for friendliness—to make you comfortable as an individual in a monumental context: this is a truly Italian delight. But it is also English: in Trafalgar Square there is the poignant juxtaposition of Nelson's huge Corinthian column with the much smaller Corinthian columns of the portico of the National Gallery; these are almost country-house-domestic in their size and scale.

What I say here about urbanity and scale may seem obvious, but it implies an opposite approach to that of some recently designed galleries. The designs of urban museums in Stuttgart, Mönchengladbach, and Los Angeles employ combinations of medium-scale elements in a spatial play of pavilions and plazas to be experienced sequentially, as in a medieval village or a Hadrian's villa. In these museums scale is extended, not through the juxtaposition of big and small within the confines of the urban block but, as it was in Modern architecture, through a breaking of the limits of the urban block—skyways span streets, outdoor public routes bisect the building.

Besides these questions of the small building with architectural presence, the inviting building with windowless walls, and the urban building conforming to the ordinary spatial system of the city, there is the question of context. An urban building should be designed from the outside in as well as from the inside out—a tradition that was temporarily forgotten in the anti-urban days of Modern architecture. Attention to context in the design of urban architecture promotes harmony and a sense of the whole. Harmony can be achieved through contrast or analogy—that is, the gray suit with the gray necktie or the gray suit with the red necktie—or through both—the gray suit with the gray necktie with red polka dots. Then also there is room for disharmony in artistic, contextual composition—this to acknowledge valid contradictions and discontinuities within the whole and to make the overall harmony more sweet.

Many museum projects today are extensions of older museums. Respect for the whole in these cases is especially significant, and here the idea of the building as fragment, the building that inflects, is important. You will see that the National Gallery extension as we have designed it, although separate from the original Wilkins fabric, inflects toward the main building. It is a kind of fragment; it could not stand alone, or make sense if the old building were somehow to disappear. At the same time we hope the new building is not subservient in its acknowledgment of the old building. It forms part of a greater whole, but it is also a building on its own and of its own time, contrasting tensely with, *and* being analogous to, the original building.

Lastly, symbolism and graphics. Today's art museum with its changing shows is like a theater and needs graphics, outside and in, that are sometimes the equivalent of a marquee—or should the graphics outside be explicitly instructive like the billboard facade of the Bibliothèque Sainte-Geneviève engraved with the names of hundreds of scholars? I also like the old, now destroyed, Neue Pinakothek in Munich with its great mosaic depiction of a picture on its front facade. But don't worry, we've not tried these graphic ideas out on the National Gallery extension; Trafalgar Square is not to become Leicester Square.

This paper has been full of conjunctive yets and buts—but that's natural in any analysis of a current urban art museum which is popular *yet* esoteric, closed *but* open, monumental *yet* inviting, an accommodating setting for the art *but* a work of art itself, and so on, and so on.

I shall conclude with a short description of an architectural idea that is good to remind ourselves of—and which, as I have said, might be taken as an anticipatory apologia for aspects of our National Gallery design.

The idea is that today's deviation is tomorrow's convention. I shall refer to a few evolutionary changes as I see them within the history of Classical architecture. The emphasis will be less on any consistency of the elements of Classicism or rigidity of their rules of combination, and more on their inherent flexibility and their potential for achieving lively art.

Here are some now familiar Classical conformations involving more or less symbolism and form:

The pilaster: What did the first critic who saw one of these say? What! A column stuck on a wall—a structural element as a decoration—what kind of oxymoron is this—or is it a joke? (Perhaps artists are never so serious as when they are accused of joking.)

The giant order: Juxtaposed pilasters of different sizes and orders! How confusing the forms and scale! (But this Michelangelo outrage initiated *the* monumental tradition for promoting hierarchies of scale for aesthetic and civic expression in architecture.)

And then there is *St. Martin-in-the-Fields*—a medieval spire atop a Roman temple? How uncomfortable! (But didn't it become *the* archetypal church of the later eighteenth and early nineteenth centuries in the United States?)

A church as a basilica? How can a Roman law court correspond to a Christian sanctuary?

Superimposed temples reflecting the basilica inside? Muddling through, Italian style!

An archaic temple as a Christian Church? Good gods!

Malcontenta—a country house with a temple front!—which became a prototype for stately houses and Southern plantations.

Frank Lloyd Wright said of *St. Peter's:* Michelangelo built a temple, slung the Pantheon on top and called it a day. (Actually, Brunelleschi did it first.)

Reclining *figures on a pediment?* I hope they don't doze off and fall down.

A broken pediment? 'Tis pity she's a half.

Classical cornices designed to control dripping rain and modulate shadows in the sun—inside? Another one of those architects' tricks.

Delicate *interior Roman plaster work*—on the outside? How fussy, Mr. Adam.

And lastly, if I may consider Mies van der Rohe a Classical architect in spirit: an old-fashioned *industrial vernacular* vocabulary for a modern civic building?

We now love these examples of what were once deviations but have become archetypes; but let us remember that evolutionary variation is sometimes harder to accept than revolutionary invention in architecture.

You will note that I have not included mannerist deviations that did not become archetypes. Mannerist architecture is architecture that was strange then and is now. This is because in mannerist architecture deviation is intrinsic; deviations in mannerist buildings are usually system-wide rather than expedient; they form part of a whole approach to composition that embraces the strange or ambiguous.

You will note lastly that many of the examples illustrated above are British. The genius of British Classicism in architecture derives largely from its deviations from the norm. Some of the deviations accommodate the intrusion of circumstance, while others represent evolutions that shift the norm. All Classical architecture balances the particular and the individual against the general and the universal. In Britain, the balance is often subtle and oscillating; the incursion of the exceptional, even the idiosyncratic, on the elemental and abstract is barely resolved, and equilibrium is precariously maintained. As a result, a tension and richness of composition are achieved that enliven the basic Classical vocabulary and make British Classicism supremely vivid and poignant.

In this context, the essential purism of Lord Burlington and his circle is an exception within a tradition that is more accurately represented by the mannerist (not Mannerist) tendencies of Wren, Hawksmoor, Vanbrugh, Archer, Soane, Greek Thomson, and the Lutyens of "the high game"—architects beloved to me.

---

1. Sylvia Lavin, "Interiors Platforms," *Interiors,* November 1986, p. 15.

NOTE ON THE BELOVED PRINCETON CAMPUS AS A BASIS FOR A PROPOSED PLANNING STUDY

Written 1993.

Why does everyone love the Princeton campus and why is it uniquely distinguished as a setting for institutional life?

I think one reason is that the architecture there is both good and varied in its generic manifestations—Georgian, Tuscan villa, Ruskinian Gothic, and Collegiate Gothic—and in its easy evolutions combining analogous and contrasting relationships among buildings and styles.

Another reason is that the spaces among buildings on this campus are consistently unified and artfully pedestrian in their quality and scale as they evolve from space punctuated by buildings, in the earlier decades, to space directed or enclosed by buildings in later decades.

Campus planning at Princeton has historically combined, balanced, and integrated two approaches that can be distinctly defined. The first is characterized by the original Nassau Hall complex of buildings that projects unifying axes and balancing symmetry among Classical forms as points in space; the second is characterized by the Holder-Hamilton Hall complex where picturesque and continuous form directs and encloses space and is perceived as evolving over time. Both ways are adorable to Princetonians as they richly acknowledge and tensely juxtapose the ideal and the pragmatic, the Classical and the Romantic, the formal and the picturesque. But it is important to remember that the various combinings of these two ways in the history of the overall planning of the Princeton campus have been directed distinctly pragmatically rather than grandiosely. Does this make of the campus plan a kind of incomplete and therefore ironical whole at any one time?

And there have consistently evolved appropriate balances between growth via expansion at the edges of the campus and growth by infill within the fabric of the campus—and between attention to the whole (not domineering) and to the details (not fussy).

While Princeton's configurations of space, form, and symbol enhance the aura of the campus, they work too to accommodate institutional programs via various manifestations of generic architecture. And how the connections between form and program acknowledge symbolic content at Princeton was brilliantly analyzed by my mentor, the historian Donald Drew Egbert, in *The Modern Princeton* (Princeton University Press, 1947).

During the planning study questions about the ethos and nature of the place and institution must be subtly posed and carefully analyzed among the planners and the users to understand where Princeton is coming from, in order to continue, via the campus plan, to accommodate change and growth for a dynamic and complex future.

The heritage that is Princeton's and that will be a basis for its future is fragile as well as precious, and, strangely, it is as vulnerable to erosion through analogous relationships within its existing campus fabric as it is to destruction via contrasting relationships. Let us heed the warning of the evolution of the "grounds" of the University of Virginia since its glorious beginning as the Lawn. At that complex by Thomas Jefferson—one of the sublime configurations, educational and architectural, of all time—it's been downhill ever since.

MORE THOUGHTS ON CONTEXT AND FUNCTION: THE AMERICAN CAMPUS IN THE AMERICAN TOWN

Excerpts from an Essay as Part of the Submission for a Competition for the Design of the Undergraduate Sciences Teaching Building at Brown University Which We Didn't Win

Written 1993.

Building and place	It could be said that this project involves *building* and *place:*
New and old	A new building in an old place.
Generic architecture	The *building* seen as a generic entity accommodating interior needs, specific and general; connecting with its neighboring Geo-Chem Building, programmatically, spatially, and aesthetically; and acknowledging exterior context—the place it is in—while enhancing that place.
Brown and Providence together	The *place* seen as two things at once: as part of an American university campus, with its rural reference, and as part of an American city with its gridiron plan—acknowledging thereby the qualities of Brown *and* Providence.
The building: flexibility, rhythm, background, in the generic tradition	As a generic type, a sciences teaching building is composed of hierarchies of repetitive spaces arranged to form an order that matches the working needs of a variety of users and can accommodate changes in particular uses and relationships over

time. This building should fall within the distinguished tradition, represented at Brown by University Hall, of buildings that acknowledge evolution over time and serve, inside and out, as rhythmic backgrounds for academic work and life.

Unobtrusive background for concentration: mess and inspiration

The building's generic loft form would suit the specifics of the teaching laboratory program by providing adaptability to changes, now and over time, in use, space requirements, and mechanical systems. In general, the loft offers an ideal background for creative work—for the artist's attic or the scientist's laboratory. It is a generous and unobtrusive workplace that can accommodate order and mess, inspiration and concentration.

Accommodating communication—explicit and incidental—to enhance community

But the need for communication as well as concentration must be satisfied if the building is to house and support an academic community. Communication may be incidental as well as explicit. It may occur "by accident" in and off the corridor as well as in the classroom and the lecture hall. Nooks and eddies for meeting should be subtly integrated both within and as exceptions to the building's spatial order and circulation system.

Consistency and exceptions

The building should achieve architectural quality via consistency *and* exception. In our sketches of the typical floor plan, the principal exception within the order is a casual meeting place located at the end of the main corridor near the elevators and the connection to the Geo-Chem Building—both circulation-intensive spots. As you approach and enter this well-lit area, you aren't required to make too explicit a social commitment; the irregular shape in plan and the built-in window seats imply that this is not a room but an attractive spatial incident.

The place: the American gridiron plan and the American rural campus

The *town:* the traditional American gridiron plan manifests—*pace* a few urban theorists and designers—some glorious dimensions, spatially and symbolically. It embraces consistency and richness, order and growth, hierarchy and equality. Given its consistency, buildings within it cannot acquire hierarchical quality from location but depend for their differentiation on size and the architectural qualities of scale and symbolism. The egalitarianism of the grid accommodates diversity and consistency; within its system growth can be inherent and constant; its open-ended streets suggest an eternal frontier.

The *gown:* the prototypical American college or university campus is rural—at least in its imagery and symbolism, if sometimes ultimately less so in its location and density.

Town and gown at Brown

The institutional and urban juxtapositions of Brown and Providence are particularly tense and poignant. These qualities should be acknowledged and understood:

The block and the corner

The *place*—the corner of George and Thayer streets and the inner block formed by George, Thayer, Waterman, and Brook streets—embraces both campus, inside the block, and town, at the corner.

The *inner block.* Owing to existing pedestrian circulation patterns, the main entrance to the new building will probably be from the interior court it helps to define. This will orient the building toward the campus interior and enhance activity within the block. The single-loaded corridor of the new building will help to enliven this part of the campus as its glass wall will expose building activity to view.

Street and inner block

The architectural contrast between the two main fa-cades of this building is derived from interior re-quirements, but it works as well to articulate differences between exterior street and interior block in a place that is at once campus and town and has obligations to both—to suggest an urban envi-ronment on the street and a "campus" within the block.

The corner

This element of both town and campus is considered very important by Brown—and we agree. As it now exists, there is at this corner a gentle coming-together of eighteenth- and nineteenth-century clapboard residential buildings, the Kasser and How-ell houses, and of delicately scaled institutional buildings. The earlier domestic buildings sit closer to the street than the larger institutional ones. De-spite the charm of this urban composition, a case can be made for replacing Howell House: it is a less than distinguished example of a Queen Anne Revival Style house, and its adaptation to new programmatic requirements, current codes, and the floor levels of the Geo-Chem Building would be difficult.

Order and variety

A new complex on the northeast corner could en-hance this significant intersection of town and cam-pus. We think of the new building as a space definer rather than a sculptural entity; its linear form directs space on the street and encloses space within the block. The gently consistent rhythms of its brick fa-cade will enhance the identity of Thayer Street and define the quality of the place it encloses. At the same time varieties of rhythms, scales, articulations, and inflections at the eastern end of the building—exterior manifestations of student-faculty meeting places and ground-floor access—break the continuous rhythms of the facade and reinforce the urban quality of the corner.

Height and bulk   We think the perceived height of this five-story building can be better reduced by setting back the top floor, to give an apparent height of four stories when seen from ground level, than by simulating the profile of residential roofs, as was done in the Geo-Chem Building. The building's bulk is minimized by its single-loaded corridor plan and by the articulations at its ends; its compact footprint lessens its impact on existing open space, landscape, pathways, and vegetation and permits it to set back from the sidewalk to approximate the alignments of other university buildings nearby.

Vitality and growth   This approach seeks to derive harmony from both contrast and analogy. It admits the tension characteristic of, indeed inevitable in, a complex urban situation where growth must be accommodated—and tries to make this tension wonderful.

A complex harmony . . .   We hope this new building will be workable inside and effective outside—and, through its inflection, its combination of order and exception, and its richness of hierarchy and scale, can achieve a complex harmony, an aesthetic tension, and a vitality deriving from realities of growth in this historic and beautiful place.

. . . With what's there   As designers, we start with what's there, we love what's there, and we go from there.

GENERAL THOUGHTS CONCERNING DESIGNING FOR ARCHITECTURE ON AMERICAN CAMPUSES

Written 1992.

Most campus academic buildings want to be generic architecturally, sometimes specifically loftlike, to be flexible inside physically and spatially over time for evolving uses. In this way they acknowledge the continuity that is characteristic of an institution—life within the building goes on beyond the lives of the individual academics that make up the institution; such buildings also want a dignity and generosity of scale appropriate for generic institutional uses; such buildings want also to be kickable—tough so they wear well with their hard use over time—and they must mellow with age; such loftlike buildings want their architectural quality to be recessive, not intrusive—to be an ideal background for work and concentration; such buildings also want to accommodate incidental interaction, to promote community and communication implicitly in the character of their circulation. If such buildings want to work as recessive backgrounds inside, they largely want to be the same in terms of their context outside. These buildings that are workplaces and dignified at the same time must not be architecturally trendy, but rather, as we've said, generic, and therefore most likely to extend harmony within their campuses and to acknowledge context via analogy more than via contrast—an academic building cannot succumb to the hyped sensibility of this moment or be a product to promote the great architect who creates it. Those kicks the architect more responsibly derives not on a campus.

It is ironic that most of the work of our office consists of institutional-civic buildings that often pertain to campuses and require contextual analogy over contextual contrast; we are thereby out of step in terms of the sensibility of our time, which is hyped—listen to loud music, flex your padded shoulders, watch commercial sound bites. Within the cycle of taste our perceptual expectations involve big scale, bold forms and colors and contrasts. But we resist this natural contemporary inclination so as to be good architect-artists, making our art appropriate rather than arbitrary—suiting the circumstances rather than artistic inclinations. I say "ironic" because I know about the general appropriateness of hype in our time: was it not I who said in the mid-sixties: "less is a bore"?—although now I wonder if more is a bore. I would love to build hype, but only as appropriate to the job.

TALKING BACK

BEING REPULSIVE: AS I TRAVEL I SEE ELEMENTS OF BUILDINGS FROM MY HOTEL WINDOW THAT ORIGINATED IN MY/OUR WORK AND HAVE BEEN EXPLOITED ALL OVER

A Recording of Current Banalities as Former Outrages—In No Particular Order

Written 1994.

1. The hierarchical facade with a base, a middle, and a top—as articulated in the Guild House Housing for the Elderly of the early sixties—via decorative patterns in the facade as areas and stripes and as openings in the base and the lunette window at the top.

2. Chain link fence not in the back yard—as in the gardens of Guild House up front.

3. Duality in the composition—as defined via the fat column—at the entrance to Guild House.

4. A fat column—as at the Guild House—which articulates duality in its composition.

5. Sculpture on the building rather than in front of it—as in the sculptural antenna on Guild House.

6. Windows that were not disguised as absence of wall, strip in wall, or empty hole in wall: windows with multiple panes defined by mullions and muntins that remind you of windows—as in Guild House and first employed (courageously, believe it or not) in mother's house.

7. The ordinary element as objet trouvé—as in the representational sculpture as TV antenna at Guild House.

8. Multiple scales as little building with big scale via elements that are not consistently "human scale"—as in all the early buildings that are small.

9. Ornament—as in the applied arch in mother's house entrance and North Penn Visiting Nurses Association entrance and in moldings that border windows there too.

10. Redundancy—as in decorative arch juxtaposed on functional lintel in mother's house entrance.

11. Symbolism: mother's house looks like a house: ordinary, familiar, conventional, nonoriginal are not bad.

12. Admit and celebrate entrance intrusion in facade: entrance is not just a shadow as absence of wall.

13. Go back to a pediment that you see on the front facade, not a flat roof or a shed roof—as in mother's house.

14. A broken pediment, at that.

15. Stripes, borders, colors as ornament!—as in all over.

16. The front is different from the back—as in mother's house, Guild House.

17. A building doesn't have to look original—as in Columbus Fire Station and Nantucket houses.

18. Historical reference, but relevant to place as context—as in the houses that look different in terms of where they are.

19. Building not in space, but makes space, acknowledging an urban tradition rather than a suburban, Ville Radieuse, superblock ideal or Broadacre City tradition—as in the NPVNA building that defines its adjacent parking lot as a positive spatial element.

20. The building as a fragment: see above.

21. Your vocabulary doesn't have to pretend to be industrial—as in mother's house.

22. Nonindustrial chimneys are OK; don't have to be pipes or stunted—as in the beach house.

23. An arch can be ornamental to symbolize and celebrate entrance—as in the NPVNA building.

24. In the end, your forms can be symbolic—not original, not industrial—and they can be different in different contexts: they can also include big signs—as in the Football Hall of Fame project.

Note: I refer to first buildings:

1. NPVNA Building

2. Mother's house

3. Guild House

4. Columbus Fire Station

5. Trubek-Wislocki Houses

6. Football Hall of Fame project.

72
Sketches

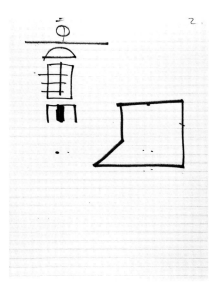

WINDOWS—c. '65

Published in "The Architecture of the Window," a special issue of *A + U,* December 1995.

I rediscovered windows! How hard it is now to remember how taboo it was then to do windows—that is, when I started out when architecture was Modern with a vengeance.

In the early days of the International Style you did find some windows as holes in the wall, as in Mies van der Rohe's great Afrikaner Strasse Housing in Berlin or Le Corbusier's great Villa Savoye, but they were disguised in their combinations as strip windows that articulated the walls as essentially long vertical planes and that did not "violate the integrity"—the formal and structural image—of the wall as a simple and abstract element.

Windows as stripes more than as openings could be not only horizontal but also vertical in the less industrial-referenced Modernism of American skyscrapers—as in the Rockefeller Center complex where the spandrel dividing the real but unacknowledged windows occurred below and above them rather than beside them.

And then there was the *brise-soleil* of Le Corbusier, which dominated the facade by its geometric force and thereby disguised the windows behind it and hid them as well by means of shadows—in the end less to keep the sun out of the inside and more to block the window out from the outside.

The concept of window as absence of wall had become almost universal, as "flowing space" that eschewed enclosure in architecture and encouraged ambiguity between the inside and the outside came to predominate. The unobtrusive glass walls connecting disconnected planar walls of Mies's Barcelona Pavilion came to exemplify the window as pariah—although we must remember the window disguised as shadow below the hovering horizontal planes as roof overhangs that dominated Frank Lloyd Wright's Prairie Style houses some decades before.

I describe the concept of architecture sans window in terms of formal perception, but it applies as vividly within a symbolic dimension involving association. The actual elements in this kind of architecture that consisted of frames and glass to keep out the cold and the rain and to look through—these elements were designed not to look familiar, not to have qualities or imagery that resembled or even reminded you of windows as you knew them from past association—from, heaven forbid, history; therefore modern sliding windows were in. The previous invention of plate glass allowing big sheets helped here, of course.

But as important as were these aesthetic bases—structural, spatial, and symbolic—for denying the window in the wall was a philosophical basis: Modern architecture was progressive, if not revolutionary; its forms had to look different, if not new, in their often pure and minimalist abstractions—and thereby entirely free of historical precedent. And it helped if the architecture looked outrageous, which increased its chance of being avant-gardely correct. I have written elsewhere of the International Style's implicit reference to an industrial vernacular architecture, which Le Corbusier acknowledges in his references to American grain elevators in *Vers une architecture*. (For Gropius, thank God, his seminal Fagus Shoe Works happened to really be a factory!)

Louis Kahn's late work contains eloquent holes in walls but they are significantly abstract and made more so by their circular and triangular shapes that reinforce their quality as holes and diminish their reference to windows.

So it turned out by the early and mid-sixties that I was revolutionary in not being revolutionary; in employing reference and association, if not symbolism; in eschewing abstract, progressive, by-then-old-fashioned Modernism;

and in making the little houses and fire stations I could get as commissions not outrageous but familiar and conventional. Being outrageous by not being outrageous sounds not outrageous now, but it *was* outrageous. And one of the ways was to make a house look like a house and a fire station look like a fire station—to make them represent what they were via association rather than to functionalize them, so to speak.

And that's how I came to make a generic window—a window that looked like a window, that was symbolically a window as well as formally a window in my second building, my mother's house. (My first building, the North Penn Visiting Nurses center in Ambler, Pennsylvania, had an entrance that looked like an entrance by sporting in the facade a frankly decorative decorative-arch.)

Yes, it took courage in the early sixties—construction was completed in the spring of '64—to make that hole in the wall on the left side of the front facade of my mother's house—and then as well to insert a window in it by persuading, with some difficulty, the Arcadia Sliding Glass Door Company to insert a horizontal muntin! This window was followed by double-hung windows with a central vertical muntin in the Guild House facades—an even more literal representation of a conventional window of the United States—and then in the Trubek-Wislocki Houses and others, sometimes in the form of casements, and then on and on until this classic window became the universal trademark of some other architects. And then there is the literal universal trademark of now—Windows '95!

In the end, architects might have to adore windows as elements that create and modulate light inside and are perhaps the single most important architectural element signifying historically the quality of a building and the character of a style.

ARCHITECTURE AS ELEMENTAL SHELTER, THE CITY AS VALID DECON

By Robert Venturi and Denise Scott Brown. Originally delivered as the Outside Architecture Lecture in honor of Reyner Banham at the Architectural Association, London, May 2, 1991; then published in *Architectural Design* Profile 94 (1991), pp. 8–13.

We were asked specifically to speak about issues outside architecture: if that means, "don't show slides of your work," we're OK. If it means relate architecture to literary criticism, semiotics, philosophical theory, psychology, and strange ideas about perception, we're in trouble because that's what we're not gonna talk about, and the significance of that avoidance is the subject of what follows.

INTRICACIES OF THE AVANT-GARDE

When we read today's architectural literature we are often confused by its obscurity, distressed by its pretension, or bored by its banality. Yet architecture and its perception and meaning should not be difficult to describe by an educated person to a literate reader, because architecture is a discipline that has to satisfy basic functional and structural requirements and meet obvious responsibilities, economic and social. Architecture, as the most social and prevalent of the arts, must sublimate its esoteric dimension or, at least, not *try* to be esoteric; it is inevitably a part of mass culture and as such must be likable and readable by lots of people—literate and illiterate—who have to use it and live with it over time. As we lament the current trend toward simplistic, if obscure, ideology we are reminded of a statement by Sir Edwin Lutyens on Sir Herbert Baker: "God asked Adam to name the animals *after* He created them. Baker names his animals first and then starts to create around a name and words." Ideology is an enemy of art. The trouble was once that architect-ideologues would read only one book, then name a movement; now they read too many books and drop too many names.[1]

In what follows, we hope you will understand what we say. We will try to talk about important things in an easy, straightforward way; speaking American, not translated French, German, or Italian. We have an old-fashioned belief in being understandable to others and even to ourselves, so don't hold us suspect if you find you understand us.[2]

There is, as well, a second weakness in our position: our criticism of current tendencies in architectural theory may not contain a proper amount of persuasive detail because we cannot understand a lot of what we've read or tried to read. If you can't understand it, you suspect it's not worth understanding. You may question how we can disagree with what we don't understand or have much patience with, but we would argue that this contradiction is the substance of what we are criticizing, and that, although we don't understand or agree with much of what we currently read and see, we still claim that most of it parallels what was written in *Complexity and Contradiction* 25 years ago, and *Learning from Las Vegas* 20 years ago, but—a significant but—in an extravagant or misunderstood manner: is Decon *C&C* in Modern dress?

Take the element of contradiction, which permeates and often dominates theory and practice in our time (although it is called by other names). If contradiction is consistent or constant, it results in no contradiction. As in music, all dissonance leads to no dissonance. If contradiction in architecture is everywhere, it is nowhere, for contradiction must work as an exception to a perceived order or remnant of order, no matter how faint, or to a "difficult whole" as described in *Complexity and Contradiction.* An architecture of mannerism must refer to an original order. By facing function and context as realities of experience rather than as facets of ideology, you will break open your aesthetic system, and this may be aesthetically good. Constant contradiction and consistent inconsistency, in the end, either grate on the sensibilities or bore. Contradiction cannot be forced and, by definition, cannot be total: the exception must prove, not make, the rule.

Although some of the theory we refer to, and the architecture *it* refers to, parallels that of *Complexity and Contradiction,* it ignores the warning, in the Gentle Manifesto that introduces the book, the warning against "the incoherence or arbitrariness of incompetent architecture" and "the precious intricacies of picturesqueness and expressionism," and the preference for "a complex and contradictory architecture based on the richness and ambiguity of the modern experience." It seems that the late Modern articulated Expressionism that we reacted against in the early sixties, what we called "heroic and original" architecture in *Learning from Las Vegas,* and the extremes of Postmodernism that we disassociated ourselves from in the early eighties in "Plus Ça Change"[3] have now been reinvented by the academic avant-garde (another oxymoron) as the architecture of Deconstructionism today: *encore plus ça change.*

Ubiquitous contradiction and gratuitous ambiguity that are not educed from program, structure, and meaning, or from the complexities and ambiguities inherent in modern cultural and social experience, but are instead derived from arbitrary, formalist-aesthetic games and clothed in the, by now, truly historic symbols of the late-lamented industrial revolution, or shrouded in obscure references to esoteric perceptual theory, or girded by extravagant and pretentious intellectual argumentation—these, in the end, bore more than they irritate.

Is what is wrong here the result of the age we live in or the age we are? We have an aversion to older architects' criticizing younger architects—having suffered from that when we were young—so our criticism, so far as it goes, is anguished as well as confused. On the other hand, we can ask ourselves, are we flogging a dead horse? Has Decon already self-destructed?

AGAINST MO, POMO, AND NEOMO

We have written elsewhere of the need, in our time of cultural and social diversity, for an architecture, or better, for architectures, of richness and ambiguity rather than clarity and purity, of variety rather than universality, and we have made a plea for an eclecticism of symbolic reference that accompanies a complexity and contradiction of form, and for the vernacular and the conventional over the progressive.[4] We have stood against the "shock of the new" *throughout infinity,* and against Modernism as a universal and perpetual avant-garde.[5] But we have also criticized the irrelevance of historic reference and the arbitrary employment of Neoclassical and Art Deco symbolism in much Postmodern architecture. We have written, too, of the validity of ornament, of the trouble caused by the rejection of explicit ornament and pattern by the Modernists and late Modernists, and of the trouble the consequent substitution of functional and structural expressionism gets them into. And today's Neo-Modernists are no different. What extremes the terror of ornament drives them to: they will perform structural and architectural acrobatics, vaudeville acts and extravaganzas to avoid ornament; applying a fragment of a truss here, suspending a tilted column there or creating, via glass roofs, an architectural greenhouse effect—all to catch your eye. But total bravado is no bravado. And how expensive all that trouble is. Even when colored up, is it worth it, dollar-wise and beauty-wise, when much simple pleasure can be derived from decorative pattern on the sheltering surfaces of a building and its framework, or in the decorative shapes of its details?

Neo-Modern disdain for historic reference does not extend to the Modern style, which is the symbolic basis of the NeoMo architectural vocabulary. Yet this derivation of an industrial vernacular *is* a historical style by now, no less so than is highfaluting Neoclassicism, and NeoMo offers little that is relevant to current practice in construction. Everyone else knows the industrial revolution, begun 200 years ago, is dead as a doornail and that naked iron or steel hanging dizzily from a facade or exposed ducts zigzagging through space are now, like exposed parts left out in the rain, bedraggled-looking, neither thrilling nor practical.

In their fervor to uphold Modern—its style, not its principles—against historical reference, Neo-Modernists' vehemence is almost menacing. Granted, many works of Postmodern architecture are bad and their allusions irrelevant to our era's cultural diversity, but why such emotion? Perhaps it's because the Neo-Modernists fear their lack of historical knowledge. For whatever reason, Neo-Modernists rely solely on purist Modern as a source for *their* Postmodern pastiche.

Pure pastiche is, of course, a contradiction in terms. Pastiche works only when it is diverse or impure, if not haphazard. And Modernism was based on anti-pastiche in the first place. What an irony! Modernist elements, derived from an International Style–Russian Constructivist vocabulary, are used literally but as decor rather than as rational and "honest" manifestations of function and structure—and they're colored-up at that. The effect is of a Puritan lady dancing the cancan. Would Walter Gropius have hated Decon even more than PoMo?

Those of us who respect and love the Modern architecture of 60 years ago and have learned immeasurably from it are offended by the Neo-Modern parody of it. Yet perhaps we should not be. Decon, whose decorative use of structural elements is the ultimate "construction of decoration," may be today's equivalent of Art Deco—that poignant and beautiful last attempt by the rearguard to graft the old Beaux-Arts onto the new International Style. Perhaps Art Decon is the Art Deco of PoMo. That ironical last gasp *was* effective and had its place. Is the Decon we are flailing a dying, but not dead, horse?

AGAINST ARBITRARY AMBIGUITY

So far we have criticized these easy ways out:

- theory and criticism that substitute for architectural art,

- built theory; architecture as frozen theory rather than frozen music,

- architecture as diagrams and words, used as a means to express complex meta-architectural perceptions and theories, rather than architecture as building and shelter, dedicated to use and aesthetic meanings,

- ignoring varieties of context, promoting a universal ideology,

- using poetic ambiguity as ideology rather than as a manifestation of experience and a technique of art,

- substituting boring-shocking for real avant-garde; promoting a pseudo avant-garde that is truly a central, if not rear, garde,

- demonstrating, rather than revealing, ideas,

- achieving cockeyed picturesqueness through the consistent use of contradiction,

- pretending the Modern style is not a style,

- pretending the Modern style is modern,

- promoting symbolic shapes as abstract forms while forgetting meaning (association and reference are inevitable after you're two years old and are OK, but you have to admit to symbolism in order to use it effectively),

- self-righteously denigrating the broad range of our culture and denying the significance of popular and mass culture as artistic sources in the rich mix of our arts,

- advocating a single, dominant, ominously elitist taste culture, oxymoronically avant-garde and universal—what Jim Collins refers to as a "semiotically impossible 'universal' grammar—a sole 'official' culture"[6]—within our pluralist ethos,

- substituting expressive articulation—the whole building as an ornament—for applied decoration.

Here is the inherent ambiguity of art taken to a ridiculous extreme, ambiguity for its own sake rather than to enhance richness and depth of meaning. It is based on a lack of recognition of, or accommodation to, the complexity and richness of contemporary experience, which in the end demands in its art truthful disorder, anguished disorder, an expression of chaos derived from reality not affectation, not sensationalism but vigor.

THE BUILDING AS PAVILIONS, THE BUILDING AS TOWN

In the works of architects as different as James Stirling, Peter Eisenman, and Frank Gehry there is a shared tendency to disengage parts of what would be conventionally considered a single building into separate units—to create the building as pavilions. In buildings of these architects, the separate units are connected so you don't get wet moving from one space to another, but the pavilions are articulated and the connections played down; it's as if the building is a town. This approach is for some reason strongly advocated by Leon Krier, whose buildings would all, ideally, consist of series of separate, proximate pavilions, little and low.

In our youth we risked our reputations arguing against the megastructure, where the town tried to be a building, because we felt that this approach ignored the inherent quality of a town as an incremental entity evolving in time and form, depending for its development on complex relationships among finance, technology, infrastructure, bureaucracy, function, taste, and aesthetics, not to mention cars. Now we don't think the current building-as-town has as bad problems as the town-as-building, yet the building-as-village—the village after an earthquake, the frozen image of an explosive gesture—contradicts some basic principles of architecture and common sense: think of roofing all those connected but distinct architectural phenomena, each exposed to the elements.

The building-as-town is essentially anti-urban; its fractured components contrast with, rather than reinforce, the scale of the existing city, and break the continuity of its building facades. People pass through and between the pavilions of what seems like a small-scale village within a city. But the combination is more like spaced-out rooms than pavilions and resembles Los Angeles sprawl more than it does European urbanism. Its buildings are orthodox-Modern in their separation, articulation, and expression of interior functions, but, in that their spaces are enclosed rather than free-flowing, they are anti-Modern. Also the occasional ornamentation of the pavilions, through pattern or surface articulation, accentuates their anti-Modern (that is, anti–International Style) formal and spatial disjointedness. The final effect is of Swiss Pavilions without the slabs.

OK, we love Los Angeles (and Las Vegas and Tokyo *and* Rome), but not *too* much; not to the extent of transforming our buildings into it. The house as village represents an extreme in the ranking of scatter over shelter. The spatial and sculptural articulation of virtually all spatial elements of a relatively small building is an extravagant gesture indeed.

BUILDING AS OBJECTS, BUILDING AS SCULPTURE

Beyond being a building that is not *a* building (or *a* building that is buildings), the deconstructed building is also not an architectural expression of shelter. It is an object, or rather a set of objects, left out in the rain. Or it is sculpture that is all right in the rain. It has no windows, or wished it hadn't; yet aren't windows the soul of a building, the main signifier of its character, the elemental and eloquent contradiction to the wall, and the heavenly modulator of light? Decon architecture has no eaves, or wished it hadn't; its reluctant roofs are usually of the same materials as its walls, or its walls are made of roof materials; there is aesthetically no difference between wall and roof, side and top. But this defines sculpture. Decon tends toward sculpture, not shelter, sculpture in lead-coated copper.

But you don't have to live in sculpture and you don't have to maintain it or worry if it leaks. Think of maintaining all the flashing that protects the connections that join the roofs that cover the links that connect this architecture's disconnected objects! This use of flashing promotes structural abstraction and spatial articulation, but it contradicts architecture's basic, sheltering quality, and the articulations are expensive both to construct (they have more external wall surface) and to maintain. So we suspect a flashy architecture of flashing.

Some Decon buildings are more unitary, their articulations resembling less a town and more the bumps, lumps, and carbuncles on a washed-up shipwreck. But buildings are not cities or boats; they are not even good analogies for them. For us, it is too easy to derive tension and drama from extreme forms of articulation and manipulation of volumes and spaces, or to produce picturesque compositions by setting building elements at unusual angles. We prefer to derive tension from the contradictions and ambiguities of complex architectural programs rather than by promoting exciting effects or accommodating obscure theories. Decon bores you in the way a crazy person does. Be anguished, not crazy.

AGAINST ARBITRARY DISTORTION, AGAINST ARCHITECTURE AS SCULPTURE

Contradiction has had a long history in architecture. A tendency to modify and distort the order of architectural parts is found in the angles and curves of Alvar Aalto; or in mosque complexes turned toward Mecca; or in the layouts of Renaissance palaces, distorted to accommodate to medieval sites; or, more violently, in wall dividers within a Corbusian grid; or in medieval town plans as they accommodate to the eastern orientation of a cathedral.

In our early work, starting with the North Penn Visiting Nurses center, we employed diagonals in plan to accommodate to programmatic, spatial, or contextual circumstances, and have seen this device become a characteristic architectural element of our time; but current distortions are more violent, and they have become a motival element in plan, section, and elevation. Such configurations aren't intrinsically wrong, but they generally appear to be used for little or no reason—unless you consider sensational effect and the promoting of avant-garde images or motival playfulness acceptable determinants for architecture.

So we are back to the exception that becomes the rule, the contradiction that's baseless, the constant dissonance that negates dissonance; to picturesque expressionism not based on the richness and ambiguity of experience—*plus ça change, plus c'est la même chose,* yet once again.

Architects should remember they are working for beings who walk upright and resist gravity, whose buildings should not convey only private or esoteric meanings tailored to the inside critic, writer, or reader. In fact, architecture, as the most everyday of the arts, must be readable on many levels, including the popular level. Architects should become sculptors if they want, but, if they remain architects, they should embrace the wonderful limitations of their field, loving the constrictions inherent in their medium—fighting them, once in a while, for the sake of a valid and artful tour de force, but not seeking to surmount all of the limits all of the time.

Practicing architects might have to be lawyers, businesspeople, psychiatrists, and performers to get and implement the job, but that's another matter; as designers and theorists they should not be literary critics, semiologists, psychologists, philosophers, or calculating obfuscators—they should be artist-craftspeople who love architectural detail. And the convention in their art should not be scorned on one hand or evolved into whimsy on the other; the job of an architect is to lead *and* to follow.

FOR ARCHITECTURE AS SHELTER AND THE DECON CITY

Having viewed some recent trends with alarm, let us now assert what we are for. The positive side of our argument makes the case for multiple architectural vocabularies, rich and varied tastes, historical and geographic contexts, symbolic and ornamental systems that evolve from contexts, and conventional building methods that architects specify at the risk of being thought outmoded. The positive argument sees the building as an elemental unit of shelter, and the city of now as a valid deconstruction. Recent trips to Japan and Korea have helped us to formulate this view.

[Authors' note: As it was originally delivered, this lecture went on to describe our late discovery of Japan and the richness we found to be an inspiring alternative to the theory-go-round. We take up these themes at greater length in the essay "Two Naifs in Japan," so we refer the reader to that essay, leaving the imagination to picture the present essay as not all sour but sweet, too.]

ARCHITECTURAL THEORY FOR ARCHITECTS

What we have attempted here is architectural theory of the kind traditionally enunciated by architects as a means of clarifying their work, to themselves and others, and sometimes to justify it. We did *not* promote a theory of architecture that substitutes itself for architecture, replacing architecture with arconcepture and buildings with diagrams and words, or promoting perceptual conceits or critical apparatus, belatedly and laboriously transposed from inappropriate disciplines and ending in extravagant yet boring (and frequently irrational and irresponsible) buildings. Architecture should not be frozen theory, the victim rather than the subject of theory. Buildings should not be accumulations of cheap thrills and emperors' clothing, theoretically rationalized by the journalistic rhetoric of an establishment avant-garde. Architectural theory should confront elemental architectural qualities of shelter, use, and meaning, seeing architecture as a thoughtful process of making and as a high-faluting craft, to be used and perceived through the sensibilities of everyday—to be "meaningful to the innocent eye."[7]

---

1. In a recent article of less than 1,500 words by a noted architectural academic, the following names were mentioned: Sigmund Freud, E. T. A. Hoffmann, Friedrich Schelling, Legrand du Saule, Georg Simmel, Siegfried Kracauer, Walter Benjamin, Maurice Halbwachs, Eugene Minkowski, Jean-Paul Sartre, Martin Heidegger, Homer(ic), Jean Jacques Rousseau.

2. What we are against is exemplified in the following quotation from the first five pages of an article on architecture by John Shuttleworth called "The Diffraction of Symbol and Sign: An Essay on Symbolic Thought and Semiologic Grammars" in a publication aptly called *Avant Garde* 3 (although 3, rather than 1, is perhaps an oxymoron and, if you call yourself avant-garde, perhaps you're not), (Winter 1990), pp. 54–75. The phrases quoted here are strung together by relatively few ordinary words represented by the dots:

> . . . hermeneutics and deconstructive criticism . . . logical positivism, mechanistic determinism and pragmatism . . . dialectical materialism . . . communist/socialistic or capitalistic/social theories . . . auguries of physical, quantitative, inductive, scientific thought . . . coloration [which] "reads through" almost all semiologic, structuralist and post structuralist writings . . . schism [existing] since the Ionian philosophers first broke with the Ionian tradition of the 6th century . . . emotio-logical thought . . . Freud, Jung, Levi-Strauss . . . analytic and synthetic, the motional and rational (etc.) [sic] . . . cognitive "feeling" . . . literal symbolism, polyvalence of significances . . . linear grammars . . . The symbolic plays redundancies of meanings to reveal the referent in modal terms. In this way the symbolic rectifies certain of the "hollowing-out" of the implicit meaning which quantifying sciences so arrogantly desiccate in the name of objectivity and illusory democracy . . . sociolinguistics, cultural anthropology, subjective literary criticism, psychiatry and "speculative" psychology, and philosophy . . . the unconscious, the mythic and the irrational . . . culture . . . perceptions and projections . . . formal (and non-formal) human expressive gesture . . . cultural density . . . totality of expression and perception . . . "defraction" . . . defractive conditions . . . cognitive referent . . . distorted condition . . . redundancy . . . symbolic simultaneity . . . mechanistic thought . . . theories of production . . . metaphorical association . . . the place as a substance of mythopoesis . . . hermeneutics and deconstructivism [again] . . . "undecidability of the text" . . . "parallels" and "difference" . . . recording of

intentionality . . . correlative set of associations creating a "field effect" . . . linear dissective analysis . . . interaction of imagery and figuration . . . identity spaces . . . mediative level . . . readable meaning and spatial perception . . . culture as a medium, conditioning human orientation and identity as being-in-the-world . . . defraction, as an ideology of conditioned perception . . . exposition of symbolic thought . . . structural linguistics and structuralism . . . implicit content . . . grammatical as well as syntactic operations . . . potential transformative power of word association . . . the guise of scientific or sociological egalitarianism . . . emotio-logical aspects . . . synchronistic noncorrelative association . . . essential structure exclusive of linear, operational mechanisms . . . trapped in plastic grammars . . . polyvalent associational simultaneities . . . the symbolic subtends the explicit content and becomes the overtones of thought through resonant simulcras . . . total cyclic entities . . . gnomonic expansion . . . symbolic space, conceptualized as volumetric associational articulation . . . plastic grammars . . . perceptual "coloration" of all communicative and perceptual gestures . . .

and so on for nine more pages.

3. Robert Venturi, "Diversity, Relevance and Representation in Historicism, or Plus Ça change . . . Plus a Plea for Pattern All Over Architecture with a Postscript on My Mother's House," *Architectural Record,* June 1982, pp. 114–119 (1982 Gropius Lecture at Harvard University).

4. Ibid.

5. As described by Jim Collins, *Uncommon Cultures: Popular Culture and Post-Modernism* (New York: Routledge Chapman & Hall, 1989).

6. Ibid.

7. Herbert Muschamp writing in *The New Republic.*

WISDOM VS. TREND: THE CURRENT ACADEMIZATION OF AMERICAN ARCHITECTURAL EDUCATION

Written 1995.

An architecture dean who prides himself on his vision condescendingly denies that his school is a professional school; it is, rather, an academic department. Why isn't he therefore a chairman—did you ever hear of a dean of an English department? You can't have it both ways. And if his institution as a whole is to continue to call itself a university, it has to have a modicum of professional schools to support its claim. How pretentious is the academization of architectural education, as Denise Scott Brown has pointed out:[1] the how is as important as the what and each needs the other in the educational environment and process. Ben Franklin in establishing the first university in the colonies united the "ornamental" and the "practical," eloquently acknowledging what was to become America's idealist and pragmatic genius.

When I gave my course on Theories in Architecture at Penn (out of which came *Complexity and Contradiction in Architecture*) it was the only theory course in architecture schools in the land; alas, there are like four in every school now. And remember I referred to theories (pragmatic), not theory (ideological).

---

1. See Denise Scott Brown, "Breaking Down the Barriers between Theory and Practice," *Architecture*, 84, no. 3 (March 1995), pp. 43–47.

THE VISION THING: WHY IT SUCKS

Written 1993.

Creeps who talk about a new vision make me sick—and suspicious.

I say screw you to vision; up yours to visionaries; vision sucks.

What a supreme irony that those who proclaim and pursue vision are the least likely to attain it.

Vision is not something you attain by consciously or heroically trying. It's achieved via indirection: the way not to achieve it is to seek it.

In fact, if you're at all superstitious, you should feel it's bad luck to even think about it as you work.

The more you try for it the less likely it is you'll attain it. You can't design vision.

If you're good, you focus on the realities of now and the potentials in the realities: you acknowledge the potentials of now, with perception—and the limitations of now, with grace. And then in hindsight you might have become visionary.

If you work not cynically—not expediently—not for the short run—but acknowledge simply the long run, then you can achieve vision in the long run.

Being truly visionary is being profoundly of now—and in this context being of now is being ahead of now. If you deal with the now perceptively, you deal with the future automatically—this applies if your focus on the now and on its potential involves evolutionary or revolutionary action.

What's truly visionary can be perceived only after it has been incidentally achieved. Visionaries are visionaries only in hindsight. The only way to be visionary is to have been visionary.

And—often—those who are later considered visionary were earlier considered nerds.

The heroism implied in this approach to creativity is generally false: in this context conscious heroes are pathetic weaklings. Ironically you are more likely to turn out heroic in your role as anti-hero. To be really visionary is to be truly humble.

The pursuit of vision is almost as futile as the pursuit of happiness—I excuse my architect-philosopher hero, Thomas Jefferson, his pursuit of happiness, which in the context of the late eighteenth century was effectively to counteract certain lingering dogma.

A noble quest for vision is often a disguise for a political quest—or for getting into the papers: beware of do-gooders with a vision.

Is vision the new last resort of scoundrels—or a fancy word for trend?

Oh, how pretentious *and* boring this cliché is—I understand vision has now become a verb!

"Fame comes to those who are thinking of something else"—Oliver Wendell Holmes. (Although today PR techniques can be effective, temporarily.) The same thing goes for vision—Robert Charles Venturi. (Although today journalistic techniques can be effective, temporarily.)

I loved it when Sheldon Hackney expressed his discomfort concerning the vision thing, which he associates with St. Joan.

By the way, "cutting edge" and "mission" in their current ubiquity can be almost as hollow and pretentious as "vision."

"CECI TUERA CELA" IS NOW "CELA EST DEVENU CECI": SOME THOUGHTS CONCERNING ARCHITECTURE AND MEDIA

Originally published as "Ceci Deviendra Cela" in *Lotus* 75 (February 1993), p. 127.

About 20 years ago Denise Scott Brown, Steven Izenour, and I published the book *Learning from Las Vegas*. It scandalized the architectural establishment of the time and we still suffer as advocates of vulgarity despite the title's explicit claim to learn from—not advocate—roadside commercial architecture. What an irony that today's establishment architecture, or rather today's architectural trends primarily proclaimed by the press, are based on a quality of hype that parallels that of the commercial strip. In our study on Las Vegas we focused on an architecture of meaning over expression, an architecture that acknowledged symbolism over form, whose bold quality was justified by its requirement for effective perception (through the medium of commercial signs) from a moving car at a distance. This, we believe, was a more valid basis for architecture than the need today to catch your attention at a monthly pace via the pages of periodicals whose funnily cropped, flashy colored photographs taken from weird angles seem to be the ultimate raison d'être of architecture.

A further irony lies in the Modern stylistic basis of this architecture—theorized as Deconstructivist—whose vocabulary is derived from an askew decorative revival of architecture of the 1920s and '30s, originally derived from vernacular industrial forms whose puritanical aesthetic, in turn, derived from an ideology of functional and structural "honesty"—purist and minimalist. Today's decorative Decon trusses in rainbow colors suspended askew and juxtaposed over patterned pastel panels conjure up images of Puritan ladies, wearing lipstick, dancing the cancan.

LETTER TO THE EDITOR OF THE
ARCHITECTURAL REVIEW, FEBRUARY 17, 1987

It is sad to read William J. R. Curtis's peevish assessment of the selections of the third Aga Khan Award Jury.

The makeup of that Jury was appropriately a heterogeneous mix of individuals who, in general, worked hard together, listened respectfully to each other, and gracefully influenced each other in their discussions and selections. This was because their approach was not ideological. They dealt with the particular material at hand and acknowledged a broad range of attitudes concerning aesthetic, technical, and social issues. The Jury's ultimate decisions were not based on a preconceived quota for the types, numbers, or distribution of awards—some perception of what ought to be—but on the essential quality of the material submitted. This discerning approach will, in the end, enhance the standing of the Aga Khan Award, not diminish it.

Mr. Curtis knows about the deliberations of the Jury because he was present at its final session in an official position as research advocate for one of the projects considered.

Given his role in the proceedings, I believe Mr. Curtis has misused privileged information in writing his critique. For example, he should not have revealed, as he essentially did, my individual position concerning the Bhong Mosque in Pakistan. Having done so, in fairness he should also have noted that it was I who wrote a large part of the assessment for the Jury Report supporting Sedad Eldem's Social Security Complex in Istanbul—certainly an example of the Modernism he espouses. This building, incidentally, was nominated for the two earlier Juries, but it was only ours, the Third Jury, that considered it worthy of an award. In truth, I admire both the Eldem building and the Bhong Mosque at the same time, acknowledging the formal artistic sophistication of the one, and the popular decorative vitality of the other. I supported both projects because I believe that the already diverse Islamic architectural tradition, if it is to evolve further in ways rich and relevant, should encompass, in our complicated time, a grand combination of sources, high *and* low, focused *and* broad.

Mr. Curtis appears to be blinded and somehow embittered by his ideology and by the narrow range of his tastes. Despite the wide knowledge, if not keen understanding, of Islamic architecture shown in his article, his approach is simplistic; this will work in the end to limit the scope and diminish the vitality of emerging kinds of Islamic architecture.

I hope the *Architectural Review* will, in fairness, now publish the Report of the Third Aga Khan Award Jury.

It was, by the way, the Jury, not the Steering Committee, that recommended the awards to those projects that received Honorable Mentions.

LETTER TO R. CRAIG MILLER, CURATOR OF THE DEPARTMENT OF DESIGN AND ARCHITECTURE AT THE DENVER ART MUSEUM

Written 1992.

Dear Craig,

May I respond privately to the review of my lecture in *Neos?* What I write I hope will explain, and also work as an excuse for, the condescending critique by the author.

First, content: the writer left out important parts of my argument involving scale and symbolism as elements of monumentality in architecture and urbanism—the latter particularly relevant for us architects to face after "abstract expressionist" Modernism. The author was also offended by my "celebration of the [commercial] strip" while not realizing that even the Las Vegas strip Denise and I "learned from" (not advocated) in the late sixties looks almost blandly tasteful compared with much of the hype-trendy, sometimes-called Deconstructivist architecture the author's sensibility ironically accommodates today.

Second: "Unfortunately much of his remaining discussion veered away from addressing the public realm and rather seemed a promotion of his private interest with the possibility of future commissions." What the heck—even the patrician H. H. Richardson, first American to study at the Ecole des Beaux-Arts, said "the first principle of architecture for architects is to get the job." Also I think I "apologized" adequately for showing our work—two relevantly monumental buildings in revealingly contrasting civic settings—and what do you *expect* when you invite a practicing architect to lecture? But that's the point—we should remember that today theory is in and building is out in architectural education and journalism: it's now arconcepture as frozen theory.

Another irony concerning erudite architects as theorists today is they're not well educated (despite an allusion or so to a Sebastiano Serlio). The writer doesn't know that I, alas, was directly involved in starting this history-theory trend of our era when I gave my course at Penn in the early sixties (out of which came *Complexity and Contradiction in Architecture*); so far as I know it was the only theory course in an architecture school in the country at that time. The pendulum has now swung to the other extreme—alas again: any attitude involving balance among extremes is hard to maintain today.

Very best,

LETTER NOT SENT TO AN ARCHITECTURE CRITIC

Written 1990.

You still don't understand that an architecture critic accepts the photographic and graphic material supplied by the architect whose building he is reviewing and he uses it to illustrate his article—this is customary and courteous. (And incidentally a critic also refers in the title of his article to the building he is reviewing rather than to a thesis he is exploiting the building to promote.) But last spring you substituted a gross and irrelevant diagram for our beautiful renderings of the Philadelphia Orchestra Hall project in your review of it. You will, as usual, condescendingly claim this was because the graphics produced by our office are naively inadequate for newsprint reproduction—yet the *New York Times* had no trouble printing even our night rendering of that building last year, and the same goes for their reproducing previously our subtle rendering of the Sainsbury Wing of the National Gallery in London. Although you rejected this rendering too, newspapers in London and elsewhere unhesitatingly and effectively printed it.

And now you substitute for our photographs of the Clinical Research Building at Penn—appropriately shot by a professional architectural photographer—an explicitly unflattering shot by a news photographer you dispatched to the site on a cloudy day to snap the building sans shadows from a lousy viewpoint that features the admittedly unfortunate bridge at the back of the building that was added to the program at the last minute, and includes a rickety temporary construction fence next door that dominates the foreground of your shot and obliterates the base of our building. Send *your* photographer to shoot the Campidoglio and it will come out a Holiday Inn; the art of architecture must meld with the art of photography if you are to illustrate architecture. If you are to judge our building as art you must treat it as art. But more important, you don't cheat to make a point.

A cheap shot, it turns out, describes your words as well as your illustration. I refer to your condescending treatment in your article of the work of a serious architect in your community whose firm is distinguished for its quality, originality, and influence; I refer also to your irresponsible, indeed inane, critique of the academic ethos of the preeminent institution of our region, the University of Pennsylvania.

Actually if your article could not have been a straightforward critique, a plain news story would have been preferable to a pretentious essay. You are right that the architecture of our new Research Building differs from that of the Richardson Medical Towers; it was I who made this comparison to you over the telephone: our building refers more to the tradition of the generic loft represented by the Medical School buildings at Penn of Cope and Stewardson of several generations ago. In the Louis Kahn building the sculptural articulations and expressionist monumentality that you extol become quite simply—in today's context and for today's academic community—unequivocally inappropriate. The very qualities you laud work against the functional and programmatic requirements of a research laboratory by constricting them within a formal and rhetorical straitjacket and minimizing the spatial flexibility necessary for dynamic work within and for the dynamic and tricky mechanical systems that work requires. The Richardson Medical Towers have been significant as a formal statement but disastrous as a useful place.

But, as important, this kind of building as a setting for research can inhibit work; when you "monumentalize" the form outside you distract the people inside. Artists tend to work in lofts less because they can't afford to rent monuments and more because it's hard to make masterpieces in someone else's masterpiece; the same goes for most creative workers, scientific as well as artistic. And scientists, like artists, are workers, not priests; they don't need a cathedral to perform rites in but a loft to do work in—a place that acknowledges the dignity of labor rather than a stage that promotes indiscriminate monumentality with its commitments to symbolism and scale.

Concerning work that's creative, you have a lot to learn. This kind of work requires concentration and eschews distraction; it requires settings flexible physically or recessive psychically. And inspiration is tricky too; when you are lucky enough to find it, it derives less from exalted settings and more from inside you—from your ability again to concentrate and then achieve momentum in the development of your work and ideas. Our approach to the workplace acknowledges the nine-tenths perspiration; "exalt learning," as you put it, but accommodate working too.

The generic loft as an architectural tradition includes in its range, besides the Cope and Stewardson medical laboratories at Penn, the New England mill of the early industrial revolution, Mies van der Rohe's work for the IIT campus, and even the prototypical Italian palazzo. And is not the "nobility" you refer to achieved in the loftlike architecture of Nassau Hall and Dartmouth Hall despite, as you would put it, their "boxy" forms and consequent "obvious" expressions of "proudly superficial aspirations"? Each of these buildings is of unquestioned quality, not rhetorical, but dignified, and is appropriate as a generic workplace within an academic community.

As I have said elsewhere, it is pattern that we have used in the design of the Clinical Research Building to promote richness and scale; this element takes the place of the sculptural-structural articulation of that other less flexible and more "monumentalized" [sic, so help me] building. And the subtle rhythm of the window configurations of the facades, with its slight exceptions, creates tension, while the plays of scale, small to large, create hierarchy and promote presence.

Now don't say I can't take criticism; this is my first and only angry letter to a critic. Actually, I delight in criticism that promotes style and sophistication over pretension and condescension—as in the rhythmic alliterations of a British critic's comment concerning our National Gallery extension in London: "instead we are to be given a vulgar American piece of Postmodern Mannerist pastiche." And how about the literary panache of the description of our facade for the same building as "picturesque mediocre slime"? Also we have even been called "those American vandals, Venturi, Scott Brownnose and Associates . . . who are pissing on Europe."

Next time, try to be less serious and more deep, or else pick on someone your own size—picayune, I mean.

Very sincerely,

J'ADORE ST. PAUL'S

Originally published in *Architectural Design* Profile 105 (September/October 1993), pp. viii–xii.

I'm afraid I can't resist responding to an article whose content and style exemplify exquisitely what's wrong with British architectural criticism. This funny article in a serious journal (*Architectural Design,* vol. 62, no. 7/8, 1992) is titled "J'Accuse St. Paul's," and I also can't resist giving my response an equally pretentious title. I write not as a scholar or historian but as a practicing architect with a reasonable aesthetic sensibility and educational background—characteristics British critics seem to lack. I quote from the article a lot because I think you will be, as they say, amused by its presumption.

The introduction describes the article as "a highly personal"—rather than a highly perverse and grammatically inept—view of St. Paul's:

> Remember this, the Ewing's [sic] massive TV ranch, Southfork, is nothing more than a screen builders' stage set. The backdrop for an endless puerile soap opera is a less than good setting for an under-budget English National Opera blue-jeans Puccini.

My friends in Dallas confirm that Southfork is a real building in a real setting, but even if the writer's assertion were less careless, what's wrong with a stage set for theatrical performances? And more to the point, what's wrong with theatrical gesture in a work of architecture—if I may anticipate this critic's condescending reference to the well-known false facades aside the nave of St. Paul's? The tired, old, literal-functionalist, Modernist ideology inherent in this stance disdains the rhetorical dimension essential to

Western architecture, whether it be the false facades of Romanesque, Renaissance, and Baroque buildings or the false storefronts of western American towns.

> . . . endless country music crooners hark back to Galveston, Phoenix [comma missing] Arizona and Tulsa—wherever they are. . . .

> As for Dallas there is a great deal more to it than Ewing, a pair of cowboy boots and a ten-gallon hat. It won its spurs, as Oliver Stone has recently reminded us through movie force-feeding, on 22nd November 1963.

> . . . on that fateful day when JFK slumped the remainder of his skull into Jackie's arms and the darling of the liberal west—who . . . invented the two-button suit and besported the prototype-yuppy wife. . . .

"The gauche, naively pompous Kennedy," this writer later calls him. This series of combinations of condescension and pretension—tasteless, illiterate, irrelevant, and tiresomely anti-American even by British journalistic standards—terminates with:

> [The] vast cadaver [of Winston Churchill]. . .

> . . . conveyed in state to St. Paul's [where the ensuing entombment] . . . finally ratified Churchill's role in establishing the Cathedral, not as a work of architecture, but as an icon of British nationalism. . . . He . . . was no lover of architecture. Politicians . . . seldom are [wasn't it Churchill who said "First we shape our buildings, then they shape us"?]. . . . Hitler's war machine succeeded where St Paul's architect, Sir Christopher Wren, had failed. The flames and smoke of the Blitz transformed an unloved hulk into a potent symbol of nationalism and resistance.

Wonder at these forced and tenuous connections among Southern country music, Southfork Ranch, Kennedy's assassination, Churchill's funeral, a famous wedding (this comes up later), and a Baroque cathedral is followed by perplexity as you realize the author equates such items of "popular mythology" with St. Paul's.

OK, if you say so, but St. Paul's as "unloved hulk" is historically false. Granted any work of art 300 years old has succumbed to periods of disfavor within cycles of taste; nevertheless the extensive influence of the design of this building is well known: for instance, its highly original columned drum, which generates its consummate floating dome, was the inspiration for the dome of Jacques-Germain Soufflot's Panthéon (originally the church of Ste.-Geneviève) and thereby represents a significant English influence on French architecture, perhaps the only influence in architectural history before the *jardin anglais*. In the United States the same composition became the prototype for the drum and dome of the typical state capitol as well as for the national capitol itself.

Following a snide biographical outline of Wren's accomplishments in anatomy and astronomy, the author continues:

> Then came architecture, the missing ingredient in the Renaissance cocktail. It was comparatively simple to apply mathematics and draughtsmanship, through the craft skills of the mason, to the art of architecture. Wren supplied the logic and the learning, the stone masons knew how to put it all together and round it off with all the latest detailing.

One understands this author's underestimation of the role of learning in architecture in light of his apparent lack of it. Next:

> He attracted the very best patrons with the plum commissions—family background . . . launched [him].

May I remind the author how few of us architects get started without some support of "family background," extraordinary luck, or any other means that can compensate for lack of experience at the beginning of our careers?

He ended his days an outcast of society. . . . [He] would sit unnoticed and unrecognized in the nave of his unfinished cathedral.

Of course: he was a good architect who had worked in England.

What we see today, years later, is not what it seems, not what we think, and not what it ought to be. Tuesday 14th January 1992 *J'accuse:*

The Jacuzzi of accusations that follow—a veritable bubble bath—raises doubts whether Tuesday 14th January 1992 will go down in history. Culprits include "The wedding of the Prince and Princess of Wales . . . of Hollywood proportions with a theatrical setting to match." But St. Paul's is the chief target:

Its inflated reputation is seriously damaging this country's architectural health.

. . . It is, in truth, second-rate architecture. . . .

. . . Firstly it is dishonest architecture and a medieval botch masquerading as genuine Classicism. Great architecture has integrity, and St Paul's has about as much architectural integrity as the castles of Disneyland or a set for Grand Opera. Secondly I am much concerned about the way in which St Paul's has become a rallying point for those who want to hold Britain back in a sterile museum culture.

Ah, here it's out, the British critical curse, aesthetic ideology: in this case a promotion of naive Modernism, tiresome demands for expressionistic integrity as a substitute for aesthetic sensibility or regard for meaning in architecture, plus a snippet of conspiracy theory, plus an ever-present touch of anti-Americanism.

Wren was determined that his dome would dominate London's skyline. . . .

The use of the possessive implicates the designer's ego; yet acknowledging hierarchy among buildings, especially in the design of a cathedral, does not necessarily imply egotism; rather, it conforms to urbanistic practice and established convention in Renaissance and post-Renaissance cities.

Then follows a "revelation," an architectural equivalent of a twentieth century tabloid scandal:

> But a dome of the scale and shape of his design clearly would not carry the weight of the lantern on top, so this plan involved a series of deceptions. On the outside there is the familiar, huge, ballooning dome, covered in lead and apparently supporting the lantern. But beneath the skin things are not what they seem. The lead dome is carried on a false timber structure, rather like a stage set, making the dome pure theatre.

Here we go again: "stage set," "pure theatre." This critic fails to acknowledge the contradictions between form and symbol that are inevitable in an urban architecture of richly layered dimensions, encompassing tension and depth in its effects. Also I had hoped *Complexity and Contradiction* had settled for our time that the outside could be different from the inside, and that a natural contradiction between the two could be acknowledged and accommodated in architecture, when urban contexts make especially significant demands from the "outside."

Then more righteous outrage:

> . . . yet another dome . . . made out of brickwork and stone lashed together with chains . . . to carry . . . the lantern above.

Ho hum, why don't you blame Michaelangelo for doing it in St. Peter's a century earlier—the way Frank Lloyd Wright did quite a while ago? Then:

> This second inner dome is not even the one you see down below in the cathedral and the fakery gets worse still.

Oh my: but these pre-Moderns who disguise structure when it contradicts their symbolism are arguably no worse than the Neo-Moderns who inflate, distort, and flaunt structure for surreptitious symbolic effect and as a substitute for decoration.

> Yet another dome, equally contrived and equally false, to cover up the structural necessity of [etc., etc., etc.]. . . . What an incredible disappointment. Wren's great dome ended up as . . . visual trickery-pokery . . . to fool the eye.

Again, the use of multiple domes for the sake of varying perceptual needs inside and outside has a long and respectable history: when you condemn the domes of St. Paul's *vous accusez* 200 years of previous architecture in Italy and France. Ruskin might have done this given his anti-Renaissance bias but he would have known better than to pick exclusively on St. Paul's.

So, excuse me, but what insufferably boring sanctimony lies in this long-discredited, old-fashioned, naive, Modernist, literalist "honesty." Fooling the eye is what visual art is about: are you gonna condemn those fussy Greeks for their entasis?

> . . . and that was not the end to the dilemma of the dome.

> Wren had to reconcile the irreconcilable—a dome over a Latin cross. Of course it did not work. . . .

Again he makes it sound as if Wren were a unique villain rather than a member of a pack—oh, what lack of education! Did you ever hear of Brunelleschi in Florence? His cathedral established the Latin cross plan with a dome over the crossing as *the* generic form for Renaissance churches. There were over 200 years of precedent for St. Paul's in Italy and France—it embarrasses me to refer to the obvious again.

The author goes on and on about the awkwardness at the arched crossing inside, using adjectives like "uncomfortable" and "unfamiliar," but is that famous configuration awkward? Maybe it's sophisticated. It seems mannerist ambiguity is beyond the sensibility of this critic. I, myself, visit this architecturally enigmatic crossing whenever I can, to savor its tensions. And I think of Benjamin Franklin (if I may expose my Americanism) who is said to have said, "Beauty is not in being perfect, beauty is in knowing how to make the design so the imperfections are unimportant."

Then the west front, which

> should have been a grand Classical portico and a magnificent pediment. . . . But what do we get? A two-storey entrance that . . . [fails] to meet the challenges of thorough Classicism

—whatever that means. And then, in triumph:

> The game is really given away up on the roof. The walls down either side of the nave are entirely false [instead of quasi-false?]. They are there just as a screen, a facade[?], to hide the real building, which is a medieval building complete with flying buttresses. . . . Wren . . . merely dressed up his medieval building in 'Classical drag'.

Again, how boring, this outmoded critique: architecture is not (cannot be) synonymous with structure except in simple building types like barns and factories. I thought this was thoroughly discussed in the 1950s. Can't we, these days, allow buildings for accommodating ceremonial ritual to be rhetorical in their expression once again?

And on:

> For the first 200 years of its life, this Cathedral church was ignored, despised and consistently treated with disrespect.

In England, perhaps; elsewhere its significant effect on religious and civic domes has been amply acknowledged.

And on:

> The Victorians cared so little about the building that they crashed an iron girder bridge across the foot of Ludgate Hill.

I would have thought that, for those whose aesthetic embraces the Lloyds Building, a structural erection at the scene of the crime would work to complement the architecture of St. Paul's.

> The world stands in awe of the staggering innovation of the Lloyds building. . . .

—which arguably represents the most retardataire example of an expressionistic tour de force based on the machine aesthetic and derived from a Russian Constructivist vocabulary both dating from the 1920s. No one with a smattering of history who is not a victim of ideology can call that particular building a "staggering innovation"—and I think there are those in the world who are not "in awe" of the other Neo-Modernist works the author mentions.

> We [British] can all be justly proud of James Gibbs' enduring monument, the church of St. Martin-in-the-Fields . . . or for that matter . . . St. George's Bloomsbury by Nicholas Hawksmoor, a pupil of Wren.

The follower's work is often sweeter than the master's—there are fewer sweat stains—but if St. Paul's is ultimately unresolved that doesn't make it less great art than Bernini's "Colonnaded Grand Piazza [sic]."

Cheer up, we're near the end:

> It is fascinating to see just how St Paul's has become a symbol of resistance to modern architecture—and I would argue, the modern world as a whole.

But liking the "modern world" does not preclude liking the old.

In sum, this contorted and pretentious ideological point-proving is sad and boring; it displaces informed analysis and sensible discovery which represent the real substance of architectural criticism; and it doesn't have much basis: in our time the "Modern" architecture argued for is no longer modern. Neo-Modernism, its current form, is sadly different from the stirring Modernism whose early stages graced the British Arts and Crafts movement, and whose heyday was in Germany, France, and the United States from the 1920s through the 1950s. The fin-de-siècle Modern advocated by this critic is either a decadent revival or a retardataire survival: the industrial revolution is long gone.

And what irony: by setting Wren in an historical vacuum and then blaming him for almost everything wrong, the author builds him up rather than tears him down—implying he is one of the most original, if most scurrilous, architects in history!

Another irony: the British critics, even those who retain their historical perspective, seem not to comprehend the British genius for mannerism evident throughout the history of British architecture—within the evolution of its Gothic styles, the vagaries of its Elizabethan style, and the works of Inigo Jones, Wren, Gibbs, Hawksmoor, Archer, Adam, Soane, Greek Thomson, Mackintosh, and Lutyens—mannerism deriving from naivete or supreme sophistication, and at times from both at once.

Finally: wake up and grow up. The view presented as the latest thing is an old thing—proclaiming at the end of the twentieth century a simplistic expressionism derived from the structures of the nineteenth century. I say, on with richness over simplicity, ambiguity over clarity, symbolism over form, and—by implication—lots of architectural vocabularies to accommodate the multiple cultures of our time. This British Zola has neither the authority nor significance of the other one. *Tant pis!*

APHORISMS AND MISCELLANY

MAL MOTS: APHORISMS—SWEET AND SOUR— BY AN ANTI-HERO ARCHITECT

Written 1990 through 1995. Some of these aphorisms appeared in *Grand Street,* no. 54 (vol. 14, no. 2, Fall 1995).

VALID RANTINGS

Be good and pay the price.

I am always out of step.

From outré to passé—sans au courant in between: from young turk to old fogey.

Double curse in this day: an architect whose work is mannerist and well mannered.

Shall I surrender as a naive maker to become a cynical journalist, zealous bureaucrat, or pompous academic?

I am an exhibitionist: I go around exposing my doubts.

As a person I'm cynical; as an artist I'm naive.

It is better to be good than in—I think.

It's hard being gauche while in ten years everyone's doing it.

People who have never had ideas are concerned you don't have new ones every month.

How sad to have to justify rather than design.

Why is it we still have to prove more than produce?

When we were young we only had to suffer upright-uptight progressive Modernists—now we have to suffer regressive-historicist-preservationists, purist urbanists, or expressionistic egoists in architecture.

Challenge me, don't harass me!

I'm giving up being a perfectionist: no one knows the difference although they punish you for it.

We are in a field where no one knows the difference: oh, to be an athlete where one's accomplishment is simply measurable.

To be 10 percent better you have to work 100 percent harder—and they don't see the difference in the end.

Being better is a lot a matter of working weekends.

The unforgiving medium: you can't modify or edit it once it's up.

If we had time to write in the late twentieth century, we would write less.

If I weren't paranoid I'd be crazy.

For me to sparkle I need some light to reflect off of.

Am I being sour?—yes, but also sweet as that combination works to illuminate.

It's OK to be cranky if you're perky too.

In America you can tell the workers—they're the ones who're talking and laughing while the customers are nuisances.

Shall we admire Italy more for Michelangelo or cappuccino?

There's no place like Rome.

Viva architects, not opportunists.

Architecture requires heart and soul—and sweat.

Am I the marginal nerd?

Remember, my positivity complements my negativity and, I hope, embraces wit.

HYPE CRITICS: JOURNALISM

Journalists like spectacular architecture: it makes their job easier.

It's no longer what's good, but what's new.

We're not in, we're good.

It is better to be good than original.

If you're original you're good, if you're outlandish you're a genius.

Getting an original idea is the easy part: you have to sweat to make it good.

Original is good; good is better.

Work hard to be good—not marketably avant-garde.

Be good and ask for trouble.

One way to distinguish good people from mediocre people is how much they are in trouble.

Good art cannot be universally liked in its time: the issue is, do the right people hate it?

You're known by your enemies.

Beware of the monthly flavor you suck as you act as critic.

Those who don't receive official recognition are not necessarily twerps and those who receive official recognition are not necessarily twerps.

What's retardataire is sometimes avant-garde.

Kinds of answers in the late twentieth century include: (1) the answer that is no answer, (2) the answer that shows what you've asked is wrong, (3) the answer that shows what you've asked is obvious.

The "of course so," "of course not" generation converses in a spirit of one-upmanship and confrontation rather than of cooperation and collaboration.

Journalist-critics—shrill and boring.

Proposal: architects set up a rating system assessing critics in terms of how stupid, crazy, and/or mean they are and plot their degrees of cynicism, condescension, and lack of cultivation in inverse ratio to their sophistication.

Stupid, crazy, mean—you can deal with a combination of any two but not all three.

If British critics don't like your design, it doesn't necessarily mean it's good.

"Fair play" invented out of necessity by the English, who must articulate what doesn't come naturally.

To condescending critics: at your age I'd turned architecture around.

Architectural sensibility over journalistic sensation.

A bas opportunistic architecture—designed to make the covers of architectural magazines.

Criticism can create a sublime confluence of sensibility, understanding, and knowledge and of complex in-between positions—not simplistic extremes that end up ideological declarations.

A critique that serves a critic's interest neither promotes understanding nor enhances sensibility.

Critics are not critics but ideologues—usually.

Critics win points rather than assess art.

Purposeful misunderstanding can be a technique of criticism.

There is little understanding of architecture these days—the art of it, the sweat, the subtlety.

Most good art is not liked at first—even Michelangelo had this problem with his *Ascension*.

My favorite thing is when a critic accuses you of not doing such and such when you introduced the idea of such and such in the first place.

Our architecture is always transitional and therefore critically problematic.

HYPE THEORIES: AVANT-GARDE

What's with this artistic originality stuff that the Modernists (who copied factories) derived from the Romantic movement—when the history of architecture is dominated by: sublime English Gothic derived from the French, sublime French Renaissance derived from the Italians, sublime Italian Renaissance derived from ancient Rome, sublime ancient Roman architecture derived from Greece; why can't our architecture derive from and represent all kinds of things for our complex and contradictory age of multiversalism?

The avant-garde of today: it is easier to be outrageous than conventional; everyone knows the avant-garde *was* the good guys—has no one noticed the avant-garde *is* the rear-guard: is it time to *épater* the avant-garde?

If you're really avant-garde you don't know it.

L'avant-garde est devenue les pompiers.

Down with architecture schools that proclaim they are academic departments rather than professional schools (did you ever hear of a dean of an English department?)—a pretentious neo-Modern trend that ironically contradicts the ideals of Modern architecture and denies the essence of the institutions they are part of: remember, universities as defined by Benjamin Franklin embrace the "ornamental and the practical" and acknowledge the how as well as the why.

Architecture as ultimately a professional art sings: architecture as ultimately an academic discipline sucks.

Liberal education—not ideological indoctrination.

Academic tenure deadens—encouraging not freedom of expression but freedom from responsibility—and creativity.

Theory-go-round in the current theory boom.

Beware of ideology: don't go too far with your own ideas.

Theory in the cause of art vs. art in the cause of theory; the latter leads to ideology.

Academic Modernists are now being sold Freudian surrealism—after Jakobsonian semantics (25 years ago) and Derridian deconstruction (10 years ago)—oh, for the fin-de-siècle of *our* century an Architecture for Architecture's sake.

True Postmodernism embraces representation—not replication.

Good architecture involves fractions of inches as well as ideas.

Trust your intuitions over their ideologies.

Viva complexity that comes naturally over complexity that comes ideologically.

I'll take the vulgar over the pretentious any day.

Viva architecture as a high-faluting craft rather than a philosophical whim.

Beware architecture as frozen theory.

Beware architects who quote complex philosophies and promote simple-minded connections and pretentious parallels.

Rich reality vs. simplistic ideology.

No God in the details today—only ideology in the concepts.

Ideology is the last refuge of scoundrels.

Architecture as accumulations of ideas is no good.

Complexity and Contradiction in Architecture is pragmatic, not ideological.

Theory should not become art; art should not become theory.

The trouble used to be that architects read only one book—now they read too many books (or pretend to).

Thirty years ago Serge Chermayeff called me the guru of chaos—little did he know.

The confusionist approach to architecture impresses some—and intimidates all.

Peter Eisenman says he gets his best ideas in the shower, or does he get them from books he hasn't read all of?

Let us remember our American genius for plain speech and pragmatic content—that of Emerson, Thoreau, Lincoln, Hemingway—which must not be substituted by perfumed shit.

I am sorry if you understand what I'm writing—please don't hold it against me or it.

You can't understand it means it's profound?

Ambiguity rather than obscurity.

Here is a less outlandish approach to so-called signature architecture: mount the architect's signature in neon across the facade—at least its pretension is thereby exposed only at night.

A commercial electronic aesthetic for now is no worse than an industrial machine aesthetic of then.

Two things we love to acknowledge are the sublime ordinary and the vital vulgar; no wonder we're hard to take if you're avant-garde.

Ambiguity in art is good, ambiguity in theory is bad.

Exceptional exceptions are nice, exceptions galore are a vice.

Beware those who flaunt their vision before they meet the challenge—and thereby really promote their ideology.

HYPE BUILDINGS: DECON-ISM

Our fin-de-siècle decadence: Mod Deco.

Mod Deco like Art Deco is a last-gasp—ironically and ornamentally based on the vocabulary of the International Style, rather than that of the Beaux-Arts.

It has been said that the in, Neo-Modern vocabulary of today or that of Deconstructivism represents a revival—that of the International Style, itself derived from an early twentieth-century industrial vernacular—and sits at home as a style therefore within the reviled context of Postmodernism—and accommodates at the same time the hype sensibility of today, promoting punk and blue trusses as appliqué and floors and walls as ramps: it engages the vulgarity of Las Vegas in terms of hype forms rather than commercial symbols—it represents the easy heroic stance of today—evoking a kind of Poussin landscape with plastic gods or an Arcadian Disneyland.

Modernism today is a representation of a style.

Late Modernism—like late English Gothic—can be called Decorated Modern.

From gingerbread Gothic to gingerbread Modern.

From *béton brut* to metal brew.

The International Style colored in and shaken up.

From late Modernist dull dry to Neo-Modernist dull hype.

The current aesthetic based on CAD wire frame imagery or that based on steel truss imagery—what's the difference irrelevancy-wise?

Why isn't applied steel structure an aesthetic oxymoron, even in our post-Miesian age?

Industrial frames stuck on the outside can look kind of sadistic even when cheerfully tinted.

Exposed steel is no less historical and no more relevant an architectural material than brick—and harder to maintain.

There are guy wires galore in today's industrial-rococo style: thank goodness there are yet no decorative rivets promoting a rivet revival.

Why don't the Decons acknowledge industrial rocaille as perverse ornament?

Those critics who are offended by the decorated shed don't blink an eye at structural exhibitionism involving sloping floors, slanting windows, and decorative trusses.

Pattern as decor is no worse than frame as decor—and cheaper to build and easier to maintain.

It is better to ornament shelter with ornament than with engineering.

Viva elemental shelter over decorative frame.

In *our* architecture we don't expose our mechanicals.

Nostalgic-industrial and expressionistic-technological imagery, ho-hum.

Be anguished, not crazy.

Exceptions ought to be exceptional.

The exception proves the rule, not makes the rule.

Motival exceptions should be oxymoronic.

Where contradiction becomes consistent and exception becomes motival—beware.

Hype, like discord, is OK, just so it's not all there is.

All bravado is no bravado.

Consistent dissonance creates not a difficult whole but a boring mess.

Just as all contradiction is no contradiction, all ambiguity is not ambiguity and all discord is not discord.

Architecture is not an aria all the time playing.

Evolve genuinely at a natural pace—rather than revolt journalistically at a hype pace.

Down with buildings as architects' orgasms.

Decon, the architecture of distraction—that drives you to distraction.

Beware of taste that stifles nerve—but also of verve that promotes pretension.

It's easy to go too far and make the journals.

The journalistic appeal of the extremist position.

"No, Peter, I was not trying to shock in *Complexity and Contradiction*—I was just trying to make sense."

Monitor what turns you on—but discount cheap thrills.

Oh, how we would love to show off architecturally—but we must do it only when and if it is appropriate: the majority of our work is for institutions where we make reticent backgrounds, or for museums where we avoid one-upping the art.

Zaha Hadid's critique of the Sainsbury Wing: "It's . . . it's . . . not . . . it's not . . . exciting": *c'est vrai.*

The Sainsbury Wing in its mannerism involves joy—can it be Decon involves jokes?

The cathedral St. Etienne in Toulouse represents valid Decon and heaven on earth.

Decon distortions of the whole are OK for sculpture, but irresponsible in architecture; you achieve that kind of jazz in architecture as applied sign.

If you are not turned on by the idea of shelter, you should probably not be an architect but a sculptor or a philosopher.

Architecture as sculpture with a resented roof.

Architecture as tumbled pieces of sculpture left out in the rain.

Architecture as a village after an earthquake designed by a god.

Decon as earthquake-spoof architecture.

Scale via detail is out.

Tired of architecture that looks good as a model from above on a conference table rather than as a building up close at eye level.

Decon in architecture needs less tenuous wacko and more genuine whammo.

Is reference to the current flight path in Columbus, Ohio, wacko—*not* the equivalent of eastern orientation of apses or the equivalent toward Mecca?

An ultimate oxymoron: Neo-Modern?

Oh, to be genuine modern rather than revival-Modern.

Down with Retro-Modern—from PoMo to Retro.

I'm modern if modern (as opposed to Modern) is not an old style but a way of architecture.

Let our art derive from authentic complex and contradictory experience— not from expressionistic complex and contradictory ideology.

Architecture for now—over architecture for Wow!

Is Decon *C&C* gone awry?

Modernist modular architecture: geometry sans exceptions—*C&C* architecture: geometry cum exceptions—Decon architecture: geometry as exceptions.

Picturesque expressionism seems easier to take than valid iconography.

Sagging wire in tension—that is, guy wire that is ornamental—whose catenary curves recall fifties architecture and McDonald's, is an oxymoron par excellence.

Romanesque, yes; Modernesque, no.

I LOVE MANNERISM

Don't be obviously different—be it ambiguously: mannerism.

Irony is often inevitable.

Much good art is an acquired taste.

Break the rules, not out of ignorance or perversity, but to acknowledge sensibility toward a complex whole and create liveliness and tension.

Viva a fragment that refers to a whole.

The job of bureaucrats and the effect of do-gooders is often to thwart accomplishment.

Today architects submit to taste qualification committees set up by architects who haven't made it representing community groups who don't get it.

For bureaucratic committees intellectual dimensions threaten and artistic dimensions elude.

The only thing worse than a corrupt bureaucracy is a zealous bureaucracy.

The bureaucrat's main job is to look good.

A partial definition of a bureaucrat: one who disguises his inefficiency by making you look bad and delays payments with no sense of meeting a payroll.

Bureaucratic jerks frustrate creative jerks.

A bureaucrat is a scaredy cat.

In the old days when experts rather than consensus held sway you got a lot of shit, but the system did not preclude some good coming out of it.

Concerning architecture everyone's an expert—except those who practice it.

Beware of the arrogance of the ignorant.

When you work with skilled and rational people you are nice that way too.

How nice and appropriate that our leading restoration architect, David De Long of the University of Pennsylvania, has promised to restore our Sainsbury Wing design—not as a response to modifications of the building after it was built but to modifications of the design before it was built.

The only thing worse than a citizenry indifferent to public art is one committed to it.

We are in an era that values dissent over trust—thus discouraging productive action.

Generally people who berate Disney have bad taste.

The only thing worse than vulgar urbanism is tasteful urbanism.

Pseudo-urbanity—closing off streets and littering them with *objets*.

Planters as an amenity are like whipped cream on *spaghetti alle vongole*.

Pedestrian circulation that's sentimental is pedestrian.

It's hard to remember how shocking it was to design from the outside in as well as the inside out; now it's the other way round—because of urban design gone despotic.

I love Geneva where the buses are on time and you sit with workers and *grandes dames*.

What an irony that the originally progressive-radical abstraction of Modern architecture has become for civic art the safe way sans controversial symbolic content.

Beware vulgarians promoting good taste.

Beware the S word: signs are vulgar—although banners are tasteful.

CONTEXT, AGAIN

We are seldom now in America the first building on the block: context is significant.

Acknowledging context in architecture doesn't mean the new building has to look like the old ones: harmony can derive from contrast as well as from analogy—look at the Piazza San Marco; it's a question of appropriateness.

Sainsbury Wing: architectural deference—to paintings inside and Trafalgar Square outside—and to Pall Mall South.

What's the difference between the eighteenth century's motival rococo and Frank Lloyd Wright's motival organic?

We tend to forget how recent today's acknowledgment of historical architecture is: Louis Kahn in his plans for Philadelphia demolished City Hall except for the tower, and as recently as the early sixties the School of Architecture faculty at Penn had to debate whether they should take a stand concerning the demolition of the Furness Library. Alas, the pendulum, as it tends to do, has swung too far—from intolerant progressive Modernism to sanctimonious historicist restorationism, where we are contemptuous of new buildings and validly evolving settings.

Viva variety of vocabularies for context's sake: architectures, not architecture.

Accommodation to architectural context leads to nonuniversalist vocabularies.

ORIGINATORS AND FOLLOWERS

Perceptions of the originator's work alternate between outrageous at first and wimpy later on; the follower is an assured hero.

At first, first is outrageous, then is wimpy; first is sweaty, then is no-sweat; first is gross, while second is refined.

The originator can be sweaty and gauche; the follower can be polished and suave.

You have to be brave to be original—and later you look timid.

The only thing worse than being ignored is being imitated—although your followers disguise their source.

The highest compliment: when yesterday's outrage becomes today's cliché.

Followers make it beautiful.

Oh, for the finesse of the follower.

Your followers sometimes do it before you.

What a challenge—trying not to look like your followers.

Tired of losing jobs to architects who are doing our thing but better—or rather, sweeter.

I can take care of my enemies, save me from my followers.

The ordeal of trying to design your buildings so they don't look like the work of your followers.

Who are the worse followers: the Postmodernists who mistook *Complexity and Contradiction*'s method of historical analogy as its message or the Deconstructivists who ignored the warnings and substituted picturesque for real thing?

The good taken to the extreme can be as bad as the bad.

The good inevitably goes bad—as it is simplified, idealized, fantasized, ideologized by do-gooders.

If you're lucky you live long enough to see the bad results of your good ideas.

To your followers you didn't go far enough with the original idea.

Bad versions of the very good are very bad.

The fate of someone who has been influential: your original contribution has been forgotten because your idea has become pervasive—or you're blamed for the misinterpretations of it that have become pervasive.

To be probably ahead is nice in the end, but in the beginning the scorn is hard to take—along with your own doubts.

If you fail, you are not necessarily a failure.

A good designer can be a follower as well as a leader—just so he acknowledges following.

A good follower is an evolver.

The greatest unintended compliment 30 years later by someone driving by the Guild House: "You wonder what all the fuss was about."

You can only say it, while your followers can do it.

We're tired of being recommended our own ideas of years ago by jerks who don't know their origin and misapply them.

ANTI-HEROISM AND THE SUBLIME ORDINARY

The strange wonder of coming to realize what you already know.

We get some of our best ideas from our clients.

In design, often it is wrong to be correct.

Pay homage to the nerd in life and art.

Designers: remember *"ma non troppo."*

Don't name styles, evolve them.

Simpleton Postmodernism promoted seductive prettiness and nostalgic appeal but was a vulgarization of our architecture—which is ugly and ordinary or gauche and tense—and which we refuse to promote by giving it a name.

Romanticism in art tended to proclaim the artist as an outsider; Modernism in art tended to proclaim the artist as a revolutionary; does the artist tend now to be a courtier?

The universal ideal as it has emerged in architecture is more vividly observed in the fast food realm of McDonald's and Pizza Huts all over the world than in the realm of heroic architecture.

Mass culture is as relevant as high culture.

It's OK to be heroic—but not quixotic.

Incidentally heroic, yes; trying to be, no.

Innovation not for its own sake.

The job of an artist is to lead *and* follow.

We love facing rational, if severe, realities.

Getting halfway there can be an accomplishment.

Evolution from where we are can be as relevant as revolution against where we are.

It isn't necessary to screw tradition.

Evolution yes, trend no.

Work to be of your time and you will be ahead of your time.

You can't progress beyond without knowing the here and now—and then.

To be of your time, focus on being good rather than new.

Complexity and Contradiction represents the first time in centuries that a major architectural statement did not depend on or advocate a specific formal vocabulary—Alan Chimacoff said this!

I love the Swiss chalet, the generic house and barn, that exemplifies architecture as shelter at an almost Japanese extreme—and whose lyrical eaves protect people, animals, and structure below.

Decoration: applied rather than integral, witty rather than correct, selective rather than universal, representative rather than "in the nature of materials."

In architectural detailing, what is easy is usually what is good.

Express function in architecture and you probably diminish function.

Form accommodates functions—in generic architecture.

Architecture that accommodates rather than imposes.

The ordinary and the familiar can become surprising and inspiring.

The ordinary tradition: peasant tunes as scherzo movements, weeds as daffodils, bourgeois picnics and bohemian cafes as in Impressionist paintings.

The question of subject matter in painting and of heroic and conventional vocabularies in architecture can suggest the contrast between heroic gods in Arcadia and realistic Bohemians in cafes; either is OK but the question is one of appropriateness: gods can seldom be in cafes or bohemians in Arcadia.

In our work we derive tension as we push the conventional to its limits—instead of indulging originality in its extremes.

Are ordinarians the Hoppers of architecture?

Out of the ordinary is nice when you can still detect a trace of the ordinary.

All heroism is no heroism—all hype is no hype.

Architectural cowards are afraid of being ordinary.

"Original" architects are afraid to engage the ordinary.

How about: the new modesty?

Architectural vocabularies: the easiest to take in our time are heroic vocabularies; after that come vocabularies perceived as avant-garde; after that vocabularies adapting the industrial vernacular of the early twentieth century; the vocabulary that acknowledges the conventional, the ordinary, is the hardest to take although it has a glorious past, a glorious tradition.

A truly heroic and original position: that of "ugly and ordinary" architecture.

Learning from the ordinary.

Learning from the familiar.

Enhance convention.

Don't be afraid to be good and conventional.

We acknowledge convention and push it to its limits.

Make no small plans: make big plans that accommodate little plans.

Visionaries can be prettifiers.

THE BUSINESS

Who has the greater future—a young architect or a roll of toilet paper?

How to get ahead: have an answer even if it's wrong.

To be in show biz and shy is hell!

I can hardly think and draw anymore—I'm too busy promoting and complaining.

Good presenters are bad architects: architectural selection committees should choose the architect who makes the worst impression in the interview.

Do you get your kicks out of getting the job or doing the job?

We cannot spend all the time required to get the work we need because we have to do the work we have.

We architects can travel 3,000 miles for a three-quarter-hour interview where we have to be sloganeers and showmen rather than thinkers and doers.

Constantly prove yourself for interviews rather than improve yourself by work.

A phenomenon in the selection interview process: having to get on your knees to promise you'll do the kind of architecture you in fact originated.

It's hard to create *and* promote.

I am very nervous and rather intelligent—terrible characteristics for job interviews.

To be creative you have to do work; to do work you have to get work; to get work you have to wear yourself out.

The price you pay for the control of your own work as an architect by having your own office is that you have little time to do it.

Oh, to be in the drafting room and not on the road!

There are three forms of clients selecting architects today: (1) a committee of amateur experts who choose via consensus—the unusual architect whom two love and three hate is discarded for the mediocre architect everyone can take; (2) the project manager or the committee of bureaucrats to whom the client entrusts the power of selection, who picks the architect it cannot feel threatened by; (3) the client as leader working as an individual or through a committee who confidently identifies a good or unusual architect and courageously selects him or her.

Trust and cooperation are basic to civilization; professionals and artists cannot work while protecting their flanks.

Opposing and irreconcilable goals: the architect's to make the building look good, the project manager's to make himself look good.

In today's world of meetings you have to justify rather than produce, argue rather than create.

Are we witnessing the end of our profession as our creativity focuses less on design and more on accommodation to codes, law, and community supervision?

Just think of the steps surrounding the Parthenon with hand rails every few feet—so the Athenians would not sue Pallas Athena and the handrail lobby would be placated.

Prima donna used to be a soprano, now it's a consultant.

As specialists, to varying degrees, all of us, let us work together to promote in the end sensibility over consistency, to acknowledge our responsibility to the whole as well as to the part.

Not every part can be perfect in a complex whole.

Building cases rather than buildings.

If you make everyone happy during the process of design, you make no one happy in the end.

Consultants can be the enemy of the whole.

The only thing worse than not getting the job is getting the job (to paraphrase Oscar Wilde).

Remember, the more time and money an architectural firm spends on getting the job the less it will spend on doing the job—and vice versa.

Architectural process gets more complex as fees get lower.

Architecture is the profession where the more service you give, the more money you lose.

The more work you do to make it better, the more penalized you are by your lump-sum fee: should your office motto be keep your standards down?

God in the details is a victim of late twentieth-century minimalism—but this works to accommodate the minimal fees.

A new conspiracy theory: the founders of Modernism in architecture were cynics rather than idealists as they promoted simplicity, minimalism, formal abstraction, and modular consistency and demoted complexity, ornament, and iconography, thereby diminishing the amount of work they had to produce during design and in the working drawings and the amount of money they had to spend on kinds of insurance and thus increasing the profits or diminishing the losses from their fees; therefore less is more profitable, God is in less detail, and ornament was more equated for Loos with loss than with crime.

Good architects die poor: they use up their fees making it better.

An architect's fee today must anticipate: will the community bureaucracy create unanticipated work, will the project manager be a co-worker or a devil, will the contractor and subs promote skill or greed?

Being a good architect precludes being a rich architect.

Do good, make enemies; be good, pay the price; work hard, confuse bureaucrats and offend committees.

"Not only do I intend to be the greatest architect who has yet lived, but the greatest who will ever live. Yes, I intend to be the greatest architect of all time, and I do hereunto affix 'the red square' and sign my name to this warning": the self-promoting posturing reflected in this Frank Lloyd Wright quotation is perhaps the answer for our time, when otherwise committees dominate the architect and create designs that are deformed camels.

If you're good, beware of any process where your work is judged by your "peers."

ICONOGRAPHY AND TECHNOLOGY

Viva iconography *and* scenography in architecture.

Can we learn from the vivid art of advertising of today?

The effect of commercial advertising on our sensibility in our art is significant and can be good or bad.

Iconography is all over tee shirts—why not buildings?

Farewell to expressionistic industrial nostalgia in our electronic age.

Architecture can be evocative as well as expressive.

Evocative scenography over purist abstraction.

Multiculturalism can become polemical-culturalism.

How sad that when you promote multicultural iconography for civic art you invite "correct" cultural criticism and encourage safe abstract expressionism—to keep the peace.

Reference is OK in architecture; it is inevitable after you are 3 years old.

I learn from the painted surfaces of peasant furniture whose *faux* is *juste* as it imitates marble or represents flowers.

I love generic buildings in old Swiss villages on whose stucco surfaces are painted pediments, frames, and pilasters promoting practical symbolism and lyricism—and wit.

Can *faux béton brut* replace real *béton brut*—which we can't afford?

Viva the Bibliothèque Ste.-Geneviève—Henri Labrouste's cultural billboard of the nineteenth century.

Houston: a beautiful American city—except the billboards aren't big enough; how sad that legislation is at work to diminish the poignant, colorful, and scaleful juxtaposition of billboards and bungalows beyond the highways.

Billboards perversely represent the civic art of today—to be cherished 100 years from now as significant elements for historical preservation; Houston will be for billboards what Williamsburg is for Colonial.

Viva billboards, beware good taste; information can be nice; is a too-big billboard an oxymoron?

Ancient Egyptian pylons—the billboards of yesteryear—are more relevant than abstract-expressionistic acrobatic forms.

Since the late Middle Ages no vocabulary or style of architecture has been totally original or not somehow based on a style of the past—Renaissance, Baroque, Neoclassicism, Eclecticism, Modernism—the latter based on American industrial vernacular architecture or industrial engineering forms—except for Rococo, Art Nouveau, and some Frank Lloyd Wright: let us now abandon our hopeless search for new form and define the artful dimension of architecture as iconographic.

Graphics were nice etched in stone—and will be nice electronically evanescent and moving.

Today's fear of electronic technology for evolving iconographic surfaces in architecture resembles yesteryear's fear of engineering technology for a machine aesthetic.

Let us explore electronics rather than exalt engineering.

It's more responsible to promote architectural rhetoric via signage on form than via distortion of form.

A decorated shed is better than a decorative truss.

And now, from decorated shed to virtual box.

The architect is now a director more than a craftsman—who plans for iconographic content and its management process.

Light is our essential material—more than bricks (and even wire frame guy wires).

Light is our essential medium—not as "veiled" and "luminous" planes that are electric, but as vivid iconographic decor that can be electronic.

Our achitecture is post-industrial, not neo-industrial.

A bas spatial expression: viva iconographic meaning.

The city as signs as in the past (and the present), but via a new technology for a new sensibility.

Irony: you can humanize our communities via vital signs more than via expressive space.

Today change is accommodated via the spatial flexibility of generic and the iconographic flexibility of electronic architecture.

Iconography defines civic architecture for now.

The psychological need for detail—but can't detail for now include the pixels of electronics?

Virtual variety.

Light-emitting diode as the mosaic of now—its pixels corresponding to the tesserae of old.

Iconography as graffiti glorified.

Viva the art of billboards in the right landscapes.

Viva Byzantine tesserae *and* electronic pixels.

LEARNING FROM NOW

Learning from everything.

I love the art that can evolve.

Within a process bad ideas can lead to good ideas.

Art is making substance out of bullshit.

Flights of fancy start from the elemental fundamental.

Make no small plans but beware grandiose plans.

The assurance of the naive surrounds us.

We work to make the ordinary extraordinary and the basic classic.

It's fun to recall with this 42nd Street revival my extraordinary benign reference to Times Square in *Complexity and Contradiction in Architecture*—in the mid-sixties!

EPILOGUE

INTRODUCTION TO MY M.F.A. THESIS

As I've said elsewhere, most of the material in this collection of essays was written in the recent past. This last work is an exception because it represents my Princeton M.F.A. thesis of 1950—slightly edited but still somewhat awkward in its style; it is accompanied by some of the illustrative material that composed the body of the thesis. My jury included Louis Kahn, whom I had met the summer before in Philadelphia, and George Howe. I am sorry the graphic material is incomplete, as some of it has been lost; the footnotes are also incomplete.

I include this work because its subject, context in architecture, represents almost a cliché in our field and because the origin of this idea has become almost forgotten: a Philadelphia architect, for instance, recently confidently referred to context as an architectural element that evolved in the seventies. But I vividly remember my Eureka-like response in 1949 when I came across the idea of perceptual context in Gestalt psychology as I perused a journal of psychology in the library in Eno Hall at Princeton and recognized its relevance for architecture—at a time when architecture was exclusively designed from the inside out and confidently promoted Modernism as universally applicable: to hell with all that old stuff that was, alas, still around. Hard as it is to remember, this was true with some few exceptions, as when Frank Lloyd Wright would connect with natural context—with the prairie or with a Pennsylvania waterfall (but never with that lousy architecture that preceded him). It's nice when a daring idea becomes an accepted idea but it hurts a little—especially as it is often misunderstood and ultimately misapplied.

It should also be noted that the significance of meaning as well as expression in architecture was here acknowledged for the first time in our time and that the way for plurality of cultures or multiculturalism, if not anticipated, was opened up for architecture.

You will detect a notable omission within this thesis—one that is forgivable, I trust, in the context of its time when aesthetic abstraction reigned supreme and reference, association, symbolism, or iconography was automatically shunned to the point where a youth might not dream much less acknowledge the existence of these dimensions within his medium. I refer to a lack of acknowledgment of an element's inherent characteristics and associations, which can exist independent of context or alongside of context.

Another reason for including this project is, I think 45 years later, the design of the chapel for the Episcopal Academy is darn good.

A short essay deriving from the part of this thesis on the Campidoglio was published in *Architectural Review* in 1953; it was my first publication.

CONTEXT IN ARCHITECTURAL COMPOSITION: M.F.A. THESIS, PRINCETON UNIVERSITY

Written 1950.

INTRODUCTION

Intent   The intent of this thesis problem is to demonstrate the importance of and the effect of setting on a building. It considers the art of environment; the element of environment as perceived by the eye. Specifically it deals with relationships of the part and the whole and with what architects call site planning. It attempts to evolve principles concerning these issues and ways for discussing them.

Implication   Its implication for the designer is that existing conditions around the site that should become a part of any design problem should be respected, and that through the designer's control of the relation of the old and the new he can perceptually enhance the existing by means of the new.

Content   The thesis of the problem in short is that its setting gives a building expression; its context is what gives a building its meaning. And consequently change in context causes change in meaning.

Sources

The sources of my interest in this subject are relevant. An early and direct one was my impatience with architecture design problems produced by the Beaux Arts Institute of Design of New York which I did as a student, which frequently lacked indications of the setting or background of the building to be designed or at best indicated merely the physical dimensions of the site. This implied for me a dangerous assumption that the building could be designed only for itself.

Another important source lay in certain experiences I had and my interpretation of them on a trip to France and Italy several summers ago. This was my first European trip and my approach was one of keen curiosity to discover fact and compare it with anticipation (to quote George Santayana). My anticipation was based on images derived from the usual graphic and photographic means of representing buildings. Invariably this comparison caused surprises. From these reactions and their implications I induced my thesis. The surprises as I analyzed them seldom resulted from the difference caused by the extra dimensions of space and time but from the opportunity to include and relate the individual building and the setting, to perceive in a perceptual whole. This first opportunity for an American to experience characteristic Medieval and Baroque spaces as wholes, especially those derived from piazzas, instilled an enthusiasm for them which made subsequent library research on the Roman ones extensive and stimulating.

One last source, a non-empirical one, was the subsequent discovery of Gestalt psychology as a necessary basis for a discussion of perceptual reactions and its usefulness for providing a precise vocabulary for an architect who hesitates to use some of his own worn out words. Among such words are "unity" which has lost precise meaning in criticism and "proportion" which in its usual application Frank Lloyd Wright, for one, has amusingly rendered useless.

Method

The method of organization and presentation of the material is as follows: The problem is essentially one great diagram so that the sizes and positions of words, symbols, plans, illustrations, etc. convey meaning as much as their symbolic denotations do. The problem as a diagram at the beginning consists of the two thesis statements mentioned above in architectural terms, accompanied, as paragraph headings to the left, by equivalent general statements in psychological terms, followed by amplification of these statements by means of a series of diagrams (Sheets 3 and 5). The following series of sheets (6 to 15) represents the argument of the thesis via analyses of historical architectural examples in Rome and of contemporary domestic architecture. The final series represents the application of the thesis to the design problem, the design of an Episcopal chapel for a country day school for which the rest of the thesis constitutes approach and research.

The system of the composition of the sheets as a whole should be noted: the two general thesis statements in verbal form at the beginning of the series of sheets each generate an axis of influence which extends horizontally through the series of diagrams and historical examples up to the design section. Therefore the diagrams and then the plans and sections along the upper axis are equivalent to statement one, and likewise for the second axis.

Furthermore, the relation between a diagram and the diagram below it, or a plan and the one below it, as in the Campidoglio of 1545 and the Campidoglio of 1939, is the same as the relation between initial statements one and two. The titles and subtitles of the various sections and also the series of colored round, square, and diamond symbols establish similar secondary horizontal axes of influence and equivalent relationships. The copies of engravings and the photographs of the examples from various views amplify their meaning, and their relative positions and connections via strings indicate equivalencies among illustrations. This form of organization facilitates the integration of the material.

Sheets 1 & 2

The subtitle of this part of the research might be: "The recognition of space and form as qualities of a perceptual whole." One definition of meaning is, "Meaning is what one idea is as context of another idea."[1] Its context gives an idea its meaning, and this statement in architectural terms becomes Statement 1 in the diagram. Its context gives a building expression. A building is not a self-contained object but a part in a whole composition relative to other parts and the whole in its position and in its form. Statement 2 is a consequence of Statement 1: Just as a change in context causes change in meaning in terms of ideas, change in the setting of a building causes change in expression of a building. Change of a part in its position or its form causes a change in other parts and in the whole. These two variables are related to a constant—to psychological responses, to the observer's visual reactions, to his limit of attention, to his situation, etc. By their adjustment quality can be attained among these relationships.[2]

There are properties of the whole which are distinct from properties of the part. The whole composition may possess different degrees of articulation. The more articulate the whole, the more does a change in one part affect the other parts and the whole.

Sheet 3

I have made distinct references to position and form: a building is a part in a whole composition in its *position* and in its *form*. And change of a part in its *position* and in its *form* causes change in other parts and in the whole. On the sheets are diagrams illustrating some specific conditions of organization in terms of the position of the parts and of the form of the parts and their relation to a whole. These develop further the thesis statements, help make the transition from the abstract principle to specific architectural applications, and establish a precise classification and vocabulary which can be constantly applied to them in discussion of the examples and the final design problem. This emphasis on classification does not represent an attempt at establishing an easy architectural formula. The first series of diagrams demonstrates the effect of spatial context, i.e. the space around an object. Confronted with a complex optical field one will reduce it to basic interrelationships. In the first diagram the two individual units are perceived as a whole and only postanalytically discernable as two parts. The condition, a very simple one, which relates each one perceptually is their *proximity.* Their *juxtaposition,* an obvious means of relationship and of creating a perceptual whole, is the condition indicated in the next diagram. *Parallel* is another and a typical positional relationship in architectural composition, as are the conditions of *direction* (found in streets) and *closure* (found in town squares) in the last configurations.

The diagrams along the second axis demonstrate Statement 2. In the first one, for instance, the two parts, because of their changed setting in the second axis, are perceived as farther apart. Their meaning in terms of their relative position is changed.

Sheets 4 & 5

The next series of diagrams illustrates the effect of formal context (i.e. form) on an object—on the size, shape, texture, color, and hue of an object, and the effect of change from complementary similarity to complementary contrast. In the process of these changes in position or form, properties of the part become more or less accented, properties of the whole evolve toward greater or less articulation. By their adjustment quality can be enhanced in these relationships. The architect accepts and creates context.

Sheet 6

Because this thesis is fundamental and broad—all buildings have settings—a range of examples without a limit would become ineffective. Because of my emphasis on experience and my fascination with Rome on the trip mentioned above, I chose examples from this city. I believe my enthusiasm results from the distinctly organic development expressed in Rome's planning as well as from the kind of intricate and rich spatial effects found in its quantity of 16th and 17th-century Baroque buildings and piazzas. A second category includes examples of contemporary domestic architecture because they conveniently illustrate some social implications of the thesis.

Each historical example in both series includes a building which indicates along axis Number 1 the visual conditions by which it is related to its background and along axis Number 2 the change in meaning caused by change in setting—by the consequent new conditions in the organization of its space and form—indicated by the color-shape symbols. The illustration represents either a geographical contrast as in the comparison of the Trevi Fountain and the Fontaine St. Michel, or a temporal change as in the Campidoglio before Michelangelo, after Michelangelo, and after the Victor Emmanuel Monument. The plans and sections correspond to those of the preceding diagrams. The illustrations, equivalent ones indicated by connecting black string, serve to amplify.

Sheet 7

For one whose familiarity with the Trevi Fountain is based on conventional photographs of it, it might be a dry and pompous monument. From such a source an unsuspecting American or Parisian might assume that a monument of such elaboration and size would find itself in a similarly large space probably terminating a vista or boulevard. But the fountain in relation to its setting, consisting of contrastingly small scale buildings forming a tightly enclosed space and approached from yet more confined spaces, becomes a dynamic spectacle. Indeed its surrounding space would be considered too small by traditional French planners, perhaps even by Le Corbusier who concludes that "without doubt everything is too huddled together in Rome."[3] Certainly the comparison of the effect of this fountain with that of the Fontaine St. Michel, comparable in scale and design (a fountain which forms the facade of a building), is indicative. The latter's is the archetypal 19th-century Parisian setting, a large place at the termination of an axial boulevard.

Sheet 8   The 18th-century designers of the Piazza S. Ignazio conceived of their design as a context for the existing facade of S. Ignazio. The contrastingly small size of the space emphasizes the large scale of the Baroque church. The sympathetic and receptive quality of the space is formed by the convex facades of the opposite buildings which connote enclosure and by their contrastingly delicate scale. All of this acknowledges and underscores the three-dimensionality and turgidity of the church facade opposite. It was Rococo architects who acknowledged and made articulate the Baroque facade.

Sheet 9   The example illustrating SS. Trinità before and after the Spanish Stairs demonstrates similar principles involving spatial direction and accommodation.

Sheet 10   In its history two major changes in the setting of the Campidoglio have affected its expression and quality. Michelangelo's design can be said to have constituted an enhanced setting for the existing Senatorial Palace. This building he modified almost negligibly by the addition of the pilasters, cornice, and window frames. It is the inclusion of the flanking buildings with the both contrasting and analogous aspects of their form and their unique positional arrangement that enhances the space around it by means of enclosure and direction and enriches the composition. The stepped ramp, like the stairs in the previous example, works also to direct space, direct focus, and enhance setting.

Since the erection of the proximate Victor Emmanuel Monument, one has had to approach the Campidoglio complex with eyes straight ahead preferably equipped with blinders. The monument in itself can be perceived as almost entertaining, but in relation to the Campidoglio it is calamitous, unsympathetic in every respect, in its form—size, shape, color, and texture—and by its position which makes the Campidoglio a backstage anticlimax. For this reason photographs of this complex, contrary to those of the Trevi Fountain, which can and usually do exclude the infamous monument apparent during the observer's approach, tend to convey a more powerful meaning than do actual views on site.

Perhaps as drastic has been the effect of the recent substitution of big boulevards and unenclosed vehicular spaces for the intricate small scale neighborhood spaces which composed the original setting of this complex. The former configuration's dense fabric and contrastingly small spaces afforded varied views tantalizingly interrupted which made for a powerful setting for the piazza. The removal of the congested area was of dubious social advantage and the substitution of the highway of questionable value for the circulation system of the city. The new Parisian spaces and other trimmings have robbed the buildings and their immediate exterior spaces of force. The modern designers' respect for a Michelangelo design caused them scrupulously to modify no part of the Campidoglio physically: ironically their destruction of it perceptually could compete with that of a demolition gang's. By removing its reason for being they obscured its meaning and significance.

One reason for the frequent failures of architectural eclecticism lies in its disregard of context—visual, historical, and functional. A comparison of some Pantheons is one of many which could be made and calls to mind the experience derived from Emerson's shells in his *Each and All:*

The delicate shells lay on the shore;
The bubbles of the latest wave
Fresh pearls to their enamel gave . . .
I wiped away the weeds and foam,
I fetched my sea-born treasures home;
But the poor, unsightly, noisome things
Had left their beauty on the shore . . .
All are needed by each one;
Nothing is fair or good alone.[4]

Perhaps the setting of the Pantheon is not ideal, but the small scale and close proximity of the surrounding buildings contribute to its magnitude and their angularity reinforces the dominance of its dome. Above all the shape of the enclosing piazza sets it off as a central-type building, the climax of a whole urban composition which its circular and domed form and its function demand.

McKim, Mead, and White's Philadelphia Girard Trust Bank building competes with skyscrapers, becomes one of many units in a row within a gridiron street pattern, which position denies its essential centrality. The innovative square plan below the dome partially ameliorates this condition.

Jefferson's University of Virginia rotunda, if eventually inconvenient as a library, is successful in expressing its centrality within a whole composition, as it is fortified perceptually by its subordinate flanking buildings and by its hilltop situation. A concept of the library as the heart of a university is thereby distinctly reinforced.

This thesis and its application fall within a so-called organic approach in architecture but the acknowledgement of context is not antithetical to a Classical tradition in architecture. The definition "meaning is what one idea is as context of another idea" could directly represent a Classical idea of proportion. The Classical concept does recognize context within composition—that of the building as a system of relationships of geometric shapes. But in its concept of universality and lack of emphasis on natural and architectural setting, the Classical approach disregards context from an organic standpoint.

Insofar as it is Platonic and Neo-Platonic, the Classical tradition in this consideration of context differs from the organic in its dogma. One contextual relationship or system of proportions is constantly superior to others and universally applicable, and this precludes acknowledging the varieties of settings which are inevitable and which the organic approach can exploit.

Sheets 12 & 13 Frank Lloyd Wright often mentions the important effect of its site on the design of a building. But this thesis maintains that this effect is reciprocal. And in the *Autobiography* Wright does acknowledge this idea specifically in reference to his Johnson house in Racine: "The house did something remarkable to that site. The site was not stimulating before the house went up . . . charm appeared in the landscape." The illustrations substantiate that this prairie site, negative in its aspect, later acquired a positive horizontal quality by means of the inclusion of the complementary form of the house which is sympathetically horizontal for one thing and by the use of its materials which are analogous to the site in texture and color. This kind of building can exemplify the country house situated alone which, by means of its relation to its setting, becomes a part in a perceptual whole.

The two other examples in this domestic architecture series illustrate the representative American house in a semi-urban setting c. 1835 and c. 1935, and an individual apartment house in an apartment development: they project, through their contextual relationships among themselves, social interrelationships and images.

Sheet 14

A representative early 19th-century house, the Simpson-Hoffman house in Salem, Massachusetts, is situated on Chestnut Street which is conventionally considered one of the most beautiful streets in America; it is a unit in a typical semi-gridiron planned neighborhood. In the house's absolute perpendicularity to the street and parallel relation to the neighboring houses only the crudest conditions of spatial organization are employed. The neighborhood's consequent lack of any direction or closure can indicate weak community relationships and social isolation which might be seen to foreshadow an era of "rugged individualism." The later excessive development of this type of spatial organization found in any typical suburban neighborhood in America containing individual houses illustrates explicitly these visual and social conditions. What makes this early 19th-century neighborhood composition effective is the delicate formal relationships within the compositions of the buildings.

A comparative 20th-century suburban house is represented by the Koch house, Snake Hill, Belmont, also in Massachusetts. By its relation to its architectural setting, more ideal than representative today, it employs the visual qualities of enclosure and direction and recognizes the natural quality of the site. Where the house is a distinct unit yet one within a pronounced neighborhood whole as it is here, a communal spirit acknowledging a social interdependence evolves.

Sheet 15

An extreme example in the opposite direction is illustrated in the comparison of two apartment house units similar in function, size, etc. and therefore comparable. An Aluminum Terrace apartment, Pittsburgh, c. 1940, and the Runtung apartment, Leipzig, c. 1935, are in apartment neighborhoods of similar size, each containing like units. But otherwise their settings are significantly different. A further analysis of the diagrams demonstrating spatial context would indicate that the value of a part depends on its relation to the whole; if it is within the locus of the whole it will exercise an inordinate influence upon the rest of the configuration. In the Aluminum City neighborhood composition the locus falls within a part. In whichever building within the development the observer is, he is a part of its locus, its dynamic locus. In the Leipzig apartment complex its static locus falls geometrically as well as perceptually in the center of a monumental space, not an individual part, the individual's apartment; the properties of the part are minimized, the properties of the whole are emphasized. The former can represent an ideal democratic expression of community living; each individual is important as such and as a member of an integrated community. The latter, designed in the Nazi era, can represent the opposite social emphasis—that of individual submission to an exterior authority. Significantly such apartment neighborhood organizations are typical not only of Germany.

THE DESIGN PROBLEM: A CHAPEL FOR THE EPISCOPAL ACADEMY, MERION, PA.

Sheet 17

This country day school consists of two converted, eclectic mansions, each unrelated in its position and form. The new chapel in its position and form is conceived as a changed context for this complex which causes a changed meaning:

Two mansions become one institution.

A whole is articulated by the addition of a part.

There is an actual need and there exist proposed designs for a memorial chapel for the Episcopal Academy.

Within the design for this chapel there exist two dimensions that are essential. The first includes the requirements of the program of the building itself and involves creating a building which functions as and expresses itself as an Episcopal school chapel, and includes some statistical detail (capacity, etc.) not directly relevant here. The second dimension involves principles of this thesis—this means that one not only has to consider the perceptual effects of setting on the design of the building itself but, conversely, as in Wright's Johnson house, to consider the perceptual effect of the building on its setting. This chapel in its design is conceived as a setting within the existing conditions of the site—as a changed context which will effect a changed meaning. To justify the need for this change in meaning or expression a thorough consideration of existing site and architectural conditions and their history is necessary and is explored on the sheets by means of the same diagrammatic technique as that of the historical examples.

Sheet 18

The Episcopal Academy, which had been established in the center of Philadelphia in 1785, moved to Merion in 1921 to accommodate the contemporary migration from city to suburb. It acquired two neighboring properties each containing a mansion and outbuildings and their grounds (about 19 acres) which bordered a highway, City Line Avenue. The grounds were gently sloping and well landscaped and easily converted into athletic fields. The two mansions presented a greater problem of conversion. Each was situated almost in the center of its approximately rectangular lot, perpendicular to the highway and directly oriented toward it and weakly related to the other in its next-door position. The mansions themselves in their forms are of late 19th-century vintage, both of Chestnut Hill greystone but diverse in every other respect involving form, composition, scale, and historical style—one employing a French Renaissance style and the other employing indescribable characteristics involving a kind of symmetrical medieval castle faced with a Classical antebellum columned portico. These monstrosities, examples of rugged individualism in their antagonistic competition, were not therefore visually related as two mansions either in their positions (site planning) or in their forms. They were designed essentially from the standpoint of the observer who receives visual impressions (and incidentally associative ones suggesting affluence on the part of the owners) from a point directly perpendicular to the front facades—only from the street. And each impression was for itself, entirely separate from the next in sequence; certainly there was little consideration in the site planning or building design of the visual effect from any other position, especially from within the sites or from within neighboring sites. This might involve a developed manifestation of the Simpson-Hoffman house setting. These buildings,

349

themselves and in their relationships to each other when they were individual houses, were not architecturally successful. It is evident that merely the removal of the dividing fence and the change of their function in 1921 could not and did not make them successful visually as the Upper and Lower Schools of one institution.

Since then the purchase of additional neighboring property and the erection of secondary buildings and wings such as dining halls and gymnasiums and a temporary chapel have had little effect either in improving or harming existing conditions. However, the recent aforementioned plans for the proposed memorial chapel have exposed a policy which will not improve conditions but will make bad matters worse by reinforcing them. The proposed location of the new chapel is an immediately expedient one, precisely between the two buildings, oriented also perpendicularly toward the street and thereby reinforcing existing difficulties within the site plan. The proposed location represents the addition, not the integration, of a unit. Its form is "Colonial style," very large in scale forming an uncomplementary contrast. This thesis problem represents an attempt to prevent an architectural mistake which will extend beyond the mere addition of a bad building in its effect.

In terms of this thesis my chapel is conceived and designed as a changed setting in terms of its position and its form which will promote a changed meaning within the existing setting: two mansions are to become one institution.

Sheets 19 & 20

There are two main considerations concerning the chapel's position—that is, concerning site planning—in this connection.

These two mansions made two distinct compositions prior to 1921 and were only partially successful as such because of their lack of relationship to each other, although they were often in the same field of vision. But each composition, each estate, did form within itself a more or less articulate whole whose locus fell within the mansion itself, mostly because of the symmetry within the site planning and the central position of each mansion. It has been stated that if the locus of the whole falls within a part, that part will exercise an immoderate influence upon the rest of the configuration. Because the gymnasiums and dining halls constitute wings of these buildings and because the other school buildings are relatively of no importance visually, the new complex with the addition of the chapel will consist essentially of three buildings, the Upper and Lower Schools and the chapel—none of which would or should to any marked degree exceed another in importance functionally or visually. Therefore the relative position of this new building is such that the locus of the new whole composition falls not within one of the parts but at a point outside of a part, that is, not on a building but within a space among them. This locus will cause the Upper and Lower Schools to become oriented toward each other, toward the interior of the site rather than toward the highway as formerly, and in that manner establish a whole of which they are parts. This space becomes the required memorial place marked precisely by sculpture and made monumental by its position as the locus of the new whole. This space represents also a much needed quiet spot among the athletic fields. A similar difference between loci which is indicated on the sheets[5] can be found in a comparison between Michelangelo's proposed piazza–church complex of St.

Peter's, where the locus of the whole composition falls directly upon the central church surrounded by the colonnaded piazza, and Bernini's existing scheme where the locus falls within the piazza space.

The second main consideration concerning position involves the relation of the location of the building to the path of motion of the observer. The designer's partial control of the changing visual impressions—what is seen, how it is seen, and in what sequence—can be employed for establishing harmony and expressing a whole. Through the adjustment of the exit and entrance driveways, by revising the existing one-way traffic system, and through the relation of the new building to them and the existing buildings, the chapel is to be seen first at an appropriate angle by the entering automobile and thereby through its form is to establish the architectural character of the composition as a whole and create a frame of reference for the other buildings to be seen within the whole when their forms come into view. A historical precedent occurs in the relative position of the Propylaea which acts not only as the entrance of the Acropolis but as a means to control the approach to the Parthenon. The removal of one of the side service driveways makes more immediate the relation of the Upper School to the monumental space, and makes for a new emphasis on the side entrances of the mansions. Planting also can make for a more evident orientation of the buildings toward each other, toward the central memorial space, and away from the highway in front. The indirect routes of the footpaths through the memorial space past the sculpture will contribute a sense of ceremony to the daily processions from each school building to the chapel.

Sheets 22–25

Considerations of the form of the new building in relation to these contextual problems work as follows. Because the function of the building cannot be considered separately from the form in a verbal analysis as well as in its design conception, its qualities will be included here simultaneously.

It is felt that the successful design of this chapel must produce a form which generally creates a complementary contrast between the existing buildings. The two former mansions, similar only in their pretensiousness, can be unified in form only through an additional building which is positively different, which contains none of the diverse elements of the existing buildings and which acknowledges their few similar elements.

The spatial concept of the chapel follows the contemporary tendency of identifying interior and exterior space and creating a sense of flowing space to achieve a lighter exterior expression and unconfined interior expression. The principal means here of deemphasizing interior–exterior barriers is through creating walls which express by their shape and path direction rather than closure,[6] and a roof which deemphasizes horizontality and enclosure as in many Wright buildings. By this means of conceiving of the building essentially as straight unenclosing walls, and deemphasizing the roof as enclosure, and by using similar walls for surrounding embankments and as an element of the memorial in the landscape design, a complementary contrast is effected with the other two buildings, which have the conventional spatial expression of an enclosed interior with punched-hole windows. The new building cannot conflict, therefore, because it is not a building in the same sense as the Upper and Lower Schools and not comparable as such, but a series of free-standing stone walls. On the positive side these walls, because they are of the same material as their neighbors', create a unity through the similarity of texture, hue, and value to their neighbors' form. In their positions these walls in their constant overlapping among themselves and the other buildings from most points of observation create another important means of creating visual unity. This condition has been called juxtaposition. Their parallel relationships to each other and the buildings represent another means of acquiring unity as an expression of a whole.

The memorial sculpture (Sheet 21) is juxtaposed on one of the ubiquitous stone walls, which sets it off and unifies it with the rest of the composition; it consists of an existing dead tree trunk utilized because in this setting this *objet trouvé* creates an atmosphere and an expression of war as tragic; juxtaposed upon this sculptural element is a bronze plaque containing inscriptions.

The treatment of the exterior ends of the chapel is exceptionally elaborate. They contrast with the neutral stone walls of the sides of the building to prevent an appearance of enclosure and to relieve oppressiveness which might result from this apparently entirely opaque building. These weathered copper-faced end walls are different enough from the mansions' in texture and color and structure not to compete and to promote harmony via contrast. The altar end is partly obscured by existing dense trees and the choir end is hidden by the high enclosing wall of the court so that they are never in the same field of vision of the mansions.

For functional as well as expressive reasons a belfry is required, but one which will not compete with the Lower School's tower. The resultant composition as a whole is horizontal, yet the belfry is dominant enough to express church and is integral with the interior truss system to suggest the interior treatment on the outside and increase the unity of the whole.

The doors of the chapel like its windows are determined by contextual considerations, the desire for neutrality and contrast. Like the fenestration, they are hidden on the exterior so as not to break the neutral aspect of the whole by forming a visual comparable part among the free-standing walls that would compete with the diverse doors and windows of the mansions. The shielding walls also create contrastingly flowing space, identify themselves with the garden walls, and create a form of vestibule, a contrastingly tight space which also makes the interior space appear more forceful on entering. These walls also constitute one of the few means for giving scale to the plain exterior.

The reasons for a neutral expression from the exterior of the chapel have been indicated above. However, neutrality here cannot mean negation. The building is a church of a denomination which emphasizes ritual and richness of visual expression. An additional demand for richness and poetic content derives from a recognition of the serious need for such qualities in contemporary architecture. In the recent past, a pseudo-simplicity has developed seen in deceptive surface simplicity, forced flush joints, etc. This has resulted often from a reaction against false richness or rich-mess found in buildings like those of the former mansions which make up the

metal also invisible from any normal position of the observer which reinforces the penetration of natural light. The amount of reflecting area on each side can be adjusted so that more reflection occurs on the north side and the amount of light laterally admitted can be equalized. This diffused light as well as the vibrant color combinations of the painted wood members of green and lavender, in themselves floating colors and richly contrasted with the light yellow of the thin, web-like tension rods, work to create a floating effect. The irregular profile of the built-up laminated wood members similar to those of Frank Lloyd Wright's at Taliesin West and Mackintosh's Glasgow Art School library interior creates a lightness of effect also. The color scheme of the truss effects a gaiety [sic][7] necessary in a boys' chapel. Its form is such that from the spectator's situation its points of connection with the walls for support are not in sight and for this reason, coupled with its profusion of light and color and intricate form and resultant lightness, it exhibits an element of mystery and an ethereal effect also appropriate for a religious building. If an observer could bring himself to use such a figure of speech in a chapel he could explain that the ceiling is held up from "God knows where."

For the sake of simplicity and economy the fourteen trusses are identical except for slight variations in the last bays of each end, which recognize the difference in function between each end and the interjacent nave. The roof structure is the same throughout. But in the trusses over the sanctuary clerestory windows occur in the central portion as well as at the sides to differentiate this portion from the nave space, to increase the amount of light, and to enhance the focus on the altar. Also a suspended cross is integrated with the truss and therefore associated with it. The variation in relation to the whole system caused by the belfry is explained above. Meanwhile, the varied trusses in the rear form a hanging balcony for the choir and organ pipe loft over a sunken narthex which takes advantage of a natural fall in the grade at this end.

Another determinant for the form of this truss, besides the desire for intricacy, expression of tension and lightness, and appropriate lighting, was the low height of the building demanded by contextual considerations. The exterior walls must be low to maintain their expression of unenclosing wall and identity with the garden walls explained above and to minimize conflict with the verticality and height of the mansions. The contrastingly low and high parts of the ceiling in the roof section then form a means of giving an overall interior expression of height to this necessarily low chapel—more so, it can be maintained, than if the ceiling had been physically higher but of one level. The absence of strictly horizontal planes helps also to prevent the oppressiveness possible from low ceilings. It should be mentioned here that the roof shape recognizes and is determined also by the varying functions of related areas in plan—of the nave especially. The ceiling over the sitting area—that is, the pews—is lower and more horizontal than that over the circulation area which consists of the monumental processional aisle.

The common use of this roof shape in industrial architecture assures its practicality in regard to drainage. As in similar factory roof conditions, radiant heating coils in the ceiling, which also constitute the general heating system for the building, melt the snow, and a proper roof slope takes care of drainage. The problem of the necessarily extensive use of metal flashing is gracefully resolved by the continuous use of copper as the roofing and end wall material.

Besides its conscious intricacy, dynamic suspension might be considered a structural-expressive theme of this building. The altar cross integral with the roof truss, the choir gallery which is a variation of the "floating" typical truss, and the "fins" of the exterior vestibules consist of specifically lighter but more voluminous material suspended by stronger but less voluminous material—wood members and steel bars respectively—which contribute to the floating quality characteristic of the structure and a dynamism overhead.

The opaqueness of this building, its hidden windows, etc., distinctly cut off the outside from the inside. The indefinitely defined form of the central portion of the truss section seen in shade and the space along the end portion of the truss section—only part of whose bounds is in view—produce immeasurable space and an element of mystery. This exclusion of the outside world for the worshipper creates in one sense confinement; the indefinitely defined form and the space only partially perceived can suggest paradoxically an identification with the beyond or the infinite. This combination when not employed as a couple of applied devices can create a mystical expression and can become a system and a part of a tradition in one kind of religious architecture found in Byzantine and Gothic interiors.

The profuse ceiling treatment is practical because its means are simple and conventional; it is refined in its effect because of its alleviating contrast to the simple and heavier expression of the walls and exterior; and it is appropriately religious in its expression partly because it follows in principle the systems and effects of the Gothic structures, even in their weaknesses—that is, an inherent tripartite facade problem and an elaborate roof-drainage problem. The latter, I hope, is as elegantly solved at the end walls by the modern equivalent of gargoyles in copper.

---

1. Nelson, *Gestalt Psychology.*
2. The diagram which appears under sheets 1 and 2 consisting of quotations compares the psychologist's and the architect's approaches to this idea.
3. *Towards a New Architecture.*
4. It was my mother who suggested this quotation as an appropriate analogy for my thesis.
5. All the prototype examples which will be referred to are demonstrated on the six-sided sheets and the main design conditions indicated by the symbols.
6. As in typical Mies van der Rohe buildings—see six-sided sheet.
7. [This was written 46 years ago.]

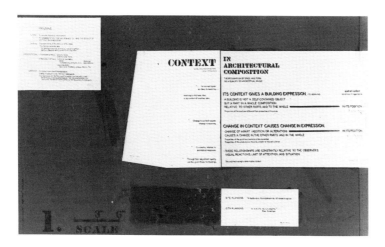

73
Graphic presentation of M.F.A. thesis,
Princeton University, 1950, Prologue and
Sheets 1 and 2

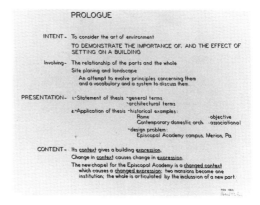

74
Graphic presentation of the thesis,
Prologue

75
Graphic presentation of the thesis, Sheet 1

76
Graphic presentation of the thesis, Sheet 2

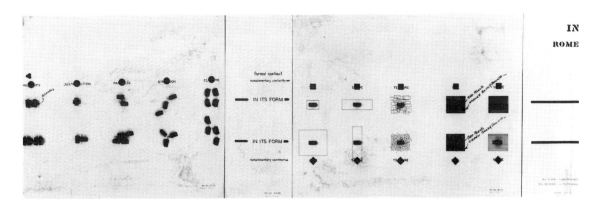

77
Graphic presentation of the thesis, Sheets
3–6

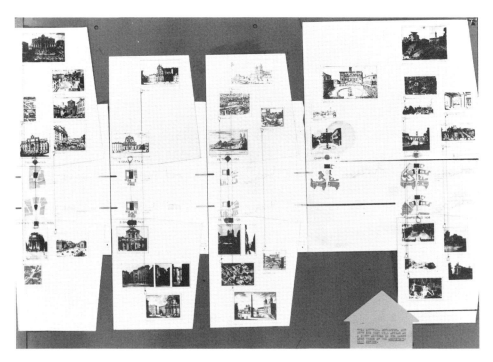

78
Excerpts of historical analysis, Sheets 7–10

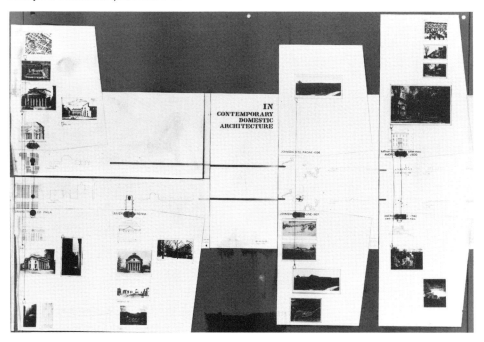

79
Excerpts of historical analysis, Sheets
11–14

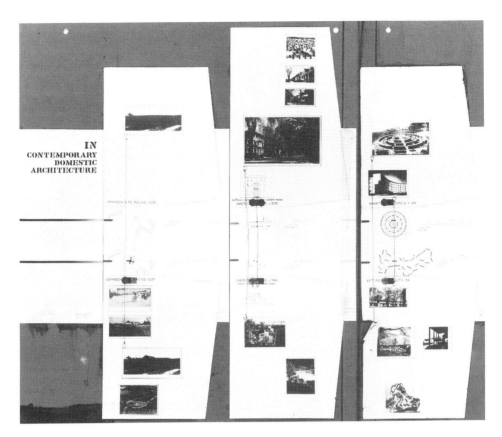

80
Excerpts of historical analysis, Sheets
12–15

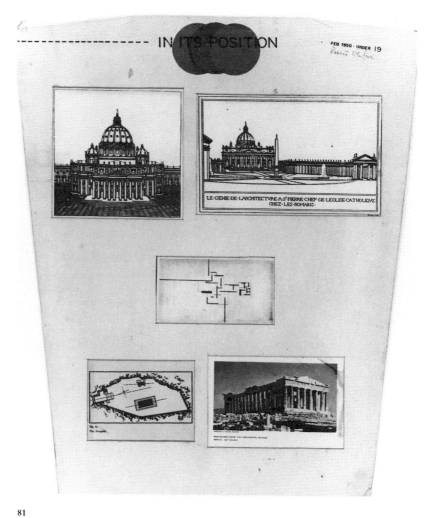

81
Excerpts of historical analysis, Sheet 19a

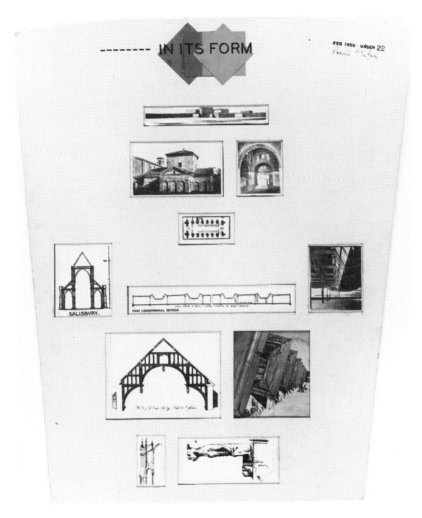

82
Excerpts of historical analysis, Sheet 22a

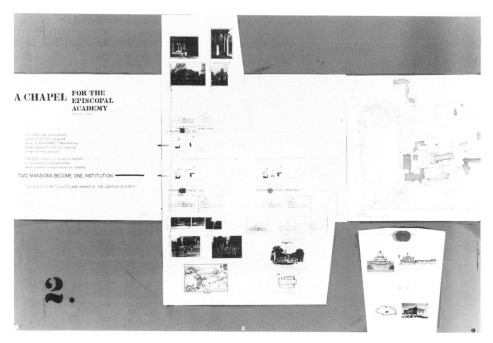

83
Design problem: A Chapel for the Episcopal Academy, Sheets 17–19

A CHAPEL FOR THE EPISCOPAL ACADEMY

MERION, PENNA

This country day school consists
essentially of TWO converted
ecclectic MANSIONS. These buildings
in their present function are unrelated
in their position and form.

The NEW CHAPEL in its position and form
is conceived as a changed context
which causes a changed expression—meaning.

TWO MANSIONS BECOME ONE INSTITUTION

THE WHOLE IS ARTICULATED AND UNIFIED BY THE ADDITION OF A PART

84
Design problem, Sheet 17

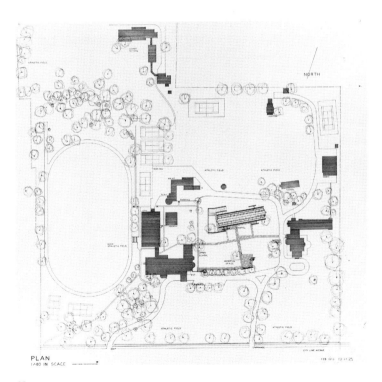

PLAN
1/40 IN SCALE

85
Design problem, Sheet 19

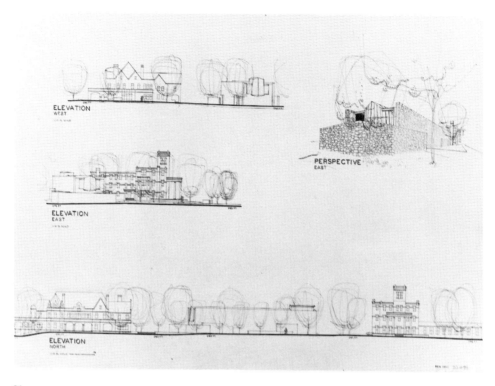

86
Design problem, Sheet 20

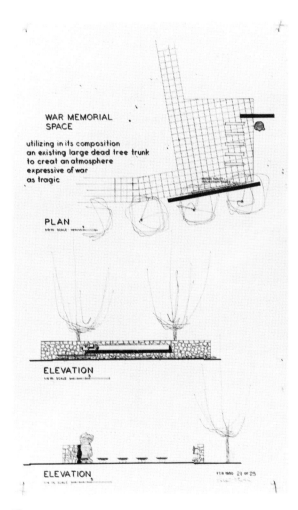

WAR MEMORIAL
SPACE

utilizing in its composition
an existing large dead tree trunk
to creat an atmosphere
expressive of war
as tragic

PLAN

ELEVATION

ELEVATION

87
Design problem, Sheet 21

EPILOGUE

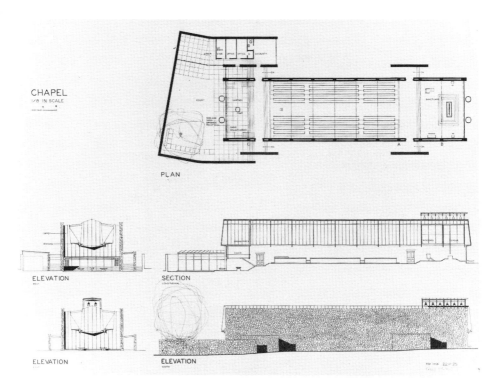

88
Design problem, Sheet 22

372

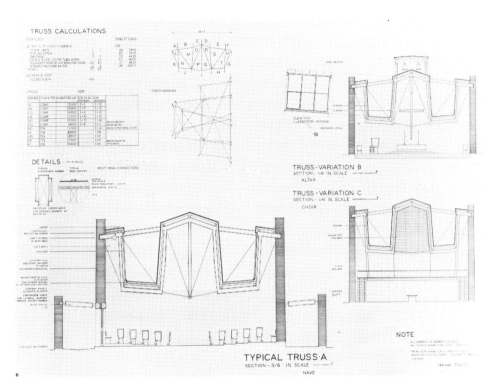

89
Design problem, Sheet 23

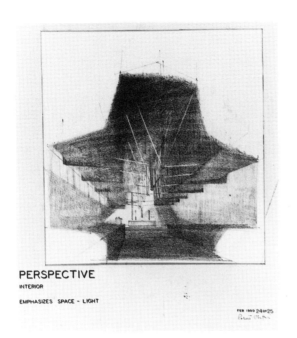

PERSPECTIVE

INTERIOR

EMPHASIZES SPACE - LIGHT

90
Design problem, Sheet 24

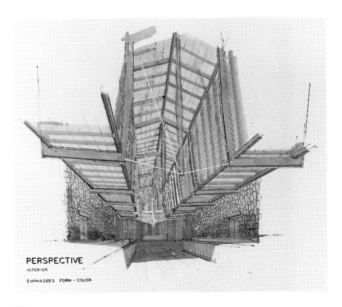

PERSPECTIVE

INTERIOR

EMPHASIZES FORM - COLOR

91
Design problem, Sheet 25